C000057200

HINTERLAND

Hinterland offers an ans
question 'what is creative
by showcasing the best n
the fields of memoir, essa
food writing, reportage, psychoscape,
biography, flash non-fiction and more.

Our pages bring together work by
established, award-winning authors
alongside new writers, many of whom
we are thrilled to publish for the first time
and whose work, we promise, will merit
your full attention.

Often, the pieces you'll find in Hinterland
will straddle the boundaries between
strands and be difficult to classify:
we see this as a strength. Hinterland
intends to challenge, move, entertain
and, above all, be a fantastic read.

WELCOME TO ISSUE 11

Advocates for Hinterland:
David Cooper, Nathan Hamilton, Kathryn Hughes, Rachel Lichtenstein,
Helen Smith, Rebecca Stott, Ian Thomson

Editorial Team
Editors-In-Chief – Yin F. Lim & Andrew Kenrick
Art Direction & Design – Tom Hutchings
Business Support – Ben Watkins
Proofreaders – Finn Brocklesby, Susan K. Burton, Aaron Deary,
                Margaret Hedderman, Stephen Massil,
                Florence Pearce-Higginson, Claire Reiderman,
                Yianni Theochari and Isabel Williams
Founding Editors – Freya Dean & Andrew Kenrick

Submissions
Hinterland is committed to paying writers and artists for all work we publish.
Please send us your work via Submittable:
hinterlandnonfiction.submittable.com
We accept submissions year-round and endeavour to reply within 4 months.
We regret we are unable to provide feedback.
There is a small fee of £3 per submission.

Subscriptions
An annual subscription to Hinterland (four issues, print and digital)
costs £40 U.K., £44 Europe, £54 Rest-of-world.
Digital subscription only, £20. Please visit our website for full details.

Distribution
Hinterland is distributed worldwide by NBN International.
For all trade orders contact +44 (0) 1752 202301
orders@nbninternational.com

Advertising
Please see our website for current rates, or to discuss sponsorship please
contact us at hinterlandnonfiction@gmail.com

Acknowledgments
The Editors gratefully acknowledge financial contributions from the UEA
Publishing Project, Manchester Metropolitan University and the National
Centre for Writing.

Find Hinterland online at
www.hinterlandnonfiction.com
or contact us: hinterlandnonfiction@gmail.com

ISBN: 978-1-913861-89-6
ISSN (Print): 2632-136X
ISSN (Online): 2632-1378

HINTERLAND

THE BEST NEW CREATIVE NON-FICTION

Issue 11
2022

Issue 11

PLACE WRITING SPECIAL

Editorial Team

Andrew Michael Hurley *(Guest Editor)* is a novelist and short story writer based in Lancashire. His debut novel, *The Loney*, won the Costa First Novel award in 2016 and the follow-up, *Devil's Day*, was jointly awarded the Royal Society of Literature's 'Encore' award for best second novel in 2018. His short fiction has appeared in Granta, the *Best British Short Stories of 2017*, the best-selling collection *The Haunting Season* and he is currently working on a series of short stories for BBC Radio 4. At Manchester Metropolitan University, Andrew is a senior lecturer in Creative Writing and a member of the Centre for Place Writing.

Tom Hutchings *(Art Direction & Design)* always struggles at this bit of the issue. Words aren't his strong point, but if you like the look of the issue, have a glance at thorngraphicdesign.com

Andrew Kenrick *(Editor-in-Chief)* has worked as an archaeologist and an archivist, a writer and an editor. He is currently studying for a PhD at the University of East Anglia, where he also teaches English Literature and Publishing.

Yin F Lim *(Editor-in-Chief)* spent many years as a journalist writing other people's stories before deciding to write her own. In 2018 she completed a Creative Non-Fiction MA at the University of East Anglia, and now mainly writes about family, food and migration.

Contributors

Alison Baxter *(El Chaltén)* has an MA in Biography and Creative Non-Fiction from the University of East Anglia and a PhD in Creative Writing from Oxford Brookes University. Her doctoral thesis explored the ambiguous boundary between fiction and non-fiction in relation to her book, *A Cornish Cargo: the untold history of a Victorian seafaring family*, published in 2020. Alison is a Fellow of the Royal Historical Society and has a particular interest in the Victorian era and the forgotten lives of so-called ordinary people. She is currently working on a new book based on a tragic story she found in the newspaper archive. She lives in Oxford.

Camilla Brueton *(Untitled #9 - The Tax Office Collages, The ridge above Cefn Onn)* is an artist and writer who is curious about place. Camilla has exhibited across the UK and currently has a public art commission, 'moss. quarry.plaque' on display in the City of Hobart's digital twin, created in collaboration with Margaret Woodward (Hobart, Tasmania). Camilla is interested in the potential of bringing words and images together through publication and performance. She lives and works in Cardiff, Wales.

Laura Cooper *(Walks Through Time)* has worked as a writer, photographer and educator in Japan, Spain and the UK. She will graduate from the UEA's MA in Creative Writing this year. Her music and travel photography has appeared on album covers and in various publications including *Time Out Tokyo* and *The Guardian*, and her portrait work has won numerous awards. Her debut novel-in-progress explores solastalgia and resilience in a speculative near-future England.

Linda Cracknell *(Crossing the Bar)* lives in Highland Perthshire and is a writer for whom place, memory and motion are important. Her non-fiction was most recently published in book form in *Doubling Back: ten paths trodden in memory* (Freight, 2014), a BBC Radio 4 Book of the Week in which she retraces memories underfoot. She has also published four works of fiction and had a number of radio plays produced. *Crossing the Bar* is extracted from a work in progress, *Three Ships: tides in the affairs of a family*, which explores her connection to the sea and her family's seafaring past. https://linktr.ee/LindaCracknellWriter

Adam Farrer *(The Californian)* is an essayist, the editor of the creative non-fiction journal *The Real Story* and the Writer in Residence for Peel Park, Salford. His manuscript, *Cold Fish Soup*, a memoir in essays about the Yorkshire coast, won the NorthBound Book Award at the 2021 Northern Writers' Awards and will be published by Saraband in August. He has been a photo lab technician, a kitchen porter, the voice of an automated phone system, an illustrator, a ceramicist, a musician, a music journalist, and currently works at the University of Salford.

Hannah Garrard *(1989)* writes creative non-fiction from her home in Norwich, where she lives with her partner and son and currently works as a programme manager at the National Centre for Writing. In 2015 she completed an MA in Creative Non-Fiction at the UEA, where she wrote an account of the Liberian civil war with help from the insights and recollections of the refugee children she taught whilst working in West Africa. Her writing has appeared in independent literary journals and news sites.

Anthony Head *(Life Is a Great Entanglement)* is a writer and editor who has lived for much of his life in Tokyo. His articles have been published in numerous journals, including *History Today, The Edinburgh Review, The London Magazine* and the *TLS*. His poetry has appeared in *Outposts, Orbis, The Frogmore Papers, Acumen* and other journals. He is the editor of three volumes of the letters and diaries of John Cowper Powys and several collections of essays by Llewelyn Powys.

Sylvia Ilahuka *(M.B.L.A)* is a Tanzanian writer now living in Uganda. Her work appears in publications such as *Lolwe, Doek!* the *Aké Review*, and *Bandcamp Daily*; she was also shortlisted for the inaugural Isele Nonfiction Prize. A graduate of Wellesley College in Massachusetts, Sylvia is the recipient of a Goethe-Institut artistic grant under which she produced photographic essays for the House of African Feminisms project.

Linda Mannheim *(Departing)* is the author of three books of fiction: *Above Sugar Hill, Risk* and *This Way to Departures*, which was shortlisted for the Edge Hill Prize in 2020. Linda's work has appeared in *The Nation, Granta, Catapult Story, 3:AM Magazine, Ambit, Alfred Hitchcock's Mystery Magazine*, and *Sight & Sound*. She has also broadcast work for BBC Witness and KCRW Berlin. Originally from New York, she lives in London and is a PhD researcher at the University of Westminster.

Jean Sprackland's *(Other Clocks)* latest book is *These Silent Mansions: a life in graveyards*, which was shortlisted for the PEN Ackerley Award in 2021. *Strands* won the Portico Prize for Non-Fiction in 2012. She is the author of five collections of poetry, including the Costa Award-winning *Tilt*. Jean is Professor of Creative Writing at Manchester Metropolitan University.

Hannah Storm *(Taking the Flak)* is an author, journalism safety expert and media consultant. Her flash fiction collection *The Thin Line Between Everything and Nothing* was published by Reflex Press and her memoir *Aftershocks* was shortlisted in the Mslexia 2021 awards. She is currently working on a novel inspired by her two decades working as a journalist. Hannah is the founder of Headlines Network, which promotes more open conversations about mental health in the media through training, tips and a podcast. She also works with newsrooms in wellbeing, safety and leadership. A keen marathon runner, Hannah lives with her family in Yorkshire.

Rebecca Thomas's *(A Mouse in Reagan Country)* work has appeared in *Prairie Schooner, ZYZZYVA, The Massachusetts Review*, among other places, and she has been nominated for a Pushcart Prize. She is a creative board member for the Ms. Aligned anthology series. Originally from Orange County, California, she now lives and teaches writing in Charlottesville, VA.

Julie Zuckerman's *(Abbaye de Valloies)* debut novel-in-stories, *The Book of Jeremiah*, was published in May 2019. Her writing has appeared in *CRAFT, Jewish Women's Archives, Crab Orchard Review, SFWP Quarterly, Atlas & Alice*, and *Sixfold*. A native of Connecticut, she now lives in Israel with her husband and four children. She is the founder of the Literary Modiin author series, connecting readers and writers of Jewish books. When she's not writing, she can be found reading, running, biking, and trying to grow things in her garden.

HINTERLAND
GIVE THE GIFT OF
CREATIVE NON-FICTION

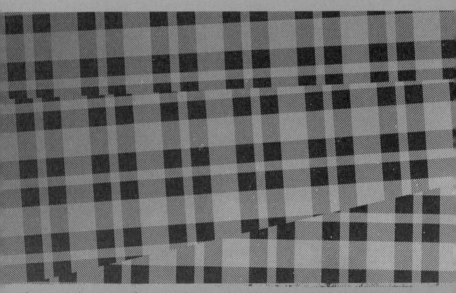

SUBSCRIPTIONS AND GIFT BUNDLES
AVAILABLE FROM OUR WEBSTORE,
GIFT-WRAPPING SERVICES AND
PERSONALISED MESSAGES
AVAILABLE ON REQUEST

Editorial

With all their associated memories and feelings, places are often the way-markers of our emotional life journeys. Special because they are where we loved, lost, received good news or bad, made mistakes or had epiphanies. But they can also be sites where we connect with stories other than our own, where we find the threads that connect us as individuals to bigger histories, as Julie Zuckerman discovers when she travels to the Abbaye De Valloires in northern France to learn more about a family member who was given sanctuary there during the Holocaust.

Sometimes, writing about place is about being a witness to history in the making. Anthony Head charts a love affair with Prague and its people against the backdrop of the Velvet Revolution. In Hannah Garrard's flash non-fiction, the same period of history is seen very differently through a child's eyes. The 7/7 bombings in London and Japan's largest earthquake are experienced first-hand by Laura Cooper, while journalist Hannah Storm depicts post-Gaddafi Benghazi as a place in flux, a place redefining itself. Full of danger but also hope.

Unpredictability of a different kind characterises the landscapes of Patagonia – a place of 'clouds, myths and tall tales' – and in the treacherous waters of the Bristol Channel, as captured respectively by Alison Baxter and Linda Cracknell. There is an instability of images and meaning, too, as Rebecca Thomas opens the cracks in the manicured fantasia of American wholesomeness that is Disneyland.

Seeing places from different perspectives can create very different feelings. From the ridge above Cefn Onn, Camilla Brueton pictures Cardiff as a magical city, silent and tiny amongst the surrounding greenery. Whereas, immersed in the grime and noise of London, the narrator of Linda Mannheim's flash piece cannot escape the harrowing absence of an unnamed 'he'.

In all of these pieces there is a sense of forces at work beyond our control; none more pressing, perhaps, than those of climate change, as witnessed by Sylvia K Ilahuka at her childhood home in Dar es Salaam and Adam Farrer on the Holderness coast of Yorkshire. Yet, in both cases, there is still optimism and determination.

We cling on to places that are significant to us, places we know. To let them go is to let part of us go too. Born by happenstance, our very existence a lottery, life is a constant struggle to make sense of what Jean Sprackland describes in her essay *Other Clocks* as the 'undrawable, unknowable scribble of coexistence of everything we are and all the ways we are living'.

And so to write about place is to try and anchor ourselves in the world somehow as it shifts endlessly around us.

Andrew Michael Hurley
Guest Editor, Place Writing Special Issue
in collaboration with Manchester Metropolitan University's Centre for Place Writing

The ridge above Cefn Onn

by Camilla Brueton

If I could take you anywhere –
I would bring you here.
Up on the ridge, above Cefn Onn.
To see the sprawl of Cardiff, and beyond.
Flat Holme and Steep Holme.
Penarth Head.
And, on a good day – Somerset.

Sunlight dances off the Bristol Channel.
A wren warbles.

Behind me is Caerphilly,
with its castle and rugby club – and Covid.*
The M4 hums in the background.

I like the view of Cardiff you get from here.

The centre, or 'town' looks so different –
like a faraway land.
Far more fantastical than it appears on the ground.
The sprawl between here and there is green.
Rooftops trace street patterns
through a canopy of trees,
with the Llanishen reservoir, a quiet void of water,
centre stage.

Cardiff is a surprisingly low-rise city.
In the north, the old Tax Office sticks out
like a sore brutalist thumb,
speaking quietly from a different era.

Every time you come up here, it's different –
the weather and the seasons doing what they do.

It's morning now – sunny and windy.
Early sun burns off cloud
from the city and the channel.

It's exposed.
I'm starting to get chilly.
It's time to run on… ▉

*This piece was written in September 2020, when Covid rates were rising and the first local
  lockdown in Wales had just been instigated in Caerphilly.

Departing

by Linda Mannheim

All that winter she saw the posters on the Underground:
'I'm not supposed to be here.' A fundraising campaign
for a cancer charity. And he was not there.

She'd board the train at Euston after work and
bright-faced survivors beamed from boards across the
tracks and the text told about the good care they'd
received from healthcare staff and the chemo that
helped them beat the odds. And he was not there.

The filth and chill of Euston was familiar and
comforting, and he'd confessed it was comforting
too when she told him. They both felt at home
in chaotic cities, wanted the oblivious crowds,
the impatiently crossed paths, the cram on the
escalators. They used to tell each other stories above
the roar at street level: the rattling traffic, the sirens,
the shouts from strangers. And he was not there.

When she stands on the Northern Line surrounded
by straphangers, she loses track of the stops,
sometimes goes too far, sometimes has to then double
back. Once she alighted in Zone 4 and, oblivious
to the transit cop blocking her way, kept walking
through the open barrier, forgetting to swipe out. And
the enforcement officer pushed her back, excoriated
her for not paying her fare and drew up the
paperwork for a fine. The bitter cold danced in damp
air and smacked her cheeks. And she couldn't explain
herself, couldn't even speak. And he was not there.

She stopped at St Paul's station twice a day when he was getting the last treatment they would try. She used to shop for ready meals at Marks & Spencer when he couldn't stand the food that Dietary sent, couldn't hide his disappointment when the metal dome was lifted from the plate. She used to get takeaway at the Italian deli downstairs where everyone was overly kind and attentive, knowing they were serving harried customers from the hospital. And he was not there.

Once, she went back after he was gone. She wanted to go to the last place she saw him, get out at that station again, climb the steps to the surface while the wind whipped down. She walked over to Barts, sat on the bench where she used to sit across from the fountain, smoked a cigarette where she used to smoke, stared at the entrance that she used to walk into to get to his ward. And he was not there.

Sometimes she stood in Euston Station remembering how they would meet there before dinner, find each other in the beautiful buzz of bustling crowds, walk around the clusters of office workers getting ready to go back to the suburbs at night. They told each other about their imagined versions of the commuters' lives: the man with slumped shoulders going back to a semi filled with fussy children, the woman in uncomfortable shoes staying with her parents while she saved, the retired man in an anorak who lost his research job because of a scandal. All those people standing there, waiting to go back to someone, their faces lifted to the departure signs. ⊞

1989

by Hannah Garrard

My twirly ballet dress was the same purple as the
birthmark on Mikhail Gorbachev's head. Mikhail
Gorbachev was our friend, my mum said. He would
stop us all from getting nuked. But even if we did, it
was OK, because we had a room under the house full
of tinned peas which would keep us going and alive.

'The youesessare is the biggest country in the
world, and everything there happens *centrally*,' Daniel,
the son of a family friend told me one day. 'The
people in the youesessare are controlled by a red
army who chuck their weight around.' He was a year
older than me, had an American mother and chewed
gum so he knew about things like the youesessare.

I asked my aunt about the youesessare and the
red army who chucked things. She'd been there, to
Moscow, with her class that year. The snow there
made it very cold, which must have had something to
do with the cold war. She explained the situation there
to me: 'You know Gorbachev? He's going to dissolve
the Soviet Union and bring democracy and decent
living standards to the people of the youesessare.' My
aunt was posting fake birthday cards to the teachers
she knew in Moscow – 'People just like you and me' –
and sellotaping British money into each one. 'To get it
past the KGB; so they can at least buy a loaf of bread
to eat.' This big place that took up half the sea was
very complicated. People had fake birthdays there.

During the summer of revolutions my parents took my brother and I to Montenegro, where I assumed there would be many kinds of eggs for us to eat. We arrived in the black of night – there were no eggs – and I remember waking to the hum of insects.

We were, my parents told me, behind the iron curtain.

Things, for me at least, were pretty good here behind the curtain. That summer I learned that I liked olives and pistachio nuts, food you could only get from going on holiday. I learned something else, I learned the colour of hungry: my parents had found us a place to eat in an outside restaurant under the shade of some ancient vines. A girl the same age as me was wandering around the restaurant all on her own going from table to table talking to strangers. I thought she was marvellous, so free and brave for talking to people she didn't know. The girl tugged at a man's sleeve. She put her hand to her mouth and mimed eating and the man handed her a paper bag of dark red cherries so bulging with fruit that the bag split. She took them in her arms and a few tumbled to the ground, there were so many. The girl came towards me popping cherries into her mouth and tugging at the stalks, one after the other until she had the dark red juice smeared across her lips and staining her fingers. Her teeth were red, her tongue and her chin, too. I studied my potential new friend hoping she would offer me a cherry. The jumper she wore had a Mickey Mouse on the front that had started to fade, so all that was left of him were his black ears and the ghost of a mousey nose. It was probably a hand-me-down, I reasoned, the receiver of many myself. Before we had a chance to make friends her mother came to collect her. As they left the courtyard the mother stooped, lowering herself to the level of the other seated diners. As she made her way through the latticed sunshine she held out her hands to make a cup.

When we returned from our holiday from behind the curtain The News showed red everywhere, in the sky and on people's hands and faces. Red was angry. Red was fury and fire. We were shown footage of a man standing in the middle of tea-and-man square with a line of tanks moving towards him like sinister, giant snails. He still had his shopping bags in his hands and I wondered what was in them when he flung them at the tanks.

Everyone in my house was angry. 'It was the iron curtain's fault!' they said. 'It has split the world in half!' And I imagined the globe like half a boiled egg. 'The young people of China want their freedom to speak and have ideas without being *harmed*.'

This cold, heavy curtain. I wanted it to come down.

And then it did – on the 9th of November. I was shocked to learn that the curtain wasn't a curtain at all but a concrete wall. 'We watched the wall come down on The News.' It sounded funny when I heard my mum say this down the phone that night. There were fireworks and people waving flags in Berlin. People laughing and holding and kissing each other and having parties in the road. They took hammers to the wall and smashed at it and when huge lumps of the wall toppled to the ground it reminded me of my birthday cake: knobbly and holey.

I noticed a woman on The News standing by the broken-up wall. She had her back to me and her wavy brown hair was a river running away behind her. Strands of it were flying about in the cold wind the way flames fling themselves at the sky. She pulled her coat tight around herself, to keep out the cold war, and turned around to look at me watching her through The News. Her cheeks were wet with many tears but her face held a smile wide enough to break it. 'That woman,' I asked my mother, 'why is she crying if she's meant to be happy?'

'Those are tears of joy,' my mother explained, 'but they come from a sad place; the world is a complicated place.' **H**

"The lecturers were excellent, the MA provided great opportunities for working on external projects and meeting students from as far away as the Bolivian Andes. Most importantly, I am now a markedly better writer and well on my way to a literary career."

Joe, Creative Non-fiction MA Student

Manchester Metropolitan University

The Manchester Writing School

Study Creative Non-Fiction
at the UK's longest running online MA/MFA programme with the Manchester Writing School at Manchester Met

- Join one of the country's largest postgraduate creative writing communities.

- Study from home with an international cohort of students via online distance learning.

- Develop your writing skills through a blend of practical and peer review workshops led by award-winning writers.

- Explore the range of sub-genres in this popular field: Autobiography, Green Writing, Literary Journalism, Nature Writing, Quest Biography, Place Writing, Memoir, Long Form Essay, Travel Writing and Historical Non-fiction.

- Examine a diverse range of twentieth and twenty-first century creative non-fiction texts with leading critical academics.

- Professional development opportunities with industry experts, and bonus sessions with published creative non-fiction authors from around the world.

Apply by end of August to guarantee a September 2022 start and by end of November for January 2023.

mmu.ac.uk/english/creative-writing

Other Clocks

by Jean Sprackland

'If time is the dimension of change,
then space is the dimension of coexisting difference.'
— Doreen Massey

1. A cottage

'Time has forgotten this place!' exclaims a voice in the lane. A woman in a fair isle beret is nodding in agreement. It may be a figure of speech, but they know what *now* looks like, and this isn't it. They spot me over the garden gate, wave and move on hastily.

It may be quiet here, but the clocks still run. And even if they stopped there would be plenty of other clocks. Paint on the window frames cracks and peels. Milk goes sour. Frogspawn bubbles between reeds at the edge of a pond.

Of course I know what he means. I too have stopped in lanes and gawped and said *What a treasure, what a wreck, oh if only, who in their right mind?* It is both enthralling and frightful to arrive at such frontiers, where the rough edges have not been smoothed by technology, and where the expected range of facilities cannot be relied upon.

On the other hand, who doesn't long to escape for a while – on holiday, on a country walk? Life is complicated and frenetic; it's normal to get nostalgic for a slower pace, a quieter environment, less *stuff*. To feel a pull of longing for the straightforwardness of our youth; or, better still, of someone else's youth. That of a grandparent, perhaps, seen in a black-and-white photograph, smiling artlessly in their one decent coat. Or, to go back further, to envy an artisan or peasant, more-or-less imaginary, who (as everyone knows) was poor but happy.

In this place where change is slow, and the passage of time can feel slippery and equivocal, I think of our cottage as a kind of clock. It was built by farm workers two hundred years ago, in a narrow, steep-sided valley in the Blackdown Hills, using whatever they could find in the fields where they laboured: walls made of chert and rubble, roof thatched with straw. It was heavy work. It stands on the springline, the point at which permeable greensand and impermeable clay sub-soils meet, squeezing water out sideways, where it wells up as springs, and forms mire and quaking bog. The land here is too wet to grow crops. A few cattle, or a few sheep, that's about it. Some vegetables, an apple tree or two. Those were the conditions then, and they remain unaltered to this day. Houses are few and it's not easy to sell them.

Those first occupants were certainly poor; whether they were happy, history does not relate. Local records tell of births and deaths within these walls. Sex out of wedlock and with the wrong brother. A ghastly accident, a fire that took the thatch, a man in uniform walking away up the lane to war. On windy days I hear their voices in the chimney, but I can't tell what they're saying. I unlatch the little iron door and put my hand into the old bread oven, feeling around in the dust for something left behind. There are marks scratched into the stone fireplace, but who knows what to read into them?

No, I said, but I spoke with the desperation of a lover already caught in the trap. *No*

The first time we saw this place, we came by taxi from the nearest town. The driver, navigating the steep, narrow, twisting lane into the valley, was appalled. '*No one* lives here,' he told us, firmly and repeatedly. It was a bleak February day, and the estate agent, impractically dressed, bouncing on his heels to keep warm, could hardly believe his luck; the place had been on and off the market for years, the owners long gone, and it was looking like a hopeless case. We pushed the gate and it dropped from its hinges. We stood and stared. The cottage, long ago rendered and roofed with tiles, was ensnared in a thicket of brambles as stout as rusted railings. Sleet ran straight off the roof and pooled on the broken concrete. Electricity wires trailed on the ground between the house and some kind of outbuilding. *No*, I said, but I spoke with the desperation of a lover already caught in the trap. *No.* In the lane behind me, the taxi driver was still attempting to turn round, clutch burning, wheels spinning uselessly in the mud.

2. A woman with a kettle

One of the places where I stopped and gawped
was a stone farmstead, high in the mountains of
Asturias in northern Spain. This was twenty years
ago; I had driven up a zigzag road from the coast
for a day's walking. There were hardly any passing
places, and my hands and jaw ached from gripping
the wheel so tightly.

At a distance I thought the house must be
abandoned, but as I drew close I could see an
elderly woman in the garden. There was a mule
tethered to the gatepost, and some sort of cart
or trap on the grass. The rope was made of jute,
the straps of leather, the upturned bucket in the
vegetable patch of galvanized iron. The woman
had filled a tin kettle at the well and was carrying
it into the house. We exchanged a greeting, and I
stood a moment admiring the garden. It took me a
minute or two to realise that there was nothing here
– no washing line or hosepipe or plant pot – made
of plastic. Yet here was this woman, cheerfully
carrying water for her tea, demonstrably as alive as
I was, and therefore belonging just as fully to the
twenty-first century as the New York skyscraper,
the suburban bungalow, or the rudimentary mobile
phone in my rucksack (useless there, since there was
no signal for many miles around).

How can there be anything that is not part of the
modern world? Modernity is not a force that sweeps
in and carries off the donkey-cart and the tin kettle
to the rubbish-heap of history. If *now* is anything
at all, it must be everything the world contains at

this moment – not a point along a line drawn to represent progress from the old ways to the new, but an undrawable, unknowable scribble of coexistence of everything we are and all the ways we are living. Why is it so hard to accept this obvious truth, this wild variousness?

There is something at stake, something personal. It confronts us with inequalities and with the randomness of circumstance. It forces us to acknowledge that there is a limitless range of possible lives each of us could be living, if we'd been born elsewhere, had different luck, made other choices. It brings us face to face with the infinite, which is always a crisis.

Hard work and ingenuity bring progress, and progress gives us such control over our destiny that we need not feel trapped in time at all

It would be more comfortable to believe in a defining 'now', of which some places fall short. To look back at the stone cottage and the cart and to be charmed by them, then to turn away with a sense of relief. There may be a long way to go, we could tell ourselves, but inconvenience and hardship are surmountable. Year by year, generation by generation, humanity is advancing towards a state of health and ease and order. Hard work and ingenuity bring progress, and progress gives us such control over our destiny that we need not feel trapped in time at all, and therefore (ah yes, now we're getting to it) *we need never die.*

3. Trees

Platanus x hispanica

Trees keep a record of the years in their rings, and measure time through leaf-fall and bud-burst and the rise of sap; and we manage them by the clock. In our London street, the first signs of spring were a council van touring the neighbourhood, and workmen who jumped out and put up notices made of yellow corrugated plastic fixed with cable ties. The notices announced the forthcoming suspension of all the parking bays for two days, purpose: Tree Works. A week or two later, as day and night moved into a state of tentative balance, it was not the first cuckoo but the first chainsaw that announced the vernal equinox. The pollarding had begun.

A traditional method of managing woodland and pasture, known since medieval times, is practised annually in those unlikely surroundings. In Middle English 'poll' meant head, and to poll was to crop the head in one way or another; a pollard might be a bull which had had its horns removed, or a deer that had shed its antlers. Or it might be a tree whose upper branches had been cut away to encourage the growth of leaves and stems for firewood, withies or animal fodder. There in our street, pollarding had a different purpose: it kept the height of the plane trees within acceptable limits, and protected them from damage in high winds.

The gang who worked the trees seemed to be made up entirely of strapping young New Zealanders, with voices that carried over the noise of the chainsaw and the wood chipper. They were dressed in Kevlar jackets and trousers, steel-capped boots, orange helmets and ear defenders; they had ropes and harnesses, spurs and pulleys and lockjacks. They worked fast and hard. One would be up in the crown of the tree, slicing through branches and slinging them down; another hefted the prunings with huge, gloved hands and fed them into the chipper. I don't know where the woodchips were destined to end up: as surfacing for paths and playgrounds in the borough's parks, maybe, or to feed a biomass boiler in a school or hospital. The street alone must have yielded many tonnes of it every pollarding, and I guess there isn't much local demand for withies or fodder.

I remember one year the tree work happened late, when the planes were already in leaf and the street was softened with lush growth and green light. There was violence, then, in the slashing back, the pulping of all that vegetation. It seemed impossible that it would ever be renewed. But these trees are veterans, planted when the estate was laid out; a few have died and been replaced with silver birch or rowan, but the rest keep growing, tough survivors of a hundred-and-thirty years of urban life.

Still, the street wore a bleak and brutalist look for a few weeks. They stood in two starkly parallel rows, and in place of their naturally rugged crowns and rustling canopies, the architecture of each tree was stripped back to a crowd of upraised fists.

Alnus glutinosa

Alder puts down its roots in mud, lives fast and dies young. It's tough and stoical in appearance, with a dark trunk, cracked and scabbed, sheened in places with lichen, flushed with red-orange sap when cut. It seeds itself profusely in the river valleys of the Blackdowns, where it helps stabilise the banks and protect against flooding. In the past this tree was tended and harvested. It played a valuable role in the local economy, linked with the lime-burning industry that sprang up here in the nineteenth century; lime-burners needed footwear that would protect them against the intense heat of the kiln, and alder was perfect for the job, because on cutting it is soft and easily worked, but in time it cures and hardens. Even alder clogs would burn through in the end, so the wood and the craftsman were in constant demand.

Alder puts down its roots in mud, lives fast and dies young. It's tough and stoical in appearance, with a dark trunk, cracked and scabbed

Our first winter here, scrambling down the riverbank with the mud sucking at my boots, I was astonished by the vivid purple of the buds. How could such a sombre tree put forth such jewels? The catkins, too, are brushed with purple, and later there are miniature cones, green at first and ripening to charcoal. Nowadays these riches are spent largely unnoticed in the trackless and shadowy seclusion of mire and carr.

But the past is not gone. Here and there along the river you can still see the outgrown remains of coppicing. Should we try to revive it? Should I teach myself to make alder clogs? When we lopped off an overhanging branch last month the cut surface, pale at first, was quickly stained with blood.

4. An old newspaper

Coexisting with difference can get extreme. In the 1930s Christiane Ritter spent a long winter in a tiny hut on the Norwegian island of Spitsbergen, and in her memoir *A Woman in the Polar Night* she describes an experience of remoteness and solitude so intense it feels like a work of fiction. Her husband and their friend Karl are often away hunting for weeks at a time, and she lives in complete isolation. The sun does not rise at all. Hunger, thirst and sleep become a way of telling the time. She crawls over the snow in the pitch dark, harnessed to a makeshift sledge carrying drinking water from the glacier. She digs through the snowdrift and excavates the frozen remnants of a long-dead seal to cook on the broken old stove. Most of the time she is fully absorbed in the moment, the task, the necessity of survival. But every now and then there are sudden, vertiginous moments of revelation, when she sees that everything she left behind in Austria is still there, that it exists and is part of the same world as this. Days after arrival, dismayed by the 'monstrous barrenness' of her surroundings, she thinks of mainland Europe: 'It seems to me now like a magic land. Flowers and fruits grow out of the earth there.

Out of the earth grows what man needs in order to live.' But later, they acquire a crumpled page of an old Tromsø newspaper that has been used as packaging, and spend hours marvelling over the advertisements for preserving sugar, coffins and electrical repairs. As time stretches, so does space.

She feels increasingly alienated from her previous way of life, and from 'civilisation' itself

She feels increasingly alienated from her previous way of life, and from 'civilisation' itself; it becomes hard to reconcile with the intensity of the Arctic experience, so that inevitably one seems more real than the other. When she arrived, Spitsbergen looked primitive, a relic of the distant past; but now she recognises it as timeless, eternal.

5. Broadband archaeology

This cottage is nothing like a hut in Spitsbergen, many days' journey from the nearest habitation, or an ancient farmstead high in the Picos. It's a little isolated, and a little wild, but only by the modest standards of twenty-first century England. Sylvia Townsend Warner, who devotes no more than a page and a half of her book *Somerset* to the Blackdown Hills, nevertheless captures them well. 'Lanes in every degree of greenness and forsaken windingness branch off the roads,' she writes, 'lanes which are rutted with cart tracks, or closed off by sagging gates, lanes whose thick hedges grow out of stony banks, lanes that disappear downhill under green tunnels. If you follow them they will entangle you in further lanes, or take you, with an artful circumvention of contours, to some farmhouse perched halfway down a hillside, with a climbing field behind it dotted with sheep'.

She was writing in 1949, but her description is as accurate now as then. The 'forsaken windingness' has so far proved an insurmountable obstacle to the provision of broadband; a couple of years ago there was talk of it, and a contractor came and painted cryptic symbols at intervals on the roads, but shortly afterwards it was pronounced impossible. A few of the symbols survive, faded to the point of archaeology. It suits us fine. When we want to send email, we walk half a mile up the lane and perch on the stile where there's usually good 4G.

It is an exceptional privilege to be able to choose where to live. We came here just because we liked it, and we live here in comfort, with central heating and electric light. We can turn on the radio whenever we want and hear all about the latest wars and floods and epidemics. The greatest freedom of all is to be able to get in the car and drive out of the valley, and if there's ice or snow or a fallen tree it's only a question of waiting till the next day.

My parents moved where the jobs were, and put down roots wherever they went. My grandparents scraped a precarious living from the same patch of land as their grandparents had. Even today, for most people in the world, choice is unthinkable. You live where you belong, where it's safe, where there's dry land, and food, where you and your sort are permitted.

7. Mire

Mountain ecosystems in northern Spain are highly vulnerable to climate disturbance. Higher temperatures and less precipitation mean reduced snow cover and some of the rarest and most fragile species have been driven to the brink. In the Picos, a project is underway to restore the old drove roads and return to the practice of moving sheep and goats between summer and winter pasture; where the animals trample and browse, biodiversity is improved.

London's plane trees scrub hundreds of tonnes of pollution from the city's air each year, and shrug it off by shedding their bark, which peels away like old wallpaper, revealing other patterns beneath. But more frequent heatwaves and droughts are starting to take their toll, thinning the canopy and making planes more susceptible to disease and felling.

The hut where Christiane Ritter lived still stands and has become an unlikely tourist attraction. You can get there relatively easily by helicopter or snowmobile these days. I feel the draw of it myself, but the thing I'd want – the chance to experience the place as Christiane did – is no longer possible. Time is the dimension of change, and Spitsbergen is on the front line of the climate crisis.

> **London's plane trees scrub hundreds of tonnes of pollution from the city's air each year, and shrug it off by shedding their bark, which peels away like old wallpaper**

Here in the Blackdowns, conversation is dominated by immortal topics: rainfall, wells, the river and its moods, the need to keep gullies clear to avoid flooding. On winter nights I am conscious of the movement of water above, around and beneath me. For months of the year, parts of the garden are impassible, reverting to mire.

Mire has long been treasured for its many curious and little-known species of moss and moth and carnivorous plant. It's also a kind of clock, measuring change, keeping a record of the past; mud cores drawn up from the local mire yielded grains of pollen deposited over the last eleven thousand years, revealing patterns and disruptions. Now there's growing recognition of its value as a carbon sink, and the farmer whose fields surround us on three sides anticipates that soon she will be paid a subsidy to manage it. Managing it essentially means leaving it alone, and in all honesty there isn't much alternative; attempting to drain it is a fool's game. Better to work round it, as people have always done.

Better to plant more alders, because the truth is that time forgets no place. Will them to grow fast and strong, grip the bank with their roots and hold it firm when the river rises. ◼

Short online creative writing courses

Book now for May!

- Study online at any time from the comfort of home
- Fully tutored, receive individual feedback on your work
- Small, friendly groups – 15 students max
- Beginner and intermediate levels available
- Co-designed with the University of East Anglia

'The materials were excellent and the tutor feedback was so helpful. I feel I have learned such a lot and my writing has definitely improved as a result.'

Lisa Tippings, Start Writing Creative Non-Fiction

nationalcentreforwriting.org.uk/creative-writing-online/

42 Hinterland

Abbaye de Valloires

by Julie Zuckerman

My son and I crisscross Gare de Lyon train station and its underbelly at least four times before we find the tiny rental car office in a small passageway across the street. We are sweaty from schlepping our luggage, our skin gritty from exhaust fumes and the August heat. I am distressed by our late start out of Paris; the booking reservation for our next accommodation states we must check in by five o'clock in the afternoon. I'm worried that we'll find ourselves stranded in the middle of the French countryside with nowhere to stay.

—

Seventy-six summers ago, another mother and son set out for the train station in Lens, three hours north of Paris. The mother is Czarna, my grandmother's elder sister, and her son is Joseph; they are 39 and 10, respectively, exactly ten years younger than we are today. Unlike ours, theirs is a hastily organized trip. As they walk through the streets, a classmate of Joseph's runs at them, screaming that he'll report them for not wearing their stars. Czarna squeezes Joseph's hand and says in a firm, calm voice, 'Ignore him and keep walking.'

When they arrive, the station is filled with children excited for a summer holiday and their grateful parents. The Red Cross is taking the children to the relative safety of the Jura mountains, into the fresh air and away from the city and the bombings.

Upon reaching his compartment on the train, Joseph bursts into tears. An only child, he harbors an acute attachment to his mother. On the platform, Czarna stands stock still, not waving, crying or showing the slightest feeling. The lack of emotion on her face will haunt Joseph for years.

———

I navigate the rental car northward, towards the Somme district, past wind farms, signs for World War I tourism destinations and the Cathedral at Amiens, where TripAdvisor reviewers urge other travelers not to miss the summer light show. We listen to a comedy album and songs my son has stored on his phone. Off the highway, we travel through fields of sunflowers, the roads so narrow that there is no room for two cars coming from opposite directions; one must pull onto the grass for the other to pass. I begin to understand why my husband's uncle, who lives a few hours away in Lille, called me 'courageous' for visiting this remote destination, though it was said in the easy way in which we throw words around these days, nothing like real courage.

—

Joseph does not stay in the mountains for long. Placed on a widower's farm, he helps with the chickens, tends the cows and works in the fields. When asked his religion, he says 'Protestant,' thinking the family is Catholic. 'Good, so are we,' they say, and thus he does not get out of attending church with them. But the family's live-in domestic is not fooled; two months into his stay, he sneaks behind a hedge to eavesdrop on a conversation between the domestic and two German soldiers who have come to flirt with her. 'I thought her pretty unpatriotic,' Joseph later writes. And when he overhears her positing his true faith to the soldiers: 'I left as quietly as I came, knowing what I needed to do.'

Joseph convinces the farmer to send him into town on errands so he can get word to the local Red Cross representative. Within a day, she removes him and two other Jewish children from nearby farms, driving them north, to the Abbaye de Valloires.

Founded by Cistercian monks in the tenth century, the abbey has become a preventorium for children prone to tuberculosis. Thérèse Papillon, a World War I nurse who runs the abbey, is one of four people who know Joseph's identity. The other Jewish children, Mina and Jules, are a sister and brother Joseph knows from home; they are instructed to never speak with each other.

—

...he pumps air into the organ, only later understanding that the adults assign him these tasks so no one will question why he doesn't take communion.

We arrive, at last, at the Abbaye de Valloires, and a young woman named Amélie accompanies us to the building where twenty monastic cells above the original refectory have been converted into guest rooms. My cousin Wendy has written ahead, asking if someone can give us a tour, and Amélie confirms our meeting with M. Cuminal, the president of the abbey, at 10am the next morning.

—

The children follow a strict regime of rest, which leaves little time for normal school subjects. Joseph excels at catechism and teaches the younger boys. During daily mass, he pumps air into the organ, only later understanding that the adults assign him these tasks so no one will question why he doesn't take communion. The abbey is near the English Channel, in the flight path of bombers. Daily, he witnesses hundreds of bombing missions and an occasional dog fight. British fighter planes shot down and pilots parachuting from the sky.

—

Our room is quaint; two single beds, a large mirror, Rococo-style wallpaper and a view of Les Jardins de Valloires, classified by the French as a Jardin Remarquable – outstanding garden – with over 5000 species. A wide walkway divides the manicured lawns, rose bushes and benches for sitting, and the perfectly symmetrical shrubbery.

We settle in, and my son finds a common area down the hall where the wifi sort of works. I wonder if we should have brought kosher food from Paris, but with the help of Google we locate a few restaurants which might have suitable vegetarian options. The first is closing; it's 7pm on a Sunday evening. The second does not seem to exist. At last, we find a charming-looking restaurant with a welcoming hostess. In my rudimentary, eleventh-grade French, I order a simple salad for myself and the owner graciously agrees to make a cheese plate for my son who, at 20, is a picky eater. The food is fresh and tasty, and we gorge ourselves on creamy, rich cheeses and jam until we can eat no more.

—

Two huge red crosses stand at either end of the abbey's main building, red bricks in a square of whitewashed stones. Perhaps these serve as markers, for the abbey is never bombed. Though the adults don't disclose much, a boy missing parts of two fingers seems to know the news and he shares it with Joseph and the other children: The Allies have landed in Normandy.

> **'Bist du ein Jude,' he asks, accusingly. Joseph understands perfectly but doesn't flinch.**

Soon after, though, the Germans arrive and begin digging a huge tunnel. The word among the boys is that they are building an underground hospital; later I read that Rommel planned to use the abbey as a general headquarters.

One day, a German soldier catches Joseph by the shoulder. 'Bist du ein Jude,' he asks, accusingly. Joseph understands perfectly but doesn't flinch. He believes the Allies will be here soon; in a flash, he calls upon a God he is no longer sure exists. He prays not to fail when he's so close to liberation. Joseph shrugs his shoulders in typical French fashion and replies, 'Je ne comprends pas.' Twice the soldier repeats his accusation, and twice Joseph repeats his lie before the soldier lets him go.

'I suddenly had a terrible dilemma,' Joseph writes later. 'Do I tell Mademoiselle Geneviève [the nurse who was his group leader] of the encounter or not? If I tell her, will they send me away some place else? Would they turn me in to save their lives and claim they didn't know I was Jewish? If I don't tell her and the soldier pursues me, they will all get shot; I'll die too … In reviewing the incident today, I certainly did the wrong thing [by not telling]. It was clearly selfish and foolish.'

—

M. Cuminal is a compact man in a navy blazer, a pin on the lapel. He meets us in the abbey's gift shop, where one can purchase tins of butter cookies, local jams and ales, postcards and books about the gardens. Siobhan, a British woman who lives nearby, joins our tour as the translator.

...we see a group of two and three-year-olds walking with their teachers. M. Cuminal stoops to say hello, tickling a few; a kindly grandfather.

Today, the abbey remains a place of shelter for children. The guest rooms seem beside the point, though I understand the charm for tourists: Une hôtellerie au cœur d'une abbaye cistercienne! Primarily it is a boarding school for at-risk boys between the ages of four and fourteen. There is another group, even younger, who have been removed from their homes because their parents are unable to care for them. The two groups do not mix. The older boys are away on a trip today, but we see a group of two and three-year-olds walking with their teachers. M. Cuminal stoops to say hello, tickling a few; a kindly grandfather.

He points to a tree under the window of the guest quarters: it is the oldest pear tree in France, planted by a monk in 1756. 'It may even be the oldest in the world,' he tells us with pride. The symbol of the pear tree is everywhere: in the emblem of the abbey and carved into decorative items inside the abbey's church. M. Cuminal and Siobhan try to draw out my son, whose eyes are red-rimmed from staying up too late playing on his phone. They assume he is a bored, uninterested youth, but I know he is absorbing everything.

—

One morning Joseph awakes to find the Germans have left overnight.

Within the week, a Canadian convoy appears outside the abbey. The line of trucks, jeeps, artillery, and tanks lasts several days, and the ebullient boys stand by the side of the road for hours on end waving to their liberators. L'Abbé, the brother of Thérèse Papillon and priest of the abbey, appears wearing an armband of the FFI. How glorious, Joseph thinks, our very own priest in the French Underground!

For the first time in three years, Joseph speaks to Mina, and they share a secret: both wish to become Catholic. Later, Joseph asks L'Abbé to baptize him. A big man, L'Abbé puts his arms around Joseph. First, we must wait for your parents to return, he says, but once you have their permission, I will be happy to do it. Joseph knows this is unlikely: the morning of his departure for the train station in

Lens, his father had spent all morning wrapped in his tallis, and when it had been time to leave, he'd gathered Joseph in his prayer shawl and whispered over and over: 'Don't ever forget you're a Jew.'

—

We are not the first visitors from the family. Cousin Wendy, first cousin to both Joseph and my father, is a French teacher, and several years ago she took it upon herself to have Thérèse Papillon and the abbey recognized for protecting Joseph during the war. Yad Vashem, the World Holocaust Remembrance Center, grants the title of 'Righteous Among Nations' to those who helped Jews in the darkest time of their history. Twice Wendy has visited the abbey: the first time in 2014, when she spoke to an audience of local journalists and dignitaries about Joseph and her research; and again in 2017, for a ceremony when the official recognition was granted. Gathered to dedicate the plaque to Thérèse Papillon were M. Cuminal; Wendy with her husband and two grandchildren; Joseph's son, daughter-in-law and their children; an elderly Jewish man who was two when his parents brought him to the abbey for safekeeping; and local French authorities and representatives of Yad Vashem and the Israeli government.

'I would love to know if the Israeli, American and French flags still fly over the Diplôme d'Honneur at the front door of the Abbaye,' Wendy emails before our trip. 'Would you give my best to M. Cuminal? I give him so much credit and appreciation for honoring Joey's memory. When you are in the chapel of the Abbey, imagine that the organist played the Israeli, American and French national anthems at the end of the ceremony. It still gives me chills.'

—

Joseph writes immediately to the family in America; Zeyde Wolf, his grandfather, and Dave, his uncle, letting them know that he is alive but that does not know the whereabouts of his parents. He expects them to return once Germany has been defeated. He does not know Zeyde Wolf passed away in 1942.

['At the shiva for Zeyde Wolf, someone said he had died because the Nazis were killing his children in Europe,' remembers my uncle, who was four at the time. When my father is born in 1944, he is given Zeyde Wolf's Hebrew and Yiddish names.]

of the 35 members of his immediate family in Europe at the start of the war, Joseph, alone, is among the living

Months pass as Joseph waits at Valloires for correspondence from his aunts and uncles in America: Wendy's father Dave, my grandmother Pearl, and two other siblings. Eventually, in the spring of 1945, a Jewish chaplain from the U.S. Army who knows the family in America comes to Valloires. He brings Joseph to live with a Jewish family in Lille while waiting for his paperwork. Each day, Joseph visits the repatriation center where names of those returning from the death camps are read aloud. Slowly the unthinkable takes shape: of the 35 members of his immediate family in Europe at the start of the war, Joseph, alone, is among the living.

—

We stop to take a picture under the Diplôme d'Honneur from Yad Vashem, one of the first things we'd seen yesterday. It hangs at the entrance of the wing with the hotel rooms.

Five months before our visit, an elderly Holocaust survivor was brutally stabbed to death in her apartment in Paris. My Facebook feed regularly features news items and pictures of defaced Jewish cemeteries and rising violence on both sides of the ocean. I am sickened by the politicians on the right and the left who support neo-Nazis and spout antisemitic tropes. We've taken pains not to pack t-shirts with Hebrew writing, and later this week when the rest of the family joins us in Paris, my husband will wear a baseball cap instead of his kippah. But here, in this remote corner of France, where surely the Jewish population is nil, the Israeli, French and American flags are displayed with pride.

I am teary with gratitude.

—

Joseph waits two years for his papers before disembarking, at last, onto the safe shores of America, where he is taken in by Czarna's remaining siblings in Bridgeport, Connecticut. He lives, for periods, with my father's family and the other aunts and uncles and cousins. The cousins are counseled not to ask questions; he does not volunteer his story to anyone.

The cousins are counseled not to ask questions; he does not volunteer his story to anyone

In due time, Joseph finishes high school and earns a degree in accounting from the University of Connecticut. He marries a Catholic woman and they have three children. All four sets of aunts and uncles and most of the cousins remain in the greater Bridgeport area, or move only as far as New York or New Jersey, but in the 1970s Joseph relocates to faraway California for work. After a divorce, he remarries and has another daughter.

—

On our tour, M. Cuminal tells us of the early monks who diverted a local river to create an underground pond beneath the courtyard from which to fish. Like my mother, a former high school history teacher, my son and I are drawn to the past, echoes of which can be found everywhere. We learn that the abbey was damaged during the Hundred Years' War and was subject to looting during the

Wars of Religion; the original church, consecrated in 1226, lasted until the eighteenth century when it collapsed. Rebuilt in 1756, it remained untouched during the French Revolution and was saved from further looting and demolition by a local landlord.

We visit grand rooms and see a painting of the 'operations' monk who oversaw the abbey's rebuilding. The interior of the church features a lavish wrought iron grid that separates the chancel from the nave, a plump pear in gold and sapphire adorning the crest. The organ stands tall behind the nave; carved onto its façade are pears and other fruit, along with figures of the sculptor's eleven children and other religious symbols. The sculptor – M. Cuminal relates, his smile mischievous – was a master Austrian woodworker who absconded to the region after killing someone in a duel, and then killed two others trying to apprehend him in France.

The sculptor... was a master Austrian woodworker who absconded to the region after killing someone in a duel

I try to picture Joseph here, hiding from sight as he pumps air into the organ. Despite the sculptor's sketchy personal history, the carved figures of children in the organ's buffet seem prescient, as if he knew the abbey would someday become an orphanage, then preventorium, and now, a home for troubled youth.

By the altar, we pay homage at the graves of Thérèse Papillon and her brother, L'Abbé, whom we learn had a wild streak and was killed in a motorcycle accident in 1957. Of Thérèse Papillon, who lived until the age of 97, the tombstone reads: 'Until her last breath, by the total gift of her character and her means, she welcomed thousands of children here and gave them spiritual and social nourishment.'

—

When Joseph meets other Jews in America, they ask where he was during the war, how he survived. He considers getting a tattoo on his arm to avoid having to explain that he spent the war in relative safety at Valloires. He doesn't feel he has a story to tell since he was not in the camps. Only when he sees a *Time* magazine article about the hidden Jewish children, three decades after the war, does he understand that there were thousands of others like him.

In 1991, on the eve of the Gulf War, as rockets are raining down on Tel Aviv and Riyadh, the sirens he hears on CNN remind Joseph of those he heard as a child. He's long promised his cousins that he will write down his wartime experiences for a family book, and he does so now, from his earliest recollections until he sets foot in America in 1947. His account closes with these lines:

'I documented my experiences for my family's sake but not with the intent to have them construed as a survivor's story. I have never felt a sense of joy or gratitude or elation at having survived. How could I? The feelings, the emotions, the enormity of the whole experience have never changed for me over the years. The question "why" is here with me every day of my life, and still there is no answer. Why? Why? Why?'

—

I've read Joseph's story in our Glantz family book dozens of times. Earlier this year, on the eve of Holocaust Remembrance Day in Israel, I read it aloud to my family. The account is twenty-two pages, single-spaced, though Joseph says that he could have gone on for a hundred. My younger children and husband eventually drift away as I read, but my son, who shares a love of family history, stays until the end.

We ourselves emigrated to Israel in the mid-1990s, and my son is the first sabra, native-born Israeli, on either side

Unlike Joseph's childhood, my son's was free: spent on the inviting playgrounds of our flourishing, verdant city in central Israel, attending school as an equal to his classmates, learning and practicing our traditions without fear. For his seventh-grade roots project, we'd made a slideshow, documenting our family's migratory moves: on my side from Russia and Poland to America, in one case via England; on my husband's side from Germany to France to Spain to Portugal to Cuba to America. We ourselves emigrated to Israel in the mid-1990s, and my son is the first sabra, native-born Israeli, on either side. He's currently serving in the Israel

Defense Forces, working as a team leader in the IT department for the Home Front Command, charged with protecting civilian lives.

At the culmination of our visit, M. Cuminal brings us to his office, where, on his desk, we find my son's glasses, mislaid in our room and deduced by the wise Amélie to belong to us. M. Cuminal has prepared snacks and an appertif of Kir; a mix of blackcurrant juice and white wine. A plaque of appreciation given by Wendy and the family hangs on the wall below a small crucifix. Below this, on a narrow side table alongside statuettes of Mary and other Christian symbols, sits a shofar decorated with silver etchings and a kiddush cup – more gifts from the family. We explain the significance of the shofar, the trumpeted wail sounded on our holiest days, but neither of us can emit the call as it's meant to be heard.

M. Cuminal presents us with a booklet from last year's ceremony. We chat about our next stop, Amiens, where he lives, as well as our plans to meet the rest of the family the next morning and travel to Normandy, where we will attempt to take in the enormity of a different angle of the war.

—

In 1999, Joseph speaks at his daughter's high school in California; it is his first time sharing his story out loud, and the first time his daughter hears his account. 'He is an example of forgiveness,' she says when introducing him. 'He always inspires me to look for the good in other people.'

—

I write M. Cuminal a long letter upon my return to Israel, sending it along with a traditional apple and honey dish and a wall hanging with a quote from Psalms 122: 'Peace be within thy walls, and prosperity within thy palaces. For my brethren and companions' sakes, I will now say, Peace be within thee.'

Six months later, I receive a note of thanks in reply. M. Cuminal's handwriting is difficult to decipher, even for my French friend to whom I show the card. But the gist is that my gifts now sit alongside the shofar, kiddush cup and plaques of appreciation.

I do not recall if I ever met Joseph before his death in 2001. My son, born in 1998, certainly did not. But when I ask my son several months later what he remembers about our visit to the abbey, he mentions the peacefulness and beauty of the place. The warm welcome we received from M. Cuminal. The sense of saintliness that continues to guide the abbey in its mission with at-risk youth. We feel honored to have visited. Extreme gratitude for Thérèse Papillon, her brother, L'Abbé, and all the Righteous Among Nations who risked their lives to protect children like Joseph during the war. Their courage inspires and lifts us up. Should he ever take *his* family on a trip to France, my son tells me, he will show them this sanctuary, this blessed place of peace. ⌗

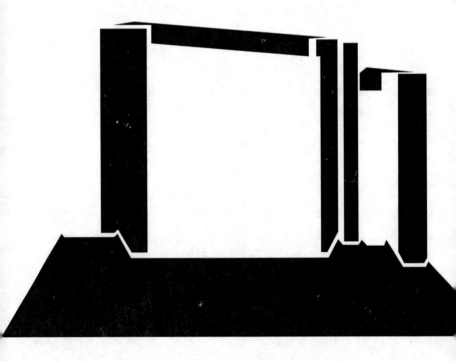

Taking the Flak

by Hannah Storm

The hotel overlooking Benghazi's corniche has seen better times. Still, it's hard not to imagine the glass shell as yet another gaudy example of a building erected in honour of the country's fallen dictator. Once it was a towering landmark for those who promenaded along the Mediterranean's edge. Now, it is a target for rebel fighters returning to Libya's second city.

Sun has fallen quickly here, and with it the heat. It's October, and daytime still brings unexpected temperatures, warm winds from the water, whipping up some of the dust from the desert that covers vast expanses of this country, turning Benghazi's streets red long before the recent bloodshed.

Inside, I know better than to stand at the full-length window overlooking the sea. Now I crouch on the floor of my hotel bedroom, the stained mattress propped against the window where I pushed it when the gunfire got so close I could feel the panes shudder. With hindsight I wonder if it was me shaking, more than the windows.

I listen to the sound of celebratory shots from the rebels returning from the frontline, shrink lower into my borrowed bulletproof jacket, turn the volume on the TV louder, trying to distract myself with news from elsewhere. But I can't make sense of the reports on the only English-language channel, or understand why there's nothing on screen about the situation here.

I tug my helmet down further, reach for my first aid pack, watch a cockroach skitter across the carpet, wonder if it's the one I saw earlier in the cracked tiles of the shower, remember how its filthy floor was plugged with pubic hair; evidence this place has not been cleaned since the exodus of Libya's migrant workers earlier in the year.

Between then and now in late 2011, Libya has become a battleground, with Benghazi the de facto capital of the rebels. But this is a city continuously conquered by different forces throughout history, and, in a country that has known no other political existence for almost half a century, it's hard to imagine how Benghazi will suddenly free itself from the iron grip of its immediate past. For now, this is a honeymoon period and there is hope. And with that hope, we have blown in.

Less than a week has passed since the capture and killing of Muammar Gaddafi, and I have just arrived here for work. I am here for what my colleagues term 'a mission'; a title that unsettles me, though we are not ministers of faith but of the Fourth Estate. We are here as international media experts to meet with representatives from a nascent

Libyan journalism industry; one that's grown out of the thirst for information after 42 years during which the only news was state-sanctioned government propaganda. Since the revolution, numerous news organisations have been formed, some of them owned by political factions, others purportedly more independent. All of them flailing a little in the space left by the removal of the regime.

If I am here for work, right now I am holding my breath, watching the cockroach creep across my bedroom. I wonder if it is undaunted by the shell it carries. I wonder if it even knows. I am anxious in my armour, feeling ill-equipped to protect myself against some of the dangers here. As the deputy director of a journalism safety charity, I wonder who signed-off on the risk assessment given this reality.

It's hours before the shots subside, hours when I fold myself foetal, counting the seconds between the shots

It's hours before the shots subside, hours when I fold myself foetal, counting the seconds between the shots, trying to recall the rare occasions when it's acceptable to use a tourniquet in first aid, hopeful I won't need it this time. I try to focus not on the grimy room or the time between bangs, but on the kind of future my colleagues say could be bright for Benghazi.

As I write this, more than a decade on, I know it is the kind of future that can only be imagined by those who avoid glancing into the corners or beneath the covers.

The next morning, I wake crumpled, craving coffee. I wet-wipe wash myself, twist deodorant on, untwist a clean shirt from my bag, long enough to cover my bottom. Downstairs, local men in white dish-dashes sit around tables with chipped vases and faded silk flowers. They puff on hookahs and cigarettes, exhaling another layer of grey to the stale air. A waiter skitters between them. A TV thumps with sound, and the men alternate their attention between it and me. I feel their eyes on my body as I creep to the back of the restaurant, searching for coffee, for a colleague.

From what I can tell, I am the only woman in this hotel, one of a group of foreign moths pulled to the flame still burning in the days after Gaddafi's death. Now, hope hangs in the musty air and we flit around, naively trying to tell a tale we will never properly understand. Having dodged the skeletons of military tanks on the airport runway and the sporadic gunfire of men in military garb, we are modern missionaries filling the vacuum between violence and peace or violence and violence, and we do so with nausea-inducing naivety.

I find a bowl of coffee granules, feel relief as I hear my name called by a colleague who has just returned from a run along the water. He is clutching a spent bullet, his eyes sparkling with the same glee my daughter shows when she picks up a penny from the pavement. He slips it into his pocket and I swallow my envy and discomfort at the ease of his experiences.

When I checked in, the man at the hotel front desk took my passport. I asked for it back when I headed to my room, but was told they needed to keep it. Now I return to the reception, steeled by coffee and a night of noise. The first man is not there.

'I do not have the key to the safe,' his substitute says, and I lower my gaze like the guide books tell me, noting it is one of the few pieces of advice still valid here from those travel tomes written for a world when Libya was still a tourist destination. In newsrooms back home, before we head to these hostile environments as journalists, we are told we should never get separated from our passports. But life is not as simple as the lessons we learn from the media safety teams who are mostly ex-military men telling us how it should be, yet failing to see how things often are for women.

Later, on the way to dinner, my bullet-wielding colleague tells me to relax, as if we are going out for a meal in Brussels, not Benghazi. His mate is whispering seductions into the satellite phone, using up the battery we're supposed to keep for emergencies to speak to the woman he loves. Both men questioned my choices when I admitted I had brought my bulletproof vest to Benghazi, so tonight I have left it back in the hotel. If I have taken leave of the safety kit, I fear they have taken leave of their senses, but I have been conditioned to go along with the men and, here especially, it does not pay to stand out. The headscarf I wear affords me some freedom to look out the window. We were supposed to be in convoy, but are driving alone, uncertain of our destination, reliant on the driver. The streets are packed with cars, the kerbs lined with the burnt or blown-up bodies of vehicles and buildings. Men squat on pavements, some of them waving weapons as if they were flags and I feel myself sweating, legs clenched, stomach churning, as if the rules of the road are as absent as the rules for war.

...I realise it's my judgement out of place here, not the desire of Libyans to chase their consumer dreams amid the chaos and uncertainty...

We are eating close to a place our local colleague tells us is known as Benghazi's Fifth Avenue. It's a far cry from Manhattan, but behind the windows there lives a world of liminal luxury. There are jewellery shops and toy stores stuffed with animals, dolls and miniature vehicles like the ones behind other windows where gaudily coloured sports cars seem to be the pick of the privileged. They are a far cry from the camouflaged, dull-hued vehicles that make up the majority on the streets now. It's as if I have slipped through a portal for a few seconds. Suddenly, I am jolted out of my window shopping by the whizz of a nearby bullet. As I hurry inside, I realise it's my judgement out of place here, not the desire of Libyans to chase their consumer dreams amid the chaos and uncertainty, even if those dreams are only affordable to a wealthy minority.

We hurry into a restaurant full of families, where tables are lined up with diners enjoying huge plates of French fries, spiced and seasoned meats, baskets with flat breads and dishes with salads and plump tomatoes, bottles of fizzy soda, sweet cakes for pudding. We spend the evening talking about music, families, homes and hopes, steering clear of conversation that might consider the real dreams of those here, just in case something said is overheard by the wrong people.

The best place to speak is in the car, though it's never that easy to concentrate on conversations when each journey seems to be a dance with death, where the soundtrack is a compilation of gunfire, horns and the ever-present music from the vehicle stereos. But it's on these journeys that I start to piece together a better picture of this place. I hear about the final weeks of Gaddafi, and the way he and his sons tormented this city.

A donkey was dressed in a football shirt, carrying Saadi's number. Days later, the leader got his revenge

On one journey, my colleague points at what was once a football ground for Al-Ahly Benghazi. He tells me the site was demolished and three fans sentenced to death on the orders of the Libyan leader. His son Saadi, who was connected with a rival side in Tripoli and head of the country's football federation, was alleged to have fixed matches to disadvantage the Benghazi team. Sick of a series of injustices against their side, local fans stormed the pitch after a game and burned a photo of the country's leader in a rare act of defiance. A donkey was dressed in a football shirt, carrying Saadi's number. Days later, the leader got his revenge. A decade on, Saadi was accused of ordering troops to shoot unarmed demonstrators, charges he denied. The story of Al-Ahly strikes me as a sign of the ruthlessness of the Gaddafi family when they ruled this land.

My Libyan colleague points out other sites where building work is planned, where international contracts are being tendered to transform this wasteland. Some construction projects seem to have stopped almost as soon as they started. Along the water's edge, development has already begun, while places that boarded their windows and shuttered themselves during the revolution are back in business. But elsewhere some will never open again.

Writing this now, I try to pinpoint on a map the restaurants, hotels, and other venues I visited during my time in Libya, knowing many will have been destroyed since that brief hiatus when we were there.

One lunch time, we are taken to a restaurant overlooking the water, not unlike places I have eaten at while on holiday in European coastal resorts. In the upstairs room of this fancy establishment overlooking the water, we are welcomed by the owner, offered platters of fresh fish and seafood. I move the food around my plate, eat little morsels, pushing down the sense of something awful so close to the surface.

A decade on, I wonder if that restaurant is still there. I suspect not.

The former Supreme Court overlooks Tahrir Square, a name given across the region where squares were renamed in honour of the 'liberation', however temporary. After the revolution, it was acquired by the rebels' National Transitional Council and a group of young volunteers transformed it into a media centre, with internet connection and a mobile phone network. We are invited inside and given a tour of the place, told how the phone lines and the internet in the city were cut to crush the spread of information and dissent, and how this centre came to offer an alternative to the official pro-government propaganda.

The walls are now decorated with satirical cartoons of Colonel Gaddafi which grossly exaggerate his features, images mocking the man who would have had people murdered for less of a crime than a caricature. Cartoons have long been an art of rebellion, a message of defiance in parts of the world where press freedom is compromised, but alongside these images are others: photos of some of the hundreds of people who have gone missing in the past few months. This is where desperate relatives and friends come, trying to find out the fate of their loved ones. It's a place that attracts international media too; this was a regular meeting place for foreign journalists covering the uprising. But the information shared here sometimes came at a cost. Mohammed 'Mo' Nabbous was one of the founders of the media centre. He launched Libya Alhurra – Free Libya – as a television channel, and was responsible for streaming the first live images to the world of the uprising in Tahrir Square. But he was killed by sniper fire when filming the fighting from the back of a truck with his mobile phone. His friends show me his photograph. He was just 28.

The pictures of others like Mo, killed in the uprising, cover the walls of Tahrir Square. It's Friday the first time we pass by, the day of prayer and, as they have every week, mourners gather to honour their sons and brothers – for they are mostly men – who died in the fighting. We decide not to stop, concerned our presence may cause a problem on this day. For the first time I am grateful for this decision, though not everyone thinks it is the right one. Later we will return and I will buy a Libyan flag, and we will walk alongside the tribute wall, noting how many of the men died on March 19, the day Gaddafi's forces started shelling the city. Like Mo, many of the dead were so young. The country's future. The country's past. My colleague tells me that those who died found purpose in their death, as if those alive are still seeking theirs. The next time we drive through these streets, I think of his words. I try to catch the expression on the faces of the young men who sit on the dusty kerbs, with their guns. Some of them must still be teenagers. They have nothing to do, but sit and wait. I wonder how many of them have already lost friends, and what the future holds for them when they do put down their weapons.

The Tibesti hotel has been long regarded as the most luxurious hotel in Benghazi. It is where some of the rest of our contingent is staying. A sign at the entrance to the lobby reminds those visiting that no guns are allowed. I watch as two men unsling their weapons, and push them through the security machine. I am beckoned around the edge of the detector with a wave of the security guard's hand; no need to remove my bag, or be scanned. I wonder how secure this place is. The lobby is full of people sitting at tables, men in shades wearing the uniform of government contractors I have seen in many places around the world. Five months earlier a bomb was detonated at almost the same spot where we have parked and this hotel made headlines, though it had long been known by journalists – and foreign diplomats – who kept it as one of their headquarters. But time is a fickle friend here, and now there is no sign of the damage caused by the bomb or any real determination on the part of the security to ensure safety.

I am increasingly worried about the dangers I face in this country and the future of the friends I have made

By the morning of our departure, I still don't have my passport. I am starting to worry I might not make my flight. I am increasingly worried about the dangers I face in this country and the future of the friends I have made. Since arriving, I have heard of other foreign female journalists who have been assaulted. We are frequently warned about the threat of kidnap but it still seems like a foreign word to my colleagues, though I sleep at night with my door locked and barricaded.

Less than a year after our visit, Benghazi will become synonymous with an attack that kills the

US ambassador. Even in the weeks that follow our visit, international organisations will start to leave because of the risks.

I remind myself the worst I can do in this situation where I need my passport is to lose my calm, so I plan my plea carefully. I remember what I learned years ago on a safety course for journalists, something about trying to find a human connection with everyone. Several minutes later, after a conversation that moves from asking after the duty manager's sister and mother, telling him I am a mother myself, and – like him – have a family to go home to, I have my passport back.

Now all that is needed is for the driver to turn up on time and to make the short journey to the airport. The man who arrives at the hotel to collect me is not the one I expect. Everything I know about security tells me this is a bad sign.

I have two options. I stay in the hotel, miss my flight and expose myself to several more days of heightening insecurity. Or I take a chance on this chauffeur, who says he has been sent by the other driver, and trust him when he says he will get me to my flight. It's a decision I hope I never have to make again.

A couple of hours later I am sitting on the plane, climbing into the clouds, the burned and battered streets of Benghazi disappearing below me. I look down at the cars creeping like insects, and those crushed and immobilised by the side of the kerbs. I think about the cockroach and wonder if it is still roaming that filthy room far below. I remember the fear I felt that first night. Grateful to escape, I know I am lucky to do so. **H**

RSL AWARDS
SUBMISSIONS SUMMER '22

The Royal Society of Literature

ALL RSL
**AWARDS &
PRIZES**

SKY ARTS RSL WRITERS AWARDS
DEADLINE: 31 JULY

IN PARTNERSHIP WITH **SKY ARTS**, THE SKY ARTS RSL WRITERS
AWARDS **CELEBRATE AND NURTURE BRITISH WRITERS OF
COLOUR** AT THE **BEGINNINGS OF THEIR CAREERS.**

- **FIVE** WINNERS, **TEN** MENTORING SESSIONS, **TWELVE** MONTHS
- **TWO** ADDITIONAL SESSIONS WITH **AWARDS AMBASSADOR AND
  RSL PRESIDENT** BERNARDINE EVARISTO
- 2022 **MENTORS**: JAY BERNARD, INUA ELLAMS, NADIFA
  MOHAMED, VINAY PATEL AND NIKESH SHUKLA

**INFO &
SUBMISSIONS**

RSL LITERATURE MATTERS AWARDS
DEADLINE: 24 AUGUST

THE **RSL LITERATURE MATTERS AWARDS** AIM TO **REWARD AND ENABLE LITERARY EXCELLENCE AND INNOVATION**.

OPEN CALL FOR PROPOSALS, AIMED AT INDIVIDUAL WRITERS OR OTHER LITERARY CREATORS
£20,000 TO BE SPLIT AMONG THE WINNERS
FINANCIAL SUPPORT TO UNDERTAKE **A PROPOSED NEW PIECE OF WRITING/LITERARY PROJECT**

2022 **JUDGES**: MELANIE ABRAHAMS, SOPHIE COLLINS AND **IAN DUHIG**

INFO & SUBMISSIONS

RSL GILES ST AUBYN AWARDS FOR NON-FICTION
DEADLINE: 14 SEPTEMBER

THE **RSL GILES ST AUBYN AWARDS** RECOGNISE **FIRST-COMMISSIONED WRITERS OF NON-FICTION** BY PROVIDING **FINANCIAL SUPPORT FOR TALENTED NEW WRITERS** TO COMPLETE THEIR FIRST BOOK FOR A MAINSTREAM AUDIENCE.

INFO & SUBMISSIONS

- **THREE AWARDS** (£10,000, £5,000, £2,500)
- 2022 **JUDGES**: HOMI K. BHABHA, FIONA BOYLE AND VIOLET MOLLER

El Chaltén

by Alison Baxter

I t was quite possibly the best ice cream I've ever had, and the most unlikely. The sharp, sweet hit of frozen lemon and ginger was just what I needed to soothe my throat and bring down my temperature. I had a cold. A bad one. It had been going around the group for a week and now it was my turn. So instead of trekking to the Fitz Roy base camp with the others I was going for my own gentle hike. To be honest, I was glad of the excuse. I've rarely felt so out of place as I did in El Chaltén. It is a destination for experienced climbers in well-worn boots, grubby shorts and faded T-shirts, displaying muscular, sunburnt arms and legs. At the end of each day, they crowd the bars and cafés, drinking beer and eating pizza, swapping stories of perilous routes and lucky escapes. I had recently turned 69 years old and although I could still walk for miles on the flat, I soon became breathless going uphill. But I was happy to be here, in this remote valley, eating Italian-quality ice cream with the jagged, steel-grey peaks of Patagonia as a backdrop.

The Andes rise in sheer granite spikes so steep that snow settles only on the very tops. It is a landscape where you quickly run out of superlatives. The small town of El Chaltén straddles the dead-end road that skirts the shore of Lago Viedma in the National Park of Los Glaciares and stops short of the Chilean border. High up in the mountains there is a lot of potential for confusion about where exactly the frontier lies, so forty years ago Argentina decided to lay visible claim to the land at the base of Mount Fitz Roy and settlers moved in to stake out their territory. The main street of El Chaltén feels familiar to anyone who has ever watched John Wayne swagger into town.

Mount Fitz Roy is the reason people come here now. Named for the captain of the *Beagle*, that extraordinary naval officer who invented the weather forecast, served for a traumatic few years as governor of New Zealand, and died by his own hand in 1865 at the age of 60, it has another identity that predates the arrival of European adventurers and colonisers. The Tehuelche call it El Chaltén: the smoking mountain. This is a land of smoke and mirrors, of clouds, myths and tall tales: Magellan's tribe of giants who gave their name to Patagonia, the pioneering pilots of the early airmail service, and numerous missing climbers.

That morning I climbed the steep path to the dramatically named lookout of the condors, the Mirador de los Cóndores. It was December and the wildflowers were in bloom, yellow citrus-scented *paramela* with ruffled green leaves like lengths of braid waiting to be stitched, silvery-grey bushes of *neneo* that could be mistaken for a sort of mutant lavender tipped with bright scarlet, and nameless purple flowers, petals thin as tissue paper, peeping from behind tufts of rough grass. Day trippers crowded the route, giggling young people slipping and sliding in their flip flops, clutching at each other, stopping for selfies at every turn, or racing up, agile in their light sneakers. I trudged behind, leaden-footed in my walking boots. I didn't want to turn my ankle on the uneven, pebble-strewn path. From time to time I stopped to look back at the neat grid of streets decreasing in size until the concrete buildings with their tin roofs resembled the miniature houses of a toy village. And on the horizon, the distinctive ziggurat of Fitz Roy and his companions.

...waves breaking on the barren shore, chunks of brilliant white ice broken off from the glacier, like scoops of sorbet drifting in the sky-blue water

The day trippers, oblivious to everything but the mountains, stopped at the viewing point, took more photos, and made their way back down to the coach park. I turned my back on Fitz Roy and walked for another half hour till I reached the second lookout, the Mirador de las Águilas. An eagle's eye view of a vast, open expanse of muddy-brown earth and sparse, grey-green scrub. Far away in the distance was Lago Viedma, waves breaking on the barren shore, chunks of brilliant white ice broken off from the glacier, like scoops of sorbet drifting in the sky-blue water. I sat down on a weathered terracotta rock, completely alone except for the dark shape that floated below me, a condor circling in the updraft, its huge wingspan dwarfed by the landscape. It was an ideal spot for peaceful meditation, with only the gusting wind for company.

It is hard to empty your mind. Thoughts crowd in to fill the space. You observe them moving across your consciousness. Gentle like grazing guanacos or fierce as mountain lions, they appear and, when they're ready, take their leave again. That day, in the foggy, feverish state that accompanied my cold, I was visited by the shadows of the missing and the dead. One of the needle points that flank Cerro Fitz Roy is named for the writer Antoine de Saint-Exupéry, who flew this route in the 1930s, in often treacherous conditions, carrying the first airmail for Aeroposta Argentina. I imagine him in the open cockpit of his single-engine Potez, armoured against the cold in helmet, goggles, scarf and gloves, gliding like a condor over the mountains. The peak next to Saint-Exupéry bears the name of chief pilot Jean Mermoz, pioneer of the daring night flying that made the airmail service competitive. He once landed on a mountain shelf just 300 metres wide and, after effecting repairs to his plane, took off again by simply rolling over the edge of the precipice. Alongside him rises another spike, named for the legendary Henri Guillaumet, who crash-landed on a frozen lake on his ninety-second flight and walked out through the mountains to safety.

I have always felt safer as a passenger in a small plane than in a modern airliner, more connected to the wings, more conscious of the cradling atmosphere that holds me up. Except once, in a thunderstorm that reduced visibility to zero and tossed us around in the clouds, preventing us from landing for a very long half hour. The early aviators risked their lives with every flight, driven by a spirit of adventure and in pursuit of commercial advantage. Mermoz, for all his skill, vanished off the African coast in 1936. These airmen faced the constant threat of mechanical failure or bad weather, as Saint-Exupéry describes in his autobiographical novel *Vol de Nuit*. We follow his fictional pilot, Fabien, in constant radio communication with the airstrips along his route, hoping for a safe landing place as the storm closes in around him, leaving him with no way out. His messages become more and more fragmented until finally he disappears from the airwaves.

The outbreak of war brought new risks for those who continued to fly. Guillaumet was shot down over the Mediterranean in 1940 and four years later Saint-Exupéry himself was lost on a reconnaissance flight from Corsica, aged 44. The wreckage of his plane was eventually identified in the sea near Marseilles and his silver bracelet dredged up in a fishing net, but no one knows why he crashed. Was it enemy action, an accident, or a deliberate decision to end his own life? As a writer, he is best known for his fable of the Little Prince, an apparently simple children's book about a boy who lives on a tiny planet with a single rose bush as his companion. Since it was first published, the year before Saint-Exupéry disappeared, adult readers have interpreted the underlying moral in myriad different ways. The author's death created a further myth to add to the multiple layers of the story.

I have the telegram, a scrap of yellowing paper in a mundane brown envelope, to mark the end of a preciouus life

Gazing out over the emptiness of the Patagonian plain, sipping cold water from my metal flask, I found myself reflecting on a painful void within my own family. Fabien fails to return from his night flight carrying the European mail to Buenos Aires. 'Failed to return' (FTR) was how the RAF recorded aircraft that never came back from more deadly missions. One of them was my uncle's Halifax bomber. During his training he wrote letters home, cheerfully describing night flying as jolly good fun. Getting lost was a game, he declared. You just landed in a field near a fine-looking house to be in with a chance of a good meal. 'Prang,' he explained with schoolboy humour, was a new verb. 'I prang, thou prangest and so on,' while in a more poetic moment he wrote of climbing up to the cool heights and peacefully gliding down. But his final landing was far from tranquil. He was still only 21 years-old when, returning from a bombing mission over the Ruhr in 1943, he was forced to ditch his plane in the North Sea. I have the telegram, a scrap of yellowing paper in a mundane brown envelope, to mark the end of a precious life.

It was an absence that haunted my childhood, although I did not fully understand the lingering distress of the grown-ups around me. 'Missing in action' is a kind of limbo. At first my grandparents wanted to believe that their boy had been taken prisoner and would return at the end of the war. But as the months went by that hope wore thin, until the most they could wish for was that the tide would wash his body ashore on a Dutch beach. Even that consolation was denied them and my uncle would never have a grave, although his name appears on the Air Forces Memorial at Runnymede. Not quite the same as having a mountain named after you, but still a kind of public remembrance.

Loss is not always so dramatic. People go missing in different ways, leaving spaces for us to fill with imagination. A lover's quarrel ends in separation, friends drift apart, families fall out. From my eyrie I watched a solitary horseman ride out from a distant cluster of buildings far below, emphasising the scale of the emptiness around him, and thought of the gaps that have appeared, like moth holes, in the fabric of my own life. One of them has now been mended, although I am still aware of it as a darn of a different texture. My cousin, who was lost, has now been found. His father chose to cut himself off from the family for reasons that no one will ever fully understand. My brother and I called him our disappearing uncle and invented all sorts of dubious life choices that might have made it necessary for him to vanish. We never imagined that he had a secret wife and a son who was just three months younger than me. I and my unknown cousin should have been playmates and friends but instead we grew up in ignorance of each other to live similar lives, both with a gift for languages and a yearning to see the world. We finally met just a year before my trip to Patagonia, a trip that my cousin was once the tour leader for. It seemed fitting that he should have been the one to tell me a story as mysterious as that of Saint-Exupéry, one that came back to haunt me as I sat on my rock, light-headed with fever, dreaming the dead back to life.

She agreed to sit and wait while the others went on up the mountain trail but when they came back down she was nowhere to be seen

My cousin and his group were making the trek that I missed up to the Fitz Roy base camp when one member of the party decided not to continue. I know virtually nothing about her, not her physical appearance nor even her name, but I imagine her as unremarkable in every way. She agreed to sit and wait while the others went on up the mountain trail but when they came back down she was nowhere to be seen. They hunted and called for her but got no reply so eventually assumed she had decided to return to the hostel on her own; not a very sensible decision but not necessarily dangerous. When they arrived back in El Chaltén they discovered she was not there either and no one had seen her. That was when my cousin started to worry that she had had an accident. Search parties were sent out to scour the mountain paths but she was never seen again.

There are so many ways you could write her story as fiction. They all exist in parallel universes, any one of them as true as the next. I shivered a little as I held my cool flask to my burning forehead and tried out various possibilities in my head. A helicopter lands on the mountainside and carries her away. A ghostly, golden puma lures her through a rent in the atmosphere to another world. A stranger pushes her over the edge of the narrow trail to an ambiguous end. Or perhaps she simply walks out of her ordinary life, not even stopping to collect her luggage, thumbing a lift with some passing motorist who, if he later hears the news of her disappearance, chooses not to get involved.

There are so many ways you could write her story as fiction. They all exist in parallel universes, any one of them as true as the next

This last scenario is almost plausible but I am not writing fiction and in the end I opt for the most obvious and saddest explanation of all. Either the woman set off to walk down the mountain and fell into a hidden crevasse, as happens even to experienced climbers. Or she chose to end her own life. I see her walking, not down towards the village but up and away from the main trail. She is thinking of Fitz Roy and the 'thing of darkness' that drove him to pick up his razor in despair, and of Saint-Exupéry, whose plane was found miles off course with no bullet holes. But she may also be remembering the story of the Little Prince, who returns to his planet and his beloved rose, taking

with him the sheep that Saint-Exupéry drew for
him. 'I will look as if I'm dead,' he says, 'but that
won't be true,' consoling his new friend with the
thought that what he will leave behind on earth is
just an empty husk. The Little Prince himself will
be back home on his asteroid, one of the multitude
of fireflies that glow in the night sky. In my version
of her story, the anonymous woman spreads her
wings and launches herself into space, trusting in
the forgiving air to catch her, cocoon her, and carry
her spirit to the stars. ◲

Life Is a Great Entanglement

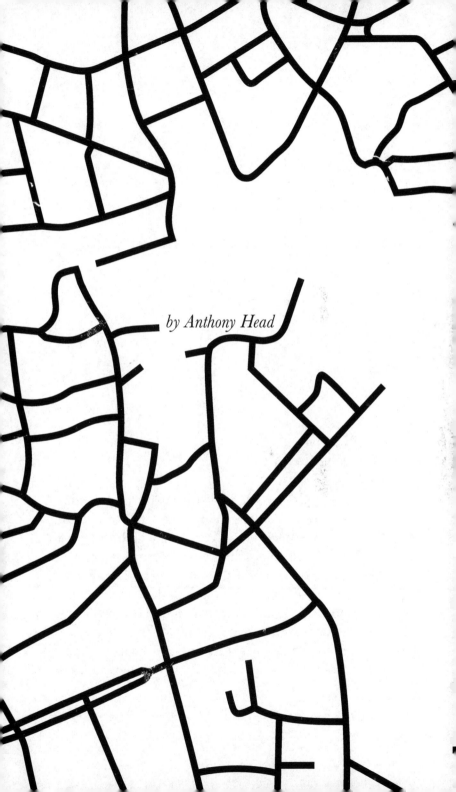

by Anthony Head

Two young women came dashing down the train corridor, laughing and exuberant, then dashing back again. When they had rushed past for the third or fourth time, Gerard, my travelling companion, and I stuck our heads out of our compartment to see what all the commotion was about. Within minutes we found ourselves engaged in conversation with the two tour guides of a group of Czech engineers visiting the Soviet Union: Jana from Prague and Miroslava from Lviv in Ukraine.

It was October 1st, 1982. We were taking a long and largely overland route back to the UK from Japan, where we had both spent a couple of years as English teachers. We were now on a slow journey from Tashkent to Samarkand, but were soon passing the hours talking, eating and drinking with the jovial Czechs in their compartments. When it transpired that we were staying at the same hotel in Samarkand, Jana and Mirka took us under their wing, effectively adding us to their tour free of charge, having us eat with them at their dinner table.

For me it was the start of several relationships that have had a profound effect on my life. Prague was on our itinerary and Jana gave us her address, insisting that we stay with her. Three weeks later we were on another train moving through the breathtaking Moravian and Bohemian countryside – thick forests of pine and the most silver birches I had ever seen, ablaze with golden leaves, tranquil lakes, green and yellow fields, an occasional house and flock of sheep. We arrived in Prague mid-afternoon and, with the help of the *Čedok* tourist agency, made our way to Jana's apartment in the Holešovice area, where we found her sitting at her kitchen window peeling potatoes. 'My boys!' she called on spotting us.

We had come via some beautiful and impressive cities – Moscow, Kiev, Sofia, Istanbul, Athens, Budapest, Vienna – but I was not prepared for Prague, for its astonishing blend of Gothic and Romanesque, of Baroque and Neoclassical, of Art Nouveau and Cubism, its churches, monasteries,

narrow cobbled alleys, gardens, bridges, town squares
and hidden courtyards. I felt that sense of wonder
most first-time visitors to the city must experience,
but something more – not déjà vu exactly, but a
sense of comfort and compatibility, a feeling of
belonging, of having arrived at a place unknown
that was somehow already and strangely *home*.

Prague is the only place that has ever impelled me, on my numerous visits over the years, to keep diaries

Prague is the only place that has ever impelled
me, on my numerous visits over the years, to keep
diaries – often a series of hurriedly scribbled notes
of conversations, people, places, sights that I don't
want ever to forget. I read these entries now and
see an unsurprising pattern in places – *knedlíky* and
Budvar in this or that pub, coffee in a courtyard
or riverside café, museums, concerts, trips to
the country or other towns and villages, and a
Beckerovka as a nightcap, or sometimes at breakfast
to start the day with a kick. Like any actual resident
of Prague, I can never number the times I have
crossed Charles Bridge or walked around Wenceslas
Square or up and down Petrin Hill. I sometimes
need to consult a map to find my way around
London, and although I have lived in Tokyo for half
my life now, it is central Prague that I have come to
know like the back of my hand.

That first visit was all too brief, though we got to
know Staré Mesto, the Old Town and Hradčany,
the Castle District, guided by Jana and her friend

Hanka, who was astonished to see us devouring *knedlíky* as she had never seen a non-Czech eat the national dumpling. One evening we visited a jazz club underground where a Dixieland band was playing acceptable music, and on the next we found ourselves in the Church of St. Nicholas, that baroque masterpiece in Malá Strana, for an organ recital – it was absolutely packed, with people squatting and lying all over the floor, mainly youths who would not have looked out of place at Woodstock. Most of another day was wasted, as was often the case in the 1980s, at a police station in Olšanská enacting a pantomime to extend our visa for an extra day. The policeman's office was bare but for his desk and chair, some pieces of crockery, and five volumes of Lenin beside his Czech-English dictionary.

But the encounter that sticks in my mind was a conversation that a lively old man struck up with us on a bridge one evening. He was 75, spoke fluent English and German, and although 'retired' still made a living from money-changing, giving most of the proceeds to his granddaughter. With us he seemed more eager to convey his hatred of the regime, denouncing socialism for depriving people of the brains and courage to start an 'uprising'. He said dictatorship requires five per cent sadists and ten per cent idiots and it will work perfectly well. He had never been a member of the Party himself, but his wife had until 1968 when she discovered what it was all about. Even Party members don't believe their own propaganda, he said, but 'This is the land of the blind where the one-eyed man is king.'

As soon as I was able to, I visited Prague again. It was August 1984. Jana was not at home when I arrived, so I waited on a wall outside. A car pulled up and a tall, attractive lady walked up the path to the apartment and rang Jana's bell.

She came back out, looked at me and smiled: 'You are Tony. You will come with me for dinner.' So began another precious friendship with Anna and her husband Otakar. At their flat in Troja we talked of films and literature. A tour guide and university teacher, Anna had three questions for me: do British people believe anything? (I think she meant religiously, but I do not recall my answer.) Do I think there will be a Third World War? (Anna did.) And what recent films have there been in Britain? (I mentioned *Chariots of Fire* and *Gandhi*, though these had not yet been shown in Prague.)

'You know Orwell,' Anna said. '*1984* is here, now. It's invisible, but it's here.' Anna and Otakar had been in England in 1968 where they had seen the Russian 'panzers' on TV and, like all other Czechs abroad at that time, faced the painful decision on whether or not to return to their homeland, knowing the likely consequences. Parental ties had settled the issue, as they had for so many, and now it was impossible for them to travel outside the Eastern Bloc. Anna and Otakar were both fluent in German, she in Danish also, and only her own exacting linguistic standards made her think her English wasn't up to scratch.

That trip was memorable for many reasons. An evening concert in the gardens of Wallenstein Palace, with the moths fluttering in the spotlights and the pinnacles of St. Vitus Cathedral and Hradčany pricking the air illuminated above, was a moment of sublimity; the ridiculous came later with Jana cursing in Italian her 'cretina politika Bolshevik' oven, which conked out one evening when she was making a pizza and couldn't be relit until it had cooled down completely. The eventual product proved tasty enough, but Jana just pointed to the sole of her shoe. She was, like many Czechs, a wonderful linguist, fluent in Russian also, and never afraid to embark on an explanation in her more limited English even if it meant completing it in sign language. My Czech was non-existent, but my Latin sometimes stood me in good stead when she lapsed into Italian in frustration and laughter.

She was, like many Czechs, a wonderful linguist, fluent in Russian also, and never afraid to embark on an explanation in her more limited English

On that trip too I made my first visit to Ústí nad Labem, at that time a depressing town marred by chemical factories, to visit Jana's sister and her three young nieces who lived in a large house on the outskirts of the town, and then the next day to Chulmec where Mirka now lived. Apart from tour guiding, Jana also worked at the mathematical faculty of Charles University. She took me there for lunch one day. One of her colleagues had set up his own bar in the machine tool factory. He had pictures of naked women and an American flag in his locker, only the latter of which he had been ordered to remove. Another colleague secretly kept posters of Ronald Reagan and Margaret Thatcher in his. And with another, Miloš, I struck up an instant rapport and spent several hours drinking beer in his office – at least, that's how it started.

'Tony,' he said, in his soothing baritone, 'we Czech people, when we drink beer, we also like to drink... rum'

'Tony,' he said, in his soothing baritone, 'we Czech people, when we drink beer, we also like to drink... rum.' He duly reappeared from beneath his desk with a bottle of the chaser, and I have no recollection or record of how I got back to Jana's flat.

I made further visits from London in 1987 and 1989 during my vacations from Tokyo, after the usual rigmarole in getting my visas issued at the Czech Embassy, each time making new acquaintances and with that sense of belonging ever more intense and mysterious.

But it is now 1990. The Velvet Revolution has taken place and Vaclav Havel is president. I arrive on August 20th and for the first time there is no obligatory money changing on the train at the Czech border, no need to reacquaint myself with the threadbare library at Olšanská police station. The train is an hour late due to an accident at

Holešovice and does not stop there as planned. It is early evening when I arrive at the central station, Hlavní nádraží, which is more crowded than I have ever seen it. I need change to make a phone call, and I am buying a snack of some sort from a kiosk when suddenly I hear my name and Anna is waving to me. Otakar has the car outside and together we drive around the city.

'Welcome back to Prague,' Anna says, with a gesture of typical inclusivity, '*our* Prague, Tony.' We park and walk.

Post-revolution Wenceslas Square is abuzz. On Charles Bridge jazz bands and Spanish guitarists vie for attention. People are singing Czech songs and passersby join in. Illuminated Hradčany towers over the city, seeming to me then as it always does the most beautiful sight in Europe. All the while Anna is feeding me with salami buns. On Hradčany the guards are wearing new uniforms; designed, Anna tells me, by Theodor Pištěk, who won the Oscar for his costumes for *Amadeus* (directed by another Czech, Miloš Forman).

'The revolution is like much theatre for Czech people,' she says. Young couples are walking hand-in-hand and looking out over the city below. 'I am optimistic again,' Anna says, 'sceptical but optimistic. I believe that Prague will again be the central point of Europe.'

Jana is away on a tour in Lithuania, so I stay with Anna and Otakar in their new house just outside the city. On television I see CNN broadcasts, the first visible sign of Western media.

Anna says, of course the Czechs know it is also propaganda of a kind – American news, American weather, American viewpoints. But Czech TV is now showing programmes about the revolution and post-war Czech history.

'Imagine, for the first time in our adult lives we can watch the truth about what has been happening, here on our own TV,' Anna says. I say they have lived through extraordinary times – to have seen 1968 *and* 1989. She nods. 'But nothing can give back Ota his health' – he had developed asthma as a result of the factory work he had to do – 'and nothing can give back the lost years.'

The next day is the 22nd anniversary of the Russian invasion. Wenceslas Square is packed. An old Russian tank turned on its side forms the backdrop to a stage where Alexander Dubcek and Havel give speeches. Havel says the first step has been made but now everyone must make the second. Walking with Anna in Malá Strana, I see some posters of Havel with imprints of lipstick on them.

'We love him,' says Anna, who had first met Havel at a friend's wedding a few years previously. 'We call him our "duckling". He looks a bit like a duck when he walks with his head forward and his bottom out.' Then after a pause: 'I have never seen *Brezhnev* kissed.'

That evening we watch a TV documentary about the Prague Spring – an endless catalogue of people who had lost their livelihoods and some, their lives. The footage shows young Soviet soldiers and everywhere, Czechs surrounding their tanks, talking to the soldiers, pleading with them to go home; they can see there is no counter-revolution. Then peace turned into violence. Hundreds were shot at, killed or injured.

'The soldiers are leaving now, next year,' says Anna. 'After 22 years, *22 years*.' She knows many of those being interviewed in the documentary. 'You are lucky I cannot speak English, because I could tell you many stories. I know many fates... terrible, terrible stories.'

'You are lucky I cannot speak English, because I could tell you many stories. I know many fates... terrible, terrible stories'

The next day we lunch in the renowned U Sixtu restaurant. People are talking at nearby tables – Spanish, Yugoslavs, Czechs. Anna smiles, listening. 'You know, these table talks, every day all over the world they are taking place, everywhere, everywhere. And they solve *nothing* ... But men like them especially. They like to show their knowledge and how they would solve all those problems ... Sometimes I feel like going over and saying "Shut up!"' She laughs. '"Shut up and *read*!"'

Jana returns for the last three days of my visit. We walk through Prague and talk and eat and drink, and laugh as ever, and again with Hanka she sees me off at the station as I leave this time for Paris.

Two years later I am back again. It is May 25th and Jana meets me at Hlavní nádraží at 9.15 am (after a sleepless journey in a carriage shared with some pleasant elderly German ladies who had wanted the window open all night). A nap and a light lunch later and we are walking through the Old Town again and across Charles Bridge to Malá Strana, where we have a beer at a roadside café. By now the changes in Prague are visible in the many new shops and renovations. My heart sinks a little at the sight of McDonalds and Chicago Pizza, and the adverts on the trams for Marlboro cigarettes. There are many more foreigners in the city now – Germans, Italians, Americans, some of them in Wenceslas Square, behaving as if they were in their own countries. The square is lively, but there's a hint of something sinister lurking. The women are as well-attired and attractive as ever but several stand apart here and there, almost inconspicuously. 'Prostitutes,' Jana says gaily, though in my naivety I would never have assumed it. The new English language newspaper *Prague Post* reports an increase in crime.

'The holiday is over for the Czechs,' Jana says. With the advent of capitalism prices have gone up (as the tourists pour in) but not Czech salaries. Most Czechs cannot afford to spend even one night in any of the city's main hotels. The average salary is about 4000 koruna a month, about 80 pounds, Jana says. I had been thinking of quitting Japan for a year or two and living in Prague, with the aim of learning Czech and writing – but I lacked the tenacity to make such a drastic change at that point in my life, when I had been settled again in Tokyo for several years and making my way into journalism and publishing. Or perhaps I felt that

Prague was already absorbing too much of the detritus of Western capitalism that would deprive it of its uniqueness. Jana says there are now too many 'stupid American films'. *Dallas* has hit the TV screens, and posters in the city centre promote the latest Schwarzenegger bloodbath.

—

In the mid-1990s I was delighted to have the chance to reciprocate and have Jana and Anna visit the UK, to show them the sights of London and the delights of the West Country. They were enchanted by the B&Bs we stayed at, the countryside, the cream tea shops, the cathedral cities; the weather was kind and we swam one sunny day in the sea at Durdle Door.

But these millennial years have passed so rapidly. The half-dozen trips I have managed have had that reassuring pattern, what Prague encourages so easefully – strolling, sitting, drinking, chatting, observing – but allied to a new confidence with the political shift from East to West.

In March 2010, just as four years after working on assignment at the World Cup in Germany, I arrived in Ústí from Berlin, making that pleasant and leisurely train trip alongside the Elbe. I was met by Jana's nieces, now grown women themselves, for a reunion in their house of laughter. In Prague, I found Jana now walking with a stick, having had five pins in her ankle and foot, but her energy undiminished. As salaries did eventually improve, and with the still-greater influx of tourists, her workload had increased, and she was now having her flat completely renovated. At an Easter Market in the Old Town Square she bought some traditional decorated eggs for my parents. I carried these home as protectively as if they had been crafted by Fabergé, a delicate balancing act compounded after Ludwig, another friend I had made through Jana, came to see me off at Ruzyně airport and suddenly handed me six bottles of Pilsner to add to my hand luggage.

Two years later, on a trip to the UK from Tokyo with my wife Kazuno, we made a quick visit to Prague, her first. Jana, Anna, Mirka, Hanka – all take her instantly to their hearts, as she takes them and Prague to hers, overwhelmed by the friendliness and beauty of it all. We promise to visit again soon, but 'life intervenes' in many ways and it is not until November 2019 that we can fly from Tokyo to Vienna (there are still no flights between Japan and the Czech Republic) and then make the four-hour journey onward by train. Jana meets us and the following day we drive with another old friend Honza to Ústí for introductions and again reunions – all the nieces now with young children of their own. The greater economic freedom for women has borne fruit in more ways than one. Around the dining table, an endless flow of talk and food and beer and wine, and suddenly the 'girls' burst into welcoming song, as I had heard them do 35-plus years ago when they were the children, and

I, at the blending of their voices again, can't stop my tears from overflowing.

With Jana and Honza we also visit Svatá Hora, the magnificent old Baroque monastery near Příbram, and spend a couple of peaceful hours there, then drive on to Tábor. Now 75, Jana relies on her stick but still exudes the enthusiasm of her younger self. But she and Honza rest at a café while we wander around that charming historic hill-top town, with its picture-postcard square and narrow cobbled streets, marking it as another place to revisit one day.

In Prague we are staying with Anna, she and Kazuno enjoying their coffee and cigarettes on the patio. Kazuno too seems very much at home – and amazed by the variety of meats and cheeses and breads at the local supermarket (almost the first thing she does on returning to Japan is sign up for some Czech lessons). We have a joyful meeting with Mirka in an antiques shop off Wenceslas Square where she now works, and another with Hanka at a café nearby, and on our last evening Jana takes us on a boat trip along the Vltava. It is overcast and drizzly, but just clear enough for a view of Hradčany towering over the far bank.

The next day, when it is time for another of the wrenching farewells I never get used to, Anna drops us at Hlavní nádraží, but doesn't stay (the explosion of traffic on the roads is another striking difference from earlier years). We meet Jana inside the station, which had for so long been perennially gloomy; now it is bright at last and easy to negotiate. We walk at Jana's pace to the platform and with kisses and waves and yet more promises, we are off back to Vienna.

The passing years had already taken their sorrowful toll, with the loss of Otakar, Miloš and Ludwig. Shortly after our return to Tokyo came the news of Jana's terminal illness. She faced it with great courage, typically organizing the funeral herself, even composing the eulogy. She had the blessing of her marvellous nieces to look after her at home, where she saw out her last days as she had wished, passing away peacefully in her sleep in the spring of 2020. Her ashes lie buried in the garden at Ústí.

I have never forgotten what Jana taught me when we first met; the saying she would get me to repeat to the great mirth of her numerous friends: *život je zašmodrchaný* – 'life is a great entanglement'. Indeed it is, and Jana's often was. She never married, though once came too close for comfort. She had her share of heartbreaks, and had broken some hearts herself. But her extraordinary vivacity was the core of her being. She would always be up early, smoking by the window, organising the day ahead, arranging something for somebody. Whenever she seemed tired, I would tell her she should take a rest. 'I shall rest in my grave' would be her response.

Of a multitude of memories, the singing and the laughter imprint themselves indelibly. On one occasion in 1987, walking with Jana and her colleagues Míša, Eva and Micheala on a cool evening in peaceful Stromovka Park, I suddenly heard the voices of angels. Softly, spontaneously, they had all begun to sing, in the easy and delightful harmonizing that seems second nature to the Czechs. I felt I was in a dream world, walking a little behind them as I savoured every syllable of this beautiful, uncomprehended language and a song I imagined to be about love or the longing for freedom.

With Jana I had a spontaneous friendship, a gift unlooked for but lovingly given and lovingly received, one that has had a deeper impact on my emotional and imaginative life than any other. I cherish the memories of all our moments together, but also her legacy to me – the many friends I made through her, and their families. I am always moved by the confluence of fates that brought us together, all stemming from the sight of two high-spirited women in the corridor of a train from Tashkent to Samarkand.

My plan to relocate to the UK as retirement looms is influenced in part by the greater proximity of Prague. For while the politicians in Europe and the systems they create will come and go, as the years pass what always remains is what Hilaire Belloc identified and so greatly prized:

> 'From quiet homes and first beginning,
> Out to the undiscovered ends,
> There's nothing worth the wear of winning,
> But laughter and the love of friends.'

This I have found more than anywhere else in my personal world in Bohemia. ◼

M.B.L.A.

by Sylvia K Ilahuka

A house stands on the Dar es Salaam coastline; white walls, brown roof tiles, coconut trees all around.

Home to a family returning home after a decade-plus abroad. Painstakingly built with remittances, in an era before the internet, which meant an extra helping of faith and trust that the sea would not swallow your money and have you washing up onto bare sand. (Sometimes it still did.)

The house is in Mbezi Beach, walking distance from the waters, in the second-last row of plots permitted before the ocean. Built in the bushes, before the masses discovered and descended upon the beauty of the 30-odd kilometres north of the city centre. So far out and made remote by the untarred roads, that the family's daughter wonders why her parents had to build so far away that her friends can't come over to play.

'Wait and see, my child; in ten years this place will be packed.'

To a child, ten years is a lifetime – and then some.

But they weren't wrong either, as fence after fence went up and mansion after mansion rose within their walls.

Still the little house stood.

If houses could talk, what would this one say?

Would it tell of the struggle to grow grass in the sandy soil, where the brackish water wouldn't let a lawn rise in peace? Or would it tell of the piles of loam soil and different varieties of manure, trucked in to coax a layer of green?

There was a tree in the yard, its branches forming a Y perfect for nestling a little girl's form. Until it had to be cut down to form the centre of a coconut thatch gazebo that the engineer father designed himself – anchoring the compass where the tree used to be, mapping out where each of the six sides would go, exactly what lengths of timber would be needed. It was exactly enough.

The perimeter coconuts, deadly when they grew taller than the fence and the wind shook them hard enough. Multipurpose trees, those: nuts with refreshing water, sweet flesh that can be squeezed into milk, husks for kindling, leaves for thatching, sap for fermenting into libation.

Would it tell of the three whole years that the garden lay dormant, grieving the death of the mother? She had been the one who talked to the plants as she watered them; in the wake of her demise no amount of rainfall or sunshine could bring forth flowers or fruit. It was three years before the family – or what was left of it – sampled a pawpaw from the backyard again.

The backyard was a mishmash of veggies, sprouted from the seeds that piggybacked out with the kitchen scraps

The triangular patch in the driveway had been planted for the daughter's First Communion, so that there'd be roses in time for the party that was thrown that Sunday afternoon. The backyard was a mishmash of veggies, sprouted from the seeds that piggybacked out with the kitchen scraps. Beans today, corn tomorrow, tomatoes every day, a random rice seedling here and there. A mint bush to soothe sore tummies and lemongrass for tea. Who-knows-what-else in the area where the chicken run used to be, the soil fertile from years of droppings. Two mango trees, one variety from each grandmother, towering over the unmarked patches where the family dogs were buried.

Would it tell of the delight that rang in the
living room when Bob Marley was played on
Saturday afternoons?
Would it tell of many a frustrated homework
session and many a stressed exam study period?
Would it tell of the cosy family times before
the furniture arrived and when power went off
for three straight weeks?
Would it tell of the beatings that resounded
when the brothers angered the father?
Would it tell of the secrets giggled during the
sister's childhood sleepovers?
Would it tell of the prayers sent up for the
cancer that wore on the mother?
Would it tell of dreams refashioned by the sour
realities of life?

Would it keep our secrets or would it spill over?

As the house grew older, it became an object of
affection. 'Mbezi Beach Luxury Apartments', the
father would jokingly term it in his correspondence
with the daughter. 'M.B.L.A'. When the daughter
went home to visit, the disrepair was jarring. It
was like someone ageing right under your nose and
you not noticing it until you haven't seen them in
a while. Lying on her childhood spring frame bed,
facing the windows on which her doctor mother
once hung IV meds for malaria, pink curtains long
faded from when said mother sewed them with a
matching bedspread, she felt a pang in her heart;
a nostalgia for bygone times paired with a stark

The newly completed house and coconut trees in the compound. Original album photos by H. Nestor Ilahuka, 1995.

The author under the two mango trees of different varieties, one from each of her grandmothers. Sylvia K. Ilahuka.

The author outside the house in Mbezi Beach, as it was in November 2019. Sylvia K. Ilahuka.

The Harvesting. H. Nestor Ilahuka, 2020.

awareness of the passage of years and the dwindling of money. The dining room cabinet, wood decaying on the inside but still housing fine dishes from a lifetime ago. A house that was once ahead of its time is now far behind.

Thirty years later, the bones of the house have long begun to show. A crack here, a leak there. What used to be a sandy neighbourhood that could absorb excess rain is now a paving-laden suburb, leaving water with nowhere to go but down towards the sea. Down towards the little house that laid low even as giants came up around it. Whose foundations carried it for as long as they could until they just gave in. One flood too many and it was now time to move on. So a buyer was found, the land sold, and the house taken apart – the pieces creatively repurposed, as minimal waste as possible. The roofing tiles, the fence spears, the window grilles, the wooden doors; all finding places in a freshly built abode in a new location, blending in but standing out just enough that someone familiar with the old would recognise them among the new. There is laughter in this home again, and life has returned to the family in the form of a second wife and more children. Nature's restorative power – the regenerative forgiveness of time – is a rare, special gift. The song by Aron Wright comes to mind; just maybe, we really do build it better the second time around.

A small house stood on the Dar es Salaam coastline; now stands a mansion in its place. ◨

The Real Story

D E V E L O P I N G   C R E A T I V E   N O N F I C T I O N
A N D   T H E   E S S A Y   I N   T H E   U K

he Real Story is a Manchester-based writer development project and
line journal devoted to promoting the form of creative nonfiction writing in
e UK. Funded by Arts Council England, we provide workshops, mentoring
d a publishing platform for both established and emerging creative
nfiction talent. We're always looking for personal essays and pitches, so
ad over to therealstory.org/submit and send us something wonderful.

Supported using public funding by

ARTS COUNCIL
ENGLAND

Crossing

the Bar

by Linda Cracknell

For tho' from out our bourne of Time and Place
The flood may bear me far,
I hope to see my Pilot face to face
When I have cross'd the bar.
– Alfred, Lord Tennyson, 'Crossing the Bar'

Our journey out towards the open sea was punctuated by landmarks I half knew from a recent visit to Braunton on the far side of the estuary. There I'd found some of our dead in the graveyards, and walked out of the village to the shore and its sentinel White House. But the land was hard to read from sea level, and from here features I thought I had fixed got shuffled. From these lower reaches of the River Torridge, I could look directly along the Taw, upstream to the White House with Braunton diminutive beyond it under green hills. To the right of the river entrance was the long dark pier at Yelland where an oil terminal used to stand and, to the left, the small, tubular steel lighthouse at Crow Point venturing way out on its pile of rocks into mud and no man's land, fending off the unwary.

The emptying estuary stretched around me an alien, changed place of mud and slick sky, kaleidoscopic fragments. Although it was May, the day was gunmetal grey, cool and windy. We were heading for the rip in the Atlantic coastline that separates Saunton Sands on the north side of the estuary from Northam Burrows on the south. We'd launched from a slipway in Appledore on the southern shore, carrying the kayaks across sticky mud and slipping over weed-draped rocks to reach the water. Once afloat, with our spraydecks tightly skirted, I saw up close the orange lifeboat that swings on its mooring just off the town. It has orientated me as I've worked my way around the hydra-shaped Taw-Torridge estuary: locus of my haphazard search for submerged family memory, an impulse at the threshold of my seventh decade that demands bodily engagement.

Our flotilla of eight kayaks from Bideford Canoe Club turned west, and was carried downstream by tide into the dancing waterways of the confluence. I hadn't been in a kayak for some time, and was glad to be travelling in a double kayak with a highly experienced paddler: club leader Pete Thorn, who matched my strokes from behind. I'd been anxious as I anticipated the trip, but the motion soon felt familiar, a rhythmic roll of the shoulders and straightening of the arms propelling the vessel, warming me inside my borrowed drysuit. My legs stretched ahead, knees wedged into the kayak's sides so my hips could tip and steer. Sitting almost below the surface, I was in a strange intimacy with the plait and shudder of currents beneath, sensing sometimes depth, sometimes sneaking shallows as recognisable land began to disappear and the sky pressed down.

The further out we paddled, the more agitated the surface became. Looking eagerly ahead, I took in a succession of channel marker buoys. First red, which, had we been a ship, we would need to pass to our port side (left), then keeping a green one to starboard. Names were displayed on the buoys – Inner Pulley and Outer Pulley – marking sandbanks ships must avoid.

> **I was in a strange intimacy with the plait and shudder of currents beneath, sensing sometimes depth, sometimes sneaking shallows...**

The Bristol Channel has the second largest tidal range in the world, caused by its funnel shape, the great massing of the Atlantic directly to the west, and the topography of rising land on either side that pipes in westerly winds, increasing inward flow. It's what makes these waters and their interaction with land so grave, the flow of the Bristol Channel so fast in either direction as it floods into or empties from the estuary. Pete told me it was challenging to find suitable waters for novice kayakers here, both because of the scale of the tides and the potential chaos beyond the Bar in any 'weather'. Trips have to be planned with care. Get it right and it's like freewheeling on a bicycle. Even a humble kayak might reach ten knots in the right circumstances. You just need to be sure it's in the intended direction.

Our trip would take two and a half hours in total, Pete said. The difference between high and low water that day was 4.72 meters, the height of a small house. On a twice-a-month 'spring' tide, when the sea floods highest and drains to its lowest, the depth of water in the channel can drop to as little as three feet: not a problem for a kayak with its tiny draft and seal-like manoeuvrability, but in a keeled vessel of any draft, precise navigation and timing have always been essential.

Low tide today was at 11.56 am. We were to travel out on the very last of the ebb from Appledore, and come back in on the flood. The idea was that the tide would carry us each way, but we had left slightly later than intended.

The name Bideford Bar – like Land's End, or Tower Ridge on Ben Nevis – rings with notoriety. Respected and feared. Without local navigation knowledge and an understanding of tides, it can be disastrous. As recently as 2014, a pleasure boat capsized on an ebbing tide and one person died. What had seemed a watery playground must have transformed abruptly into a confusion of shifting land and hissing seas.

I'm a committed walker and Ordnance Survey maps, my usual companions, leave the sea as a blank mystery. In preparing to cross this puzzle of water, sand and gravel, I'd pored over a nineteenth-century sea chart, delighting in the textured detail applied to 'non-land'. A statement cautioned that the entrance shown was no longer representative due to the shifting nature of those sandbanks. However, it gave an account of the main channel at the time, showing depths numerically, and writhing a great white loop south around the mountainous dunes of Braunton Burrows before branching dramatically north-west and south into the two rivers. Sandbanks and their associated mini-channels, which vanish at high tide, were marked with names: Sprat Ridge, Crow Ridge, Middle Ridge. A ballast heap and buoys featured, and incoming vessels were advised to align the 'lower and upper lights': two lighthouses that once stood a distance apart close to the estuary entrance. Other features on land were offered for navigational assistance: 'Watertown in line with old mill'; 'bungalow in line with Worlington houses'.

There's a map on the wall of Braunton Museum scarred with names of wrecks. Count up the ships around the estuary entrance, cast up onto Zulu Bank or breached on Saunton Sands, despite the paraphernalia of lighthouses, guiding lights, buoys and the pilots who could come aboard to take the helm with native authority; the toll is vast. An Admiralty pilot publication from 1910 advises: 'This bar is of so changeable a nature that the depths are not to be depended on; the mariner is accordingly cautioned against taking the chart…as a guide, and not to enter without local knowledge'. But of course there were those who tried to cut costs by doing so.

The interplay of river, sea, geology and moon must have dominated the lives of my grandmother Drake's family and their sail-cargo business, which continued out of Braunton into the early twentieth century. The quay, built by the seafaring community at Velator, was accessed from the estuary by a creek crossing a mile of low-lying marshland. They could only load or unload or easily reach the estuary and go out over the Bar twice a month at the new or full moon. The local story goes that if a sea captain missed his slot due to an overenthusiastic night in the Mariners Arms or a need for repairs, he would be held back for a fortnight, causing financial chaos for his family and crew. 'Master's lost his spring', was the justification a wife might take to a local shop when asking for credit on purchases: a request to be 'tided over'.

> ## 'Master's lost his spring', was the justification a wife might take to a local shop when asking for credit on purchases

Even in the estuary itself their two-masted wooden ketches needed enough water to clear the hazards beneath, the tide flowing in the right direction to travel in or out, and helpful winds. Or it would have to be oars, or some other method involving heaving an anchor forward and hauling the vessel on a line towards it, at least until engines began to be fitted to their ships. Rather than the hands on a clock face, the state of the tide would have dictated plans. It synchronised local efforts. As many as a hundred ships reputedly went out under sail in one tide, attempting not to collide.

Before investing in ketches in the late nineteenth century and focusing on coastal journeys within and beyond the Bristol Channel, my grandmother's family sailed as part of a long-standing trade taking salt from Devon to Newfoundland, salted cod from there to the Iberian Peninsula, and returning home with a hold full of wine and oranges. We think of this link between Devon and Newfoundland as Elizabethan but as recently as 1881, *Nellie*, a modest ketch belonging to my grandmother's grandfather, Francis Drake, went missing on a passage between St John in Newfoundland and Oporto, loaded with salt cod.

For the more recent coastal voyages, a knowledge of the current play of tide and the shifting channel was the difference between life and death. The means of finding the channel was handed down from those living with it and by it, generation to generation, 'like a treasured family heirloom that it undoubtedly was', according to John Whitlock in *Pilots and Pilotage on the Rivers Taw and Torridge*. Directions were oral, precise and esoteric: 'when you'm abrist the Middle Ridge, keep high light a hand spike's breadth open of the low one ...'

...a knowledge of the current play of tide and the shifting channel was the difference between life and death

Unlike Braunton folk, Appledore's inhabitants have long faced the sea, and over the centuries closely witnessed patterns of tide, current and weather. Perhaps unsurprisingly, the village produced many pilots from amongst its seafarers who kept their knowledge of the capricious monster up-to-date. This included walking the low-tide shallows after rain to see the latest effect of freshwater ingress from the surrounding hills. For voyagers, this estuary was rare shelter on a rugged, cliff-fortressed stretch of coast, especially important in the days of sail alone when wind strength and direction would determine course.

Particular local families became known for piloting, and before Trinity House regulations diminished their numbers, there would have been great competition between them to be the first to reach an incoming ship signalling for assistance. They got the work to guide the ship both into port and, later, back out. The race demanded fitness and resilience. Rowing in 'gigs' with a coxswain pressing the crew onwards, they would race other families; sometimes the rivalry led to the gigs overreaching the Bar and capsizing in its wild surf, with possible losses of several members of the same family.

Races were held between rival pilot gigs at other times, perhaps with gambling involved. Such racing for 'pleasure' died out but has recently had a great resurgence. Just as at home in Scotland, where coastal rowing has burgeoned as a community activity with a slightly different type of boat, gig-rowing with six rowers and a cox is now a popular recreation around Devon and Cornish coasts. An annual race has been established on the Taw-Torridge Estuary, men's crews starting close to Bideford Old Bridge and finishing at Barnstaple Bridge, and women racing back from there to Appledore.

Originally founded in 1855, the Appledore shipyard has survived through a declining chain of ownership, at times building ships of some size. Ferries and superyachts have launched on the turn of a high tide, always with an expert pilot. Only one pilot now remains in Appledore, doubling up as the harbourmaster, but commercial sea traffic is mainly limited to the barges that shift clay and stones. People travel and goods are carried by ring roads and bypasses and a new concrete bridge soaring across the Torridge Valley close to Bideford. But it is just within living memory that there were well-scored 'sea-roads' between the five ports of the Taw-Torridge Estuary. So I was glad to hear of the waters being plied by the small rowing craft, even if only for recreation, stitching the ports of the sprawling estuary back together again. In the past surely there were friendships forged, marriages made between its various shores?

Whilst the chart I'd studied fixed a sense of order and geometry, the complex jigsaw of water, sandbanks and shores we were moving through refused to steady. The estuary began to open out as we reached the marker buoy for Middle Ridge. Because we were low in the water, the buoys we strained to see were hidden by choppy waves ahead; the action of incoming wind against outgoing tide. I began to anticipate, as we rose up the slope of each wave, the fairground-ride-drop down the other side. The surrounding splutter and splash seemed inseparable from the motion.

The perspective stretched and shortened as we paddled towards a big sky, the open sea. Saunton Sands stretched a long yellowy strip away to our right, and beyond it stood Baggy Point, a craggy and black fortress, with Morte Point gradually amassing beyond.

I began to anticipate, as we rose up the slope of each wave, the fairground-ride-drop down the other side

Close on our left, a corrugated stretch of shingle bank humpbacked from the sea, declaring low tide. It was prickled by mussel shells and patrolled by seabirds. We pulled onto mud worked into rippling contour lines by tide and current, for a sandwich and a rest. This was Zulu Bank, I was told, a feature whose name has been ominous to seafarers through the ages, lying concealed, or acting as a natural breakwater, or breaching the surface. Depending.

After lunch some of the group turned back for Appledore. Three boats went on: ours, Simon's and Jake's, noses into increasingly lively waves, towards the Bar.

Joseph Conrad refers to the pilot as 'trustworthiness personified', unsurprising when local expertise puts so many lives in his hands. The ultimate respect seems to have been in Alfred, Lord Tennyson's mind when he wrote his poem 'Crossing the Bar' at the age of 81 from a room with a sea view in Salcombe. The central metaphor is a boat travelling out to sea on a fast-ebbing tide and crossing the bar with ease, carrying the grateful narrator over the threshold to a peaceful death. He hopes finally to meet his 'pilot' face to face.

...crossing the bar with ease, carrying the grateful narrator over the threshold to a peaceful death

Although I probably knew of this poem as a child, it was a video of The Spooky Men's Chorale singing a harmonised a cappella version of it in the Lady Chapel of Ely Cathedral that shivered me to attention. Standing to encircle their audience sitting on the floor, the music rises from the human cauldron into the dome above them. The emotion is palpable in the listening faces, and drew me back to the poem and its pairing of material and spiritual worlds.

May there be no moaning of the bar
When I put out to sea.

When I was invited by BBC Radio to write a short story in response to a classic poem for 'The Poet and the Echo' series, I knew immediately it would be Tennyson's, not least because my great-great-grandmother Emma (née) Chichester's leather-bound volume of Tennyson had recently come into my hands. I also knew that I would set my story around her homeland and the Bideford Bar, and this gave sharpened focus to my wanderings of the places close to Braunton where sea and land wrangle with each other. My imagination built upon what I found there.

The main character for the story soon materialised: an elderly woman, daughter of a local pilot. She had enjoyed independent sailing here as a child with strict respect for tidal dangers and the Bar, but was now being curtailed from even minor adventure by arthritis and the cautions of her adult children.

Writing a fictional story required me to fully imagine this territory somewhere between the White House and Crow Point, between firm sand and tidal rush, life and death. I think that engaging with it in this way, feeling it in my bones, gave me a greater degree of apprehension on this short literal journey from estuary-port to Bar.

Through spray-filled air, I could just make out last land at the 'north tail'. On the corresponding 'south tail', I saw two vertical figures. They stood, black and erect, close to the white line of water where incoming waves hit the shallow of the Bar's groundswell, making it sing out.

I stopped paddling to point them out to Pete. 'Are they surfers?'

'Birds,' said Pete over the roar.

I had the scale so wrong. When I looked again, they were exactly as he said: two cormorants, much closer than I had imagined.

There was nothing human out here and, had there been, they would soon be cut off by the incoming tide. Only two weeks before, two people had become encircled by the sea, Pete told me. The RNLI rescued them. Others try to jump the channel when it's at its narrowest, not realising its immense speed. I'd read of two nineteenth century Braunton men – James Hancock and William Murphy –

duck-trapping somewhere out here, their bodies brought in by a search party after they were cut off by the tide.

We still followed the channel, wind coming from the north-west, agitating the surface against us. As we had left slightly later than intended, the last part of our journey to the Bar was in slack water, unassisted by the ebb and slowed by the wind's opposition. Pete had warned me it could be choppy today. Sometimes water was scooped into my drysuit sleeves. As we hit the waves I took sea-slaps to my face. But now I had gathered a sense of purpose, I found myself reacting with simple exhilaration to the growing wildness.

'You should have worn swimming goggles,' shouted Jake from the kayak next to us.

And then, paddling harder against it, we left the shelter of land. Pete alerted me to the whole stretch of the bay between Morte Point to our north and south to Hartland Point, a bay holding the open Atlantic in its craggy arms. The Bar itself was now clearly visible: a stretching white line of surf just ahead underscored by something dark, and beyond it a much more confused and shifty sea. Far beyond the churn rose the pale shape of Lundy Island, fifteen miles off. Beyond it, the horizon flickered, spelling enticement and promise.

Surely my seafaring forebears had felt the thrill of their forthcoming journey each time they arrived at this point and the water livened beneath them, the air freshened, the surface grew skittish and unruly? This is where they committed, where they truly 'put out' to sea. This crossing of bad-tempered groundswell and a chaotic stretch of sea marked a necessary ordeal between two distinct worlds – the shelter of the domestic and the wild. We were approaching that ancient threshold leading into adventure and commerce; exile from home and land. The world of women and children closed in behind the Bar.

Achievement swelled in me; in being here amidst the chop and the bite of salt air to witness something of my own family story

In the lull between tides, before the water started to flood in to the estuary again, we paddled the last of our journey out. We wouldn't go beyond the Bar, not today; not in this. I felt a great thrill, face wet, eyes stinging with salt, to see the words 'Bideford Bar' growing larger on the marker buoy we headed for. It had a dark green, buoyant base with open vanes supporting a light above to make the entrance to the channel visible at night. As we bobbed around this hefty steel drum, it strained on its anchored lines, leaping above us. It brought to mind an account I'd read of the men of past times who relit it when the flame was blown out by a gale, one of them bringing the boat as close as possible to the dancing buoy and the other choosing his moment to jump.

Achievement swelled in me; in being here amidst the chop and the bite of salt air to witness something of my own family story. A story my mother didn't seem aware of and my grandmother never would have experienced. We turned the kayaks and put our backs to the wind. Simon took photos. I was suddenly too warm after the effort. Salty and grinning madly. Proud to have shaken off my own timidity, as if as a fragile child I'd let go from the side of a pool and begun to swim. But there was also relief that all the hostility was at my back and I was now facing green hills, white cottages on the shores, all the human infrastructure that I cling to. Past human lives remain scored here in hedgelines, engraved stones, houses names; at sea they leave no trace.

I tried to look at the estuary entrance now as the master of a sailing vessel might have done, coming in with the tide and wind directly behind. Driven in with stern raised, surfing with waves, rudder clearing the water; the ship would be un-steerable. A following wind would also risk an out-of-control gybe, the mainsail and boom slamming across the beam of the ship, causing chaos, flapping sails, splintering timber. Better to take the sails down and let the tide take you in, perhaps? But even then, with the tide running south to north across the estuary mouth as well as in and out of it, you might be sent onto Crow Point instead of Zulu Bank. There was a devil and there was the deep blue.

In the days of my family's ships, when the half-tide between ebb and flood was reached, safe water was indicated to incoming ships by the raising of a large black wickerwork ball at Braunton Lighthouse, visible on approach, and at night shown by a light. It was considered safe to enter with a minimum of fifteen feet of water and even then, the marked channel must be found. That the lighthouse had a mortuary with space for twelve bodies on Delabole slate slabs tells the consequences of underestimating this local hazard.

When we resumed paddling, I was surprised to find that without any effort, without noticing, we had travelled well upstream of the Bar buoy. Tide and wind had taken us. Skirls of surf were breaking over Zulu Bank where we'd had lunch. We played at catching waves until it was too shallow, even for us with our tiny draft.

A turning tide often seems to bring a change of weather and now the sun blasted into our faces. Perhaps it can also bring a shift in fortune or a different way of thinking: a reliable pendulum of change. Ahead, the White House appeared on the shore of the filling estuary to my left and behind it, the cluster of Braunton's roofs and spires. Somewhere in there was the Heanton Street house in which my grandmother grew up with a father, grandfather, brother, and countless other male relatives who repeatedly made this journey over the Bar.

This frequent act of ordinary heroism, this sailing 'close to the wind' of life itself, must once have moulded generations of men from the Taw-Torridge estuary and the families who watched and waited for and lost them. And it occurred to me now that remnants of such states may still lodge like hidden channels in their descendants. ⊞

A Mouse in Reagan Country

by *Rebecca Thomas*

'Imagine a place where dreams come true every single day, where you walk among legends, where family members become best friends, and perfect strangers become family. That place is Disneyland resort, located in sunny California.'
– From Disneyland's employment recruiting website

'Discover for yourself that the sun just seems to shine longer here. In the OC, it's forever summer.'
– From The Orange County Visitors' Association website

Main Street, USA

My husband and I walk down High Street in Morgantown, West Virginia. The air bites. It is March, and winter hangs on. The street shifts from downtown stores to homes; American Foursquare, Craftsman, Victorian. Bulbs peek out of the ground, little fingertips of green reminding us that winter won't last forever. I hold on to the spot of color, a countdown for a new season, and a promise that soon it will be warm. We walk behind the Willey House. From this angle, we can see the wooden backboards of a beaten-up basketball court. There is only a glimpse of brick, but we know on the other side is the sprawling mid-nineteenth century American Colonial where Waitman T. Willey, a prominent legislator, once lived.

My husband pauses. 'It smells like Disneyland,' he says.

'What?' I ask.

'It smells like the train.'

I stop and smell it, too, an almost basement smell of damp and plastic and electricity. Perhaps it's the carwash next to us, or the soot in the cold, winter air mixing with the smell of the Monongahela River nearby. Whatever it is, we both are suddenly transported to the Disneyland Railroad. We might be standing on cracked sidewalk next to a hundred-eighty-year-old house, but we're also on the steam locomotive, hearing Tony the Tiger's voice as he leads us into Adventureland, the first part of our grand-circle tour of the park. Suddenly, we're back home.

———

Walt Disney opened his theme park in 1955. Two years earlier, my hometown, Costa Mesa, incorporated as a city. Both are located in Orange County, California. It seems impossible to separate Disneyland from Orange County. The two are so connected, both reactions against Los Angeles, both highly designed and ordered. In a chapter on Disneyland in his book, *Popular Culture in the Age of White Flight: Fear and Fantasy in Suburban Los Angeles*, Eric Avila discusses the origins of Disney's theme park. At the time, amusement parks in cities were prominent. Places like Coney Island in Brooklyn or the Promenade in Long Beach allowed people to come and escape for a few hours. Young people flocked there, a great place for a date with plenty of dark spaces. According to Avila, Disney hated the parks, calling them full of 'dirty, phoney tough looking people'. He wanted a new type of park, one that escaped the 'urban' feeling of such places, and replaced them with a suburban version of a theme park. He wanted, in Avila's words, 'a suburban refuge'.

As Disneyland grew, people shed citrus for rectangular lawns, single-story tract houses, and wide freeways. Suburbia spread, and so did conservatism

Disney planted his refuge in the middle of what would become one of the largest counties in the country. At the time, much of the county was still farms and citrus groves. As Disneyland grew, people shed citrus for rectangular lawns, single-story tract houses, and wide freeways. Suburbia spread, and so did conservatism. The foothold the Right had on the county, earned the region the nickname 'Reagan Country'. After all, this was the county that helped Reagan get elected governor and eventually president. In the words of the former president, Orange County was 'where good Republicans go to die'. At the center of it all is the theme park, a place known for family-friendly fun, and for much of my childhood, Disneyland was one of the settings I knew best, second only to my own home, because for much of my life in Orange County, I had a Disneyland pass.

Adventureland

When I was ten and eleven, my cousins and I spent every Wednesday of our summer vacation at Disneyland. We knew the rules: we stuck by my mother until we went through the park's turnstiles; then, we could roam free, and we did, treating the park like our own backyard. We knew its hidden passages, its quiet corners of park benches and waterfalls.

Indiana Jones was still new then, and my cousins and I went on the ride almost every time we visited. The line could be long, and so Disneyland used to give out index cards with hieroglyphics on them. The line entered a faux cave complete with hidden treasures and archeological finds along the way. On the cave's walls, the designers etched symbols. Waiting, we held up our cards, trying to make out phrases. A cat-eye, a slanted h, a dash, a dot. Light flickered from fake torches. Creeping forward, we made sure we knew every artifact placed by the queue's designers. We knew the fake bamboo pole that, when shook, would make a ceiling with spikes on it suddenly drop a few inches. My stomach churned as I neared the pole. We always shook it, looking around with eager anticipation at the unsuspecting tourists.

Growing up in a land covered with strip malls and tract houses, our escapes at Disneyland felt just like that: escapes. We ran around the woods of Tom Sawyer's Island. We traveled to the South in Critter Country, to the Southwest in Frontierland. For a few hours each week, we inhabited a space where every turn offered a new view. At home, we knew our neighbors' floor plans simply because they were the same as ours, but at Disneyland, each angle offered something unique.

Of course, the nooks that my cousins and I found were designed to feel hidden. From the moment a guest enters Disneyland, every part of their experience is under tight control. Disney designed every aspect of the park, managing every view, every employee, and the layout of the lands. He used his filmmaker's knowledge and created the park as a living set, scaling the buildings on Main Street to look taller than they really were, cordoning off green spaces to create the illusion of space.

Although I'd like to think the vistas in the park that I found and the park benches I sat on were my discoveries, they weren't. At Disneyland, while there are hidden spaces, there are no private spaces. My childhood discoveries of new and secret territory around the park were only simulacrums. An idea of privacy. After all, at Disneyland, you cannot stray off the paths.

Frontierland
Walking around Disneyland, observing the rowed flowers, the hedged bushes, the draped Spanish moss, the work behind the production is obvious. The shrubs of Frontierland never lose their color. The topiaries surrounding It's a Small World never have a leaf out of place. Mickey's head is always in bloom at the park's entrance. At times, there's beauty in this: beauty in the effort that makes a row of daisies blossom at the same time. At times, it is

too much, and it becomes clear that Disneyland is like the rest of Orange County: a willful denial of a Mediterranean climate. In August, the green grass of Disneyland is too bright. It's the green of suburban lawns and of the parkways lining my undergraduate university, and I know the work it takes to keep up those lawns.

> ## It becomes clear that Disneyland is like the rest of Orange County: a willful denial of a Mediterranean climate

I went to school less than ten miles away from Disneyland. I used to walk to my campus early in the morning. It was quiet then, and it was in those moments that the university charmed me; the Victorian-style buildings, the sixties-era fountains, the statue of our founder surrounded by orange trees. Bright green grass lined the campus, though often yellow police tape surrounded large patches as the university tried to keep the lawns pristine. One morning, as I walked past, I saw a gardener spraying the grass. The lawn turned suddenly greener. Grass, now Technicolor. A thin, green line colored the edge of the sidewalk. Miracle Grow. A healthy dose weekly, and the lawns looked perfect, even in August, even in September when the sun broke the ground because it hadn't rained since March.

At times, when the façade cracked, when I was reminded that all of Disneyland is highly manufactured, I was reminded that so is Southern California. In Orange County, everything seems shiny, everything seems new, everything seems too green.

New Orleans Square

My freshman year of college, my then-boyfriend-now-husband often picked me up after a morning class. I'd walk out of my dorm, book bag in hand, get in his car, and twenty minutes later we'd be sitting in New Orleans Square, studying.

Usually, we sat at one of the wrought iron tables that lined the walkways of a fake New Orleans. Often, the coastal fog hadn't yet cleared, and the cold metal dug into my legs. I'd pull my sweatshirt around me tighter and open my notes. Bands alternated throughout the morning —first a jazz quartet, then doo-wop. Kids shrieked. Strollers clattered. The steam train honked as it stopped at the New Orleans Square Station.

We loathed the mime with his jaunty dress and oversized umbrella. He'd round the corner with his bouncy steps, and my stomach sank

I turned to the next chapter, answered the reading questions. Occasionally, we spoke, pointing out a passage, gesturing to a peculiarly dressed park-goer, but for the most part, we kept to ourselves, reading to the sounds of a theme park.

Until the mime came.

We loathed the mime with his jaunty dress and oversized umbrella. He'd round the corner with his bouncy steps, and my stomach sank. A woman with bridal Mickey ears window-shopped, and he played bashful next to her, pretending to blush.

'Jesus,' I said.

He walked up to us. Sticking his umbrella in our faces, he made kissing sounds.

We sighed. 'Yep,' my husband said. 'Kissy. Kissy.'
'Very funny,' I said.

He moved the umbrella and shook his finger at us. We raised our eyebrows and nodded.

'You caught us,' I said, and then we stared at the mime and waited in silence until he moved on.

Some days, when we saw him coming, we packed up and took a study break by riding The Haunted Mansion.

Eventually, we took to reading in Critter Country at a table by Rivers of America overlooking Tom Sawyer's Island. We liked the change in scenery, the 'river' lapping against the deck and the ducks that gathered hoping for food. We liked to watch 'nature'.

That mime got to me, though. I was indignant at his intrusions. When the mime came and interrupted our experience of Disneyland, boiling my actions down to flirtations and sex as I was reading Thomas Hardy for a Victorian Literature class, I was forced to see Disneyland as first and foremost an amusement park. I was coerced into the actor's performance. What made it worse was that I never forgot that this was just a guy getting paid to be a mime. He wasn't like the street performers at the beach. He was scheduled every day to make people feel as if they were experiencing a street performer, and each time, we witnessed the same act. When that mime came up to us, we were reminded that the whole park was one elaborate stage.

While I might have tried to pretend that the park was more than just a stage, Disneyland does not. The Disney Corporation calls its employees Cast Members; they are expected to act, to play roles. On

Disneyland's career opportunities website, a highly enthusiastic woman in a promotional video tells prospective employees that it is the Cast Members who create the magical Disneyland experience, or 'The Show'. As she speaks, Cast Members work both on 'stage' and off, looking entirely satisfied with their choice of employment. They smile constantly, and they all have, as Disney's website puts it, 'The Disney Look'. This means they are all 'clean, natural, polished and professional'. There are no '"cutting edge" trends or extreme styles' – bright nail polish, unnatural hair color, or facial hair that's longer than 'a quarter on an inch in length.'

I knew this. My husband once worked at Disneyland, as did my college roommate. One of my best friends met her husband while working there. I knew about 'the Disney Show'. I knew how strict they were. If you work for Disney, everything counts – from how you look, to how often you smile, to the fact that your cell phone must be out of sight from the park's guests. Disney reminds its employees that 'all of this adds up to one of the most important aspects of your role in our show: good stage presence.' And I knew that if you didn't have good stage presence, if too many guests complained, if you were called in too many times, if you didn't hide your tattoos or piercings, you were asked to leave the show. I knew all of this, but I still tried to pretend that Disneyland wasn't a stage. I tried to create a space for myself at Disneyland, a space that felt authentic and my own. And then, the mime would come and ruin it.

In Orange County, too, it seemed impossible to escape the stage of our landscape. Hollywood isn't confined to a small strip of land in Los Angeles. It spills all over the Southland. At times, it was magical to stumble on a film set. But at times, the show got tiring. Our suspension of disbelief when watching films was constantly shattered. Saudi Arabia was really the road to Palm Springs. The news announced freeway closures for filming. My college campus became overrun with elderly people as they shot the next *American Pie*. I had to quietly go the long way to class as actors pushed walkers across our quad. In high school, I signed up as an extra for an MTV rooftop celebrity basketball tournament. On top of a building in Downtown

> **Hollywood isn't confined to a small strip of land in Los Angeles ... At times, it was magical to stumble on a film set. But at times, the show got tiring**

LA, I sat in a bikini top and board shorts and watched girls fight over Tyrese's dirty towel. I was cold. We couldn't take bathroom breaks. In Orange County, in Southern California, we cannot escape the amount of work it takes to keep up the show.

Fantasyland

My husband and I sat in Carnation Plaza at the park with walkie-talkies and a master list of nearly two hundred eighth graders. We were chaperones for the day, and in exchange for the price of admission, we had to ride a bus with a group of teenagers and then man the emergency table for two hours. We were about to move to West Virginia, and this was our last chance to go to the park; or more importantly, go for free. There was still a price to be paid: a busload of eighth graders singing Katy Perry's *California Gurls* on the 57 Freeway.

Mickey and Minnie stood behind the bride and groom. Minnie clutched her hands to her chest. At times, she took Mickey's arm, clearly moved

Our seats overlooked the bridge that connected Main Street, USA with Cinderella's Castle. We sat directly across from a small patch of green grass. It was fenced, of course. The grassy spaces at Disneyland are not for the walking public. They usually remain empty, a brief catch of color, a small blank space that gives the illusion that the park is less crowded than it is. However, this time, people milled about on the grass. Cast Members guarded the area. A table sat off to the side with a cake on it. A photographer stood testing the light. A videographer shot b-roll. Next to him, another man in a suit and a woman with a harp. She began to play.

And then Mickey and Minnie appeared, followed by a couple. The man in a suit. The woman, a long, white dress. Mickey and Minnie wore their formal wear – a tuxedo for Mickey with a pale gold bow tie, a light yellow dress for Minnie.

My husband and I looked at each other. We looked around for other guests, other members of the wedding, but there was no one. The officiant began. Mickey and Minnie stood behind the bride and groom. Minnie clutched her hands to her chest. At times, she took Mickey's arm, clearly moved. A crowd of park-goers gathered behind a gold chain that the Cast Members put up for the occasion. The couple was married. They kissed. Everyone applauded, including the mice.

The videographer walked between Mickey and Minnie, the two hamming it up for the camera. He walked in front of the newlyweds, the two kissing. Mickey and Minnie covered their eyes. The couple blushed. They cut the cake. Mickey and Minnie mimed that they should stuff the cake in each other's faces. The couple didn't. They had their first dance, and Mickey and Minnie danced next to them. In the middle of the song, they switched partners, everything captured on video. Fifteen minutes after it started, it was over, and they left. We watched as new Cast Members removed the barriers, cleaned away all evidence of the wedding before disappearing. Then, it was just a grassy space, a good spot to take a picture by the castle.

We told everyone we knew, emphasizing the oddity of having two cartoon characters as your only wedding guests, the strangeness of the video. Who would watch it? What would they say? It all seemed so elaborately over the top, so ridiculous that it felt unreal.

But maybe the wedding just highlighted the absurdity of Disneyland. Everything in the park is highly produced. A team of construction workers comes in after the park closes to fix any new imperfections. Doors and trim are repainted. Shelves restocked. A flower wilts during the day and is changed that night. The trick of Disneyland, like the trick of filmmaking, is to never ruin the illusion.

Tomorrowland

Disneyland is a park built on nostalgia and optimism. Disney tried to capture views from his small-town childhood and offered idealistic dreams of the future – dreams rooted in capitalism and paternalism as we saw in the now-defunct House of the Future ride where companies provided model appliances. The park willfully denies any 'real' darkness. At Disneyland, darkness comes in the form of fables, and it is always vanquished. Even the hitchhiking ghosts in The Haunted Mansion are friendly.

But in reality, darkness cannot be banished. While we may try to hide it, it can bubble up in the form of hatred and bigotry and violence. Like most suburbs, White Flight created Orange County. The draw of the region was the appeal to live in a land away from Los Angeles, in a 'suburban refuge'. As the county formed, it became a conservative refuge, too. Tension between conservative Orange County and liberal Los Angeles lurked in the land all throughout my childhood, and when that tension erupted, when anger or hatred spilled over into everyday life, it was unsettling.

In 2000, in my history class, we discussed the upcoming proposition on the ballot: Prop. 22, a ballot initiative about the definition of marriage. We debated.

'Shouldn't we treat others equally?' I asked.

The girl who sat next to me shot back Bible verses.

'I'm a Christian, too,' I said, 'but –'

'If you believe in gay marriage, then you aren't a Christian,' she said. Her words spat at me. I stared at her, her face firm and unyielding. I remember nothing else from that day, just her words and her face. Before this, I'd thought we were friends. 'Then you aren't a Christian,' she said. Her simple definition of who she thought I was stayed with me like a bad perm.

This is the problem with living in a place that tries to live in the past: when the future comes, the illusion of cohesion falls apart

And then eight years later, the same fight again. I drove home from teaching the Thursday before the 2008 election. I was tired of the election season, tired of listening to students spout hate, denouncing homosexuality. Driving home, I waited at a stop light by a community college. On all sides of the street, people carried yellow signs supporting Proposition 8. People honked in support of 'traditional marriage'. The protesters chanted, crossing the intersections, waving their signs. Kids followed their parents. I felt sick to my stomach as I drove on, getting on the freeway, listening to projections on the radio. This feeling wasn't new. I'd felt sick to my stomach for months before the election as I drove around our block, yellow sign after yellow sign reminding me where I was living. And then the election came and Proposition 8 passed and my heart sank lower yet. The yellow signs slowly came down, but a few stayed on lawns like mold.

This is the problem with living in a place that tries to live in the past: when the future comes, the illusion of cohesion falls apart.

California Adventure

Before children, my husband and I visited home during Christmas. One night, after dinner, my in-laws left for a walk. We joined them. They live in a neighborhood of tract houses, the streets snaking around each other. We circled the neighborhood, passing single-story after single-story, the houses the same only colored differently – tan, then white, then beige, then clay. The front yards the same lawn with different plant accents: jacarandas, bougainvillea, or cactus, maybe a rose. But always grass. Always Bermuda. Always bright green. Our feet did not stumble on the sidewalk. It was smooth, newly repaved after the telephone company put in fiber-optic cable. Like Disneyland, all phone lines had been buried underground. That night, the air was crisp, and so smoke lingered from fireplaces. Temperatures were only in the forties, but people were excited to have a chance to pretend winter for a night. A nativity scene blinked on a rooftop.

> **I stand on the sidewalk breathing in, hoping to hold on to that vision of Disneyland and home for just a while longer**

We covered the block in ten minutes. I crossed the street back to the house, but my in-laws kept going. This was their after-dinner walk, an occasion. Ten minutes wouldn't do, so I rejoined them, and we continued, circling a second time, passing the same two-car driveways, the same blinking Christmas lights, the same chimneys. After the second turn, we went back to the house – ours identified by the honeysuckle out front.

When my family walks in West Virginia now, we trip over the sidewalk and the rutted streets. We always check the weather, unsure when a storm will blow in. We love this, the unpredictability of what we'll see: a deer in our neighbor's yard, the first daffodils of spring, a slick patch of ice that hasn't yet thawed. And yet, I find myself seeing Disneyland everywhere. When we stand by the Willey House, transported to the Disneyland Railroad by a smell in the air, I feel an ache, a longing. I stand on the sidewalk breathing in, hoping to hold on to that vision of Disneyland and home for just a while longer. But then, we move on. **H**

The Californian

by Adam Farrer

I first heard about the Withernsea whales on Christmas Day of 2020, when my mother called me on WhatsApp video to wish me a Merry Christmas and show me the knickers that she'd received that morning.

'They've got Captain America on them,' she said unnecessarily as she hoisted her skirt, the image of a red, white and blue shield hurtling past her crotch.

'Lovely,' I replied, long used to this sort of thing. Since she began her burlesque career at the age of 63, the sight of my mother's underwear has become as familiar to me as my own. Despite this, she can still find ways to surprise me.

'There are ten dead whales on the beach!' she said. Her words were delivered like a newsflash, but coming off the back of 'Look at my knickers!', they sounded like a non sequitur.

'Really!?' I replied.

'It's true,' she said. 'Ten! They washed up on Christmas Eve. It's all over the news.'

Withernsea rarely makes the mainstream media, and now that I live in Manchester, what little news I do get about my hometown tends to arrive through the prism of my mother. Her reports are amped up and storified, the boring parts cut away until only the juicy anecdote remains. But on this occasion, it seemed that the unedited truth would do just fine. A whole pod of whales coming to die on Withernsea's beleaguered sands in the aftermath of the Government's decision to cancel Christmas; it was story enough. And the mental image of it shook me.

I thought of the animal size chart I'd had pinned to my bedroom wall as a child, which featured a human, a lion, an elephant and a whale, each compared alongside one another. The whale topped the chart by some considerable distance and easily measured the length of five elephants. And now here were ten whales, equal to fifty elephants, stranded on Withernsea beach and rolling in the shallows. The idea of this was startling. The biggest thing I'd ever seen on that beach had been my own body, during an unhappy period of my life when my weight ballooned to 19 stone. What did ten whales equate to when converted into sad Adams? Five hundred? A thousand? All of them marble-skinned and helplessly gasping their last on the freezing sands. It didn't bear thinking about, but I thought about it anyway. I would probably have carried on thinking about it until the day I died, had my mother not changed the subject.

'So, what do you have planned for today?'

I issued a list of the few activities open to me

that day: phoning friends. Watching *The Muppets Christmas Carol*. Eating until I was sore. But, if I'd answered honestly, I'd have said: 'I'm going to fret about the whales, maybe have a little nap, then fret some more.' And, true to those unspoken words, I did just that.

Watching a report on California's wildfires, I saw some footage of a twisting column of flame, referred to as a 'firenado'

It's important to mention here that, during the pandemic, with time on my hands and apparently believing that the threat of an acute respiratory virus was not scary enough, I'd developed a morbid fascination with complete global and environmental collapse. Most of the non-COVID news seemed to be about a planet that was alternately bursting into flames, disappearing under flood waters or, in the case of Siberia, both. Watching a report on California's wildfires, I saw some footage of a twisting column of flame, referred to as a 'firenado'. Hearing this word out of context I'd have assumed it was the title of a Jason Statham movie, but presented on the news it became a tipping point, throwing me into a full-scale panic about imminent global end times. I began to chain-watch distressing documentaries about melting permafrost, microplastics in the food chain and degraded agricultural land, certain that I'd soon receive a concerned email from Netflix, asking me if everything was OK. But what I got was ten whales turning up and dying in what I still thought of as my backyard, an occurrence I could only interpret as a grim environmental portent.

I wanted to know how the whales had ended up on the beach, and couldn't rest until I had an explanation. Ideally, a comforting one, rather than the news that the sea had been transformed into an uninhabitable poison. So, I spent the Christmas holidays reading news websites, refreshing them several times an hour on the off chance they'd update with a satisfactory answer. Instead, I got images. Lots of them. A close-up of a whale, its skin the grey-pink of short-dated oyster flesh, mouth open in what looked to me like shock. Another draped across the groynes, so grim and snotty looking you could believe that Neptune had risen from the waters and cleared it from his sinuses. What I *did* learn was that there were only *seven* whales, which makes it slightly less heart breaking but really, there's no such thing as *only* seven dead whales. That's still a good seven hundred sad Adams and while, yes, I'm biased, I don't think that's insignificant. It also raises the question: *how did anyone lose count?* But these numbers didn't seem so important once the reports began to focus on the emergence of 'dead whale tourism'.

It seems that, robbed of the usual options of panto or Christmas markets, large numbers of people had transferred their attentions onto the whale news and decided to visit Withernsea, disregarding the COVID travel restrictions in their desperation to witness the rare and tragic spectacle on the sands.

At first, they stood in curious groups on the promenade, peering down at the whales in something approaching solemn contemplation. Over time though, they grew bolder, less respectful, creeping down onto the sands to take a closer look, prodding in fascination at the barnacled and glistening skin. Before long the beach was alive with content creators, taking selfies for Instagram and posing against the beached bodies like hunters who'd just bagged the biggest game of all. For most, the appeal of this was limited, and they'd only stick around for so long before heading off to grab fish and chips or a hot drink from a seafront café, the local economy benefitting from the morbid boon of rotting sea giants. But rumours would soon spread that some of these tourists had grown a little too fascinated, removing teeth from the gaping jaws to keep as gruesome souvenirs of a Christmas like no other. Not quite believing this, I asked my mother to clarify.

'Yes,' she said, 'It's true. It's all over Facebook. Someone sawed off a whole jaw.'

I tried to imagine the kind of person who would take a saw to the beach and found that I could only picture notable serial killers, a legion of Jeffrey Dahmer lookalikes strolling the sands of my hometown. I was relieved to see the news in early January that the whales were finally being removed. By that time, I'd already learned the most likely theory about the whales: that they took a wrong turn while hunting for squid off the coast of Norway and ended up struggling in the shallow waters of the North Sea where, too hungry and weak to avoid their fate, they became stranded on the beach.

Having found an answer, I relaxed a little and gradually, the whales slipped to the back of my mind. I didn't give them much thought until the summer, when during a visit to see my family, my brother-in-law explained that two of the whales were still on the beach.

Faced with the might of the North Sea, the fragile clay cliffs show all the resilience of a twice-dunked rich tea biscuit...

'They got washed past the groynes to the edge of town,' he said, 'so the council doesn't have to do anything about them.'

'So, they're just being left there to rot?'

'Yeah, they're in no-man's land,' he said.

'Oh god,' my mother said, sensing where this was going. 'You're going to *look* at them, aren't you?'

'Yes,' I said, 'Do you want to come?'

'No,' she replied, 'it's too sad.'

I put my coat on and headed down to the beach, sad to be going alone but understanding her reluctance. After all, environmental tragedies tend to lose their novelty when you're living in one and trying your hardest not to think about that.

Withernsea is located on East Yorkshire's Holderness coast, the fastest eroding area of the UK. Faced with the might of the North Sea, the fragile clay cliffs show all the resilience of a twice-dunked rich tea biscuit, collapsing into the waters at a rate of roughly ten foot a year. The town's fate has become so compelling that it's now taught to GCSE Geography pupils, allowing them to study a high-speed geological phenomenon. I could not take you to the clifftop places where I stood thirty years ago, when I first moved to Withernsea, because those places no longer exist. Long swallowed up by the sea, they remain only as The Ghosts of Cliffs Past, floating out above the water. And beyond them lie the dozens of lost towns and villages that have tumbled into the sea over the years and now have more in common with the horizon than the land. Each day more of the coastline dissolves into the waters, creating the distinctive cocoa-coloured waves that lap the beaches. In time, Withernsea too will fall beneath these waves and disappear from the map altogether.

Long swallowed up by the sea, they remain only as The Ghosts of Cliffs Past, floating out above the water

You'd think that this fate would make living in the town unbearable, but Withernsea is by some distance the most hopeful place I've ever known. A tired but once-prosperous seaside resort, it's inhabited by a community that is far more interested in restoring the town's former glories than pondering its future status as East Yorkshire's answer to Atlantis. Most of the local energy is centred on attracting holidaymakers and turning around the local economy; it's hoped this will be achieved with the construction of a new pier.

The previous one was destroyed during the late nineteenth century in a series of nautical disasters, leaving only the crenelated entranceway standing. In the same manner that past calamities haven't deterred the building of a *Titanic II*, a committee of Withernsea locals began raising funds for an ambitious new structure, reaching 560ft out to sea and topped off with a hydroelectric restaurant, for which they've secured a 99-year lease. This could seem like a hope too far, given that in 99 years, it's speculated Withernsea may have already dissolved into the sea, its pier only accessible by boat from the UK coast, rapidly receding into the distance. Still, this kind of hope is infectious, and as soon as I heard that a GoFundMe campaign had been set up to pay for it, I found myself donating £50. The rational part of my brain yelled 'why don't you just cut out the middleman and throw your wallet into the sea?' but the alternative would be to give in and embrace doom, and that's not really the way things are done in Withernsea. So, we ignore the threats and hope that someone will come up with a solution. And when whales start washing up on the beach, the arrangement of their bodies seeming to spell out 'YOU'RE NEXT,' we ignore that too.

It took me a good twenty minutes of walking to reach the final groyne on the edge of town, by which point the beach was empty, save for me and another man who was sitting in the opening of a tent set up against the sea wall, sheltering from the winds. He called out to me as I passed.

'Going to see the whales?'

'Yes,' I called back to him, 'How did you know?'

'That's the only reason anyone goes that way,' he said. 'Just make sure you leave them in one piece.'

I promised him I would, then continued on my way, annoyed at his inference that I was the sort of person who might interfere with a dead whale. But as I vaulted the groyne and found myself suddenly confronted with their bodies, partially swallowed by the sands, I felt exactly like that sort of person. I'd come to the whales in search of something, and worse than the trophy hunters, I wasn't even sure what that something was. I guess what I had in mind was an epiphany. That, by spending time with them, I'd gain some meaningful level of understanding and acceptance around the inevitability of ecological collapse. It was a lot to ask of a corpse, especially these two, that had already gone through so much. What with the starving, the washing up on Withernsea beach, where they'd been prodded and posed with. And then the final indignity, of me arriving to say, 'I hope you don't mind, but I have a few questions about the environment…'

I'd also had the vague, foolish idea that, once dead, a whale was basically soluble, the lapping of the sea quickly reducing it to a skeleton, the way a cartoon cat will dunk a fish into its mouth and suck it down to its bones. So, it was a shock to see them like this after eight months, their bodies still largely intact, save for the occasional rib or oven-sized chunk of vertebrae poking through rips in their now tanned, leathery skin. I had no interest in seeing them like this, so irreversibly dead. What I'd *really* wanted was to have been on this spot last December, saving the day.

So, why wouldn't I be able to roll a whale back into the sea? If I'd managed that, then all this drama could have been avoided

I do this a lot, mentally overplay my capabilities. Convince myself that, given the right set of circumstances, I could arrive on a scene and make everything better. So, were it not for the inconvenience of COVID, I'd have been on that beach on Christmas Eve, helping the RNLI wrestle the whales into the sea and happily back to Norway. It's odd but, while I'm always doubtful of my proven abilities, I have absolutely no trouble speculating about the ones that haven't been tested yet. So, why wouldn't I be able to roll a whale back into the sea? If I'd managed that, then all this drama could have been avoided. The sadness, the environmental concerns, the dark tourism. And with the whales safely out of the way, I could get to work on rebuilding the coastline, scraping the collapsed cliffs off the beach and patting them back into place, one filthy handful at a time, saving Withernsea from its watery fate. But instead, this being the real world, I was just a guy standing beside two dead whales and staring up at the crumbling cliffs, wondering if it might be easier if we all just evolved gills.

My mobile rang. It was my mother, wondering if I wanted anything to eat before I drove back to Manchester.

'Did you find the whales?' she added.

'Yeah,' I said, 'I'm with them now.'

'How do you feel?'

'Terrible.'

'Well, I could have told you that,' she said. 'Come home, I'm heating up a quiche.'

I said I'd be there soon, but hung around a while longer, thinking about this town I loved, with its hope, its grand plans and its 99-year lease on the future, wondering if it would one day make a decent subject for an environmental disaster documentary. A cautionary tale about the dangers of false hope, with a title like 'Withernsea: A Town on the Edge'.

And I thought of how it might appeal to my Californian equivalent, someone anxious about the incoming wildfires and scrolling Netflix for a distraction. I pictured them clicking play on the trailer, where an aerial shot slowly tracks the Holderness coastline, capturing me as it passes. Just a speck on the beach, two dead whales at my side, the three of us caught between a town and the waves. Intrigued, the Californian settles in to watch this tale about an abundance of water and a town about to be extinguished, hoping that someone will do something, while he waits for the firenados to arrive.

H

The Californian *was originally commissioned by the Portico Library and first published in 2021 as an episode of the Portico Podcast's series* Rewriting the North, *supported by Arts Council England.*

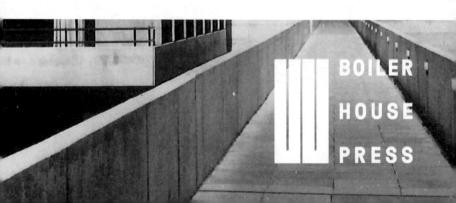

Walks Thro

ugh Time

by Laura Cooper

7th October, 2002
Chinatown to Fisherman's Wharf, San Francisco

I have the idea to go walking without a map in a city I don't know. I study my tourist map over breakfast then fold it away in my backpack, hoping my memory will navigate me to the harbour. I turn left out of my hostel and start wandering, taking lefts and rights uphill until I find a focus – a tall concrete needle. Eventually, I find myself at the top of Telegraph Hill at the foot of Coit Tower, an Art Deco column dedicated to the firemen of San Francisco. From the top – first flâneuse, now a voyeur checking their bearing – I see the city unfold. A squeaky-toy chorus of cherry-headed parakeets bursts up from the park below.

I detour down an unmarked path as a woman in an unknown place – I possess a wealth of youthful confidence – following where instinct tells me to go. I find myself on a flight of wooden steps descending a steep hill. Ahead in the distance, the shadow of the Bay Bridge emerges from the thinning morning mist. Lush gardens flank the steps: huge yellow angel trumpets dangle above the path, hot-pink bougainvillea, roses, palm trees. Birds sing. A dog barks. No one else is around.

7th July, 2005
London, UK

When it's finally safe to leave the office, my friend
and I cross the Millennium Bridge to St Paul's.
From there, we piece together our mental maps.
Half-lost, there's the frequent relief of turning a
corner to find a familiar street mixed with the eerie,
traffic-less gasp of a city in shock. On the way, we
stop for ice cream in the sun and half-pints in a
pub where everyone is oddly convivial; smiling at
strangers, wishing them luck.

11th March, 2011
Tokyo, Japan

Once it's apparent that today is cancelled, I hurry to
Shibuya. The train tracks are silent, and I have to
queue for thirty minutes to get on a bus. I'm lucky
I get there when I do – by the time my bus leaves,
rammed so full of people that one woman collapses
in the crush, the lines are hours deep.

It takes five hours standing still to get home. No
one speaks to or acknowledges other passengers,
especially those we press up against. My back aches
from tensing against other bodies. Outside the
bus, thousands of commuters walk by. Family and
friends leave messages on my voicemail ('Please call
me, I hope you're OK') but I can't call back because
the network is swamped. At the front of the bus, a
passenger with an antenna on his phone watches
TV. I squint: there's something grey, then there

are flames. Thoughts of what could be happening beyond this bus, this city, run through my mind. Only later will I find out it is so much worse. The bus is a void of jolted memories – we forgot any day could be this.

When I enter the bar where we've always agreed to meet, my friends pour me a shot of tequila and tell me I could have walked there faster. It hadn't occurred to me at any point that I could have followed the train lines back.

We stay into the early hours waiting for others to check in on their way home. We strain at every aftershock as the bottles behind the bar ding and clink behind their wires.

2nd June, 2011
Casablanca, Morocco

We are bored of the tourist market with its gaudy tagines, photogenic melon carts and spice mountains. The minaret of the Hassan II Mosque rises in the distance. Someone reckons it's a straight line from here, so we choose an alleyway and start walking.

'You don't want to go that way, my friends!' says one man from a nearby shop. But we do, and we keep going. Where we slip through a gap at the end of the alley, a large puddle of grey water stands like a warning. We jump it.

> **'You don't want to go that way, my friends!' says one man from a nearby shop. But we do, and we keep going.**

We emerge near a butcher's shop. On the side of the counter sits the head of a cow, pink tongue spilling heavily below wide eyes. Beneath the head, on the dusty floor, a small black kitten laps at a pool of blood. The air tastes metallic.

We walk across a market square where people are buying vegetables. Caged chickens cluck and murmur. A man sits next to a bucket brimming over with snails making for a slow freedom. Another sits by a pile of wire and circuit boards and watches us pass. We are conspicuous. There are no tourists here.

'Where are you going?' people ask us, and when we tell them we want to go to the mosque, they point us in the right direction, hurry us along.

27th July, 2014
Parc Guell to somewhere in Barcelona, Spain

It's best when one walks in a city to walk like you know it. In this case, I sort of do, just not this bit. I'm counting on the remnants of my photographic memory to get me back to the train station (with detours to admire graffiti).

The afternoon heat is oppressive, and my water bottle is empty. I walk in the shade of apartment buildings looking for open bodegas but everywhere is shut. I pass cool stone entranceways, catching green flashes of vegetation in interior courtyards beyond.

Then, somewhere in the doldrums of siesta, I hear live music. Music = people = liquid. I follow the sound, take a wrong turn when I follow an echo, return and round a corner. There's a square full of people swing-dancing.

I find a seat at a terrace café and order a caña and a cheese and walnut bocadillo. I pull out my map.

2017-2019
Tokyo, Japan

A Canadian tourist takes me on a date in Shibuya. It's rainy season and it hasn't let up for weeks. When we leave the pub, he asks if I'm going to the train station. The rain has stopped, but the streets are still slick and bleeding neon.

I'm walking, I decide – I haven't had a stroll for a while. He asks to join me even though he's going the opposite way.

We cut up and through Yoyogi Park. Back in the '70s, I tell him, men would come here at night to stalk couples in one of the few public spaces that provided darkness. The game would be to touch the woman without her realising it was not her lover's hands.

When we get to Harajuku, he asks if I'm taking the train.

I'm walking to Shinjuku.

We continue.

———

I tour Shinjuku with coffee and a professor of sound who has excellent taste in jackets. He wants to make a field recording of the Golden Clock in West Shinjuku Park, but every time he goes there on the hour it doesn't ring.

———

I walk Kabukicho with a man whose accent is all coastal voodoo and Spanish moss. We buy street beers and I give him the tour of the sleazy part of town, explaining host clubs and how the girls who look like hookers are just girls, but the women dressed in shades of drab are for sale. I show him the Hawaiian love hotel called Laura; the one that smells like Bali; the one that has rooms like cute English B&Bs. When we reach the four-lane carriageway and can go no further, he slides his arms around me and asks me which country I want to visit.

30th August, 2019
Sidemen, Bali

The owner of the café below my room, like some kind of seer, hands me a large walking stick as we leave: 'You'll need this.'

There's no map for this route, only the one in my guide's head. We tread the perimeter of rice fields patching the foot of Mount Agung, jump irrigation channels and tiptoe narrow paths. We pass my guide's brother, tilling his patch, calf-deep in water where ducks, frogs and plastic detritus co-exist with the communal rice harvest.

Halfway through, on the side of a culvert I just hopped, pain burns through my knee and something visibly twinges. I'm glad for the walking stick as we continue, and we must go on – we've got a funeral to get to.

Five kilometres later, we stop for the Ngaben procession. Hundreds of men in sarongs and udeng hats walk ahead of a festively upbeat gamelan troop. Behind them comes an ox-shaped sarcophagus for cremation, lines of women carrying offerings, and finally the funeral tower, where the sons of the deceased, swung about by pallbearers below, cling precariously to the sides.

Next to me, a stray dog watches the procession pass and nuzzles the chicken bone between his feet.

26th February, 2021
Mile Cross to Carrow Road, Norwich, England

Over a Christmas Zoom lunch, my mother informs me that my great-grandmother lived in Norwich. My grandmother sometimes mentioned Norfolk in stories she'd tell before bed – something about a Maltese servant at Sandringham being the reason she wasn't grey. I put down my fork and pick up a pen.

Today I google the address and set off with my route marked out on screen, detouring along the River Wensum to enjoy the sun. I exit the riverbank near the station and pass the football stadium. When I find the house, it's a slim one-up-one-down on the ring road. There's a satellite dish and new double-glazing. My mother says she has a photo somewhere of Nanny Burton standing outside. I imagine I am opposite where she once stood, separated by buses and cars and at least sixty years. I feel an urge to wave. **H**

Double page
spread,
full colour –
£350

Single page,
full colour –
£200

Half page,
full colour –
£120

Single page,
b&w – £150

Half page,
b&w – £70

To take advantage of the above rates and advertise
with Hinterland, or to discuss sponsorship
or other collaborations, please contact
Andrew Kenrick: hinterlandnonfiction@gmail.com

teach yourself

world cultures:
russia

world cultures:
russia
stephen webber and
tatyana webber

The publisher has used its best endeavours to ensure that the URLs for external websites referred to in this book are correct and active at the time of going to press. However, the publisher has no responsibility for the websites and can make no guarantee that a site will remain live or that the content is or will remain appropriate.

For UK order enquiries: please contact Bookpoint Ltd, 130 Milton Park, Abingdon, Oxon OX14 4SB. Telephone: +44 (0) 1235 827720. Fax: +44 (0) 1235 400454. Lines are open 09.00–18.00, Monday to Saturday, with a 24-hour message-answering service. Details about our titles and how to order are available at www.teachyourself.co.uk

For USA order enquiries: please contact McGraw-Hill Customer Services, PO Box 545, Blacklick, OH 43004-0545, USA. Telephone: 1-800-722-4726. Fax: 1-614-755-5645.

For Canada order enquiries: please contact McGraw-Hill Ryerson Ltd, 300 Water St, Whitby, Ontario L1N 9B6, Canada. Telephone: 905 430 5000. Fax: 905 430 5020.

Long-renowned as the authoritative source for self-guided learning – with more than 30 million copies sold worldwide – the *Teach Yourself* series includes over 300 titles in the fields of languages, crafts, hobbies, business, computing and education.

British Library Cataloguing in Publication Data: a catalogue record for this title is available from The British Library.

Library of Congress Catalog Card Number: on file.

First published in UK 2002 by Hodder Headline, 338 Euston Road, London, NW1 3BH.

First published in US 2002 by Contemporary Books, a Division of The McGraw-Hill Companies, 1 Prudential Plaza, 130 East Randolph Street, Chicago, IL 60601 USA.

This edition published 2004.

The 'Teach Yourself' name is a registered trade mark of Hodder & Stoughton Ltd.

Typeset by Transet Limited, Coventry, England.
Printed in Great Britain for Hodder & Stoughton Educational, a division of Hodder Headline, 338 Euston Road, London NW1 3BH by Cox & Wyman Ltd, Reading, Berkshire.

Papers used in this book are natural, renewable and recyclable products. They are made from wood grown in sustainable forests. The logging and manufacturing processes conform to the environmental regulations of the country of origin.

Impression number 10 9 8 7 6 5 4 3 2 1
Year   2010 2009 2008 2007 2006 2005 2004

contents

This book is designed to give you as full a basic overview as possible in its 250 or so pages of the main aspects of Russia: the country, its language, its people, their way of life and culture and what makes them tick.

You will find it a useful foundation if you are studying for examinations which require a knowledge of the background of Russia and its civilization, or if you are learning the language in, for example, an evening class and want to know more about the country and how it works. If your job involves travel and business relations, it will provide valuable and practical information about the ways and customs of the people you are working with. Or if you simply have an interest in Russia for whatever reason, it will broaden your knowledge about the country and its inhabitants.

The book is divided into three sections:

- **The making of Russia**
  Units 1–2 deal with the forces – historical, geographical, geological, demographical and linguistic – that have brought about the formation of the country we know as Russia and the language we know as Russian.

- **Creative Russia**
  Units 3–7 deal with the wealth of creative aspects of Russian culture from the beginnings to the present day. These chapters take a look at the main areas or works of literature, art and architecture, music, traditions and festivals, science and technology, fashion and food and drink, together with the people who have created and are still creating them.

- **Living in Russia now**

  Units 8–12 deal with aspects of contemporary Russian society and the practicalities of living in present-day Russia: the way the political structure of the country is organized, education, the health service, the workplace and how people spend their leisure time. Unit 11 looks at the Russian people themselves and the final chapter looks at the country's political, economic and social relations with the wider world, and takes a glance at the future.

Taking it further

Each unit ends with a section entitled 'Taking it further', where you will find useful addresses, websites, suggested places to visit and things to see and do in order to develop your interest further and increase your knowledge.

The language

Within each unit you will encounter a number of terms in Russian, which are presented in transliterated form, i.e. in Latin script, together with their meaning in English when they are first introduced. If you wish to put your knowledge into practice, we have provided at the end of each chapter a list of useful words and phrases to enable you to talk or write about the subject in question: these are presented in Cyrillic, i.e. Russian, script.

We have been careful in researching and checking facts, but please be aware that sources sometimes offer differing information. Of course a book of this length cannot contain everything you may need to know on every aspect of Russia. That is why we have provided so many pointers to where you can find further information about any aspect that you may wish to pursue in more depth. We trust that you will enjoy this introductory book, and that it will provide leads to further profitable reading, listening and visiting.

Schastlivogo puti! (Have a good trip!)

Phil Turk
Series Editor

The Cyrillic alphabet used in Russian can be transliterated with the Latin letters used in English in a variety of styles. We have employed one that should help a layperson with no knowledge of Russian to pronounce the word in a manner close to the original and be understood by native Russian speakers.

The Russian letter **e** is transliterated as [ye] in those cases where its pronunciation in the Russian word is close to the sound [ye] in the English word 'yes'. So, for example, **Егор** and **Достоевский** are transliterated as Yegor and Dostoyevskii. Where the sound is less emphatic in Russian, **e** is transliterated as [e] (e.g. **образование** becomes obrazovanie).

The soft sign **ь** is indicated by the symbol ['] in those cases where it is used to 'palatalize' or 'soften' the preceding consonant (see page 25). Where a soft sign is used in the Russian to separate the vowels **я, ю, е** and **ё** from a preceding consonant, these vowels are transliterated as [ya], [yu], [ye] and [yo]. The soft sign is not shown, as its purpose in the original Russian is already performed by the presence of the [y] sound in English, and we felt that the addition of the symbol ['] might actually make it more difficult for the reader to achieve the correct pronunciation of the word. (We do not refer to any words in the book where a hard sign **ъ** is used in the original Russian, although a similar system would be used to represent it, e.g. **объявление** would be shown as obyavlenie.)

Although the pronunciation of most Russian consonants is phonetic, i.e. they are pronounced as they are written, the letter **г** when found in the combinations **-ого-** and **-его-** is pronounced as в [English 'v']. We have transliterated these combinations as [ogo] and [ego] in line with the spelling of, rather than the pronunciation of, the Russian word, in order to show the reader how the original is spelled. However, you should bear the pronunciation rule in mind when trying to recreate the sound of these words.

Abbreviations used in Glossaries

(m.) masculine
(f.) feminine
(n.) neuter
(pl.) plural
(adj.) adjective
(vb.) verb
(colloq.) colloquial

acknowledgements

We would like to express our heartfelt gratitude to the friends and colleagues who have provided support and critical views. They are: Ol'ga Bean, Helen Grady, Julian Moss, Maureen Perrie, Michael Pursglove, Stephen Reeve, Jeremy Smith and Anastasiya Zhel'vis. Special thanks are due to Tatyana Bungey, Katerina Feoktistova, Aleksei Morozov, Vera Morozova and Alina Zil'berman, who all made a significant contribution to the development of the manuscript. As always, any remaining errors and oversights are entirely the responsibility of the authors.

We would also like to thank the excellent editorial team at Hodder & Stoughton – Phil Turk, Sue Hart and Rebecca Green – who have given us tireless encouragement and thoughtful commentary on the text, and displayed enormous patience.

The biggest thanks go to our beloved son, Alex, who has for too long now put up with us spending hours in front of the computer screen, typing away at the manuscript. He has been the source of our inspiration.

The authors

Steve Webber comes from Glastonbury, England, and is a lecturer in Russian Studies at the University of Birmingham, UK. Tatyana Webber was born and educated in Yaroslavl', Russia, and moved to England in 1990. She teaches Russian at the City Technology College in Birmingham.

01

what made Russia?

In this unit you will learn
- about the geography of Russia
- about Russia's history
- about the Soviet Union
- about the new Russia

Russia cannot be understood with the mind.
One can only believe in Russia.
Fyodor Tyutchev (19th century poet)

This famous quotation by Tyutchev has been echoed in the sentiments of many observers, both Russian and foreign, across the centuries. It reflects the sense of mystery that has been associated with Russia in the West until very recently. Russia has, directly and indirectly, exerted a huge influence on the world – yet it has remained relatively little known and little explored by outsiders. The lack of knowledge and understanding on both sides has tended to fuel suspicion and fear – and unfortunately even now, after the end of the Cold War and the lifting (or easing) of barriers to freedom of movement, communication and thought, such negative factors are still present.

Russia is a complex place, it is true, but we shouldn't be led to believe that it is impossible for someone from outside to understand the country and the people who live there. All you need is an open mind and a willingness to explore a rich and fascinating culture that is at once both familiar and different. In the following chapters we want to give you an impression of Russia in all its diversity, looking not just at the famous, but also at the not so well known, focusing not just on the key personalities and events, but also on the experience of the ordinary people. Are you ready for the journey? We'll start by looking at the making of what we now call Russia.

Geography

The vastness of Russia is hard to come to terms with, even for Russians themselves, and it's worth pausing for a moment just to contemplate its sheer scale. It is a huge country, the largest in the world, covering an area of some 17 million square kilometres (almost 1.8 times larger than the United States of America, some 70 times larger than the United Kingdom!). The current-day Russian Federation covers one-eighth of the earth's surface (the Soviet Union covered one-sixth). It stretches for some 9,000 kilometres, across 11 time zones, from the Baltic Sea in the west to the Pacific and for some 2,500–4,000 kilometres from north to south, from the White Sea to the Black Sea and borders with its neighbours in the Caucasus, Central Asia and China. While Russia's population of some 149 million people ranks fifth in the world, the density of population is just nine people per square kilometre (compared with 29 per square kilometre in the USA, and 241 per square kilometre in the UK). However, these figures are distorted somewhat by the fact that two-thirds of the country can be considered uninhabitable in any case. The majority of the population is found in the Central (European) part of Russia, west of the **Ural Mountains**, which act as a gateway to the harsher climes of **Siberia** beyond.

The landscape and the earth

Russia is a country of huge, seemingly never ending plains. In the far north, there is the arid region of *tundra*, where there is virtually no vegetation. Further south, there are the vast expanses of the *taiga*, a forest area that covers almost one-third of Russia, with a mixture of deciduous and coniferous trees in the western part, but almost entirely coniferous east of the Ural Mountains. The *vechnaya merzlota* (permafrost or ground that is perennially frozen) reaches a depth of up to 1,500 metres in parts of Siberia and is the source of ongoing fascination for scientists, searching both for evidence of life on earth (the preserved bodies of mammoths have been discovered here), and even for clues as to whether life may have existed on other planets in our solar system. Only a small proportion of Russia's territory contains fertile soil, although this includes a number of productive *chernozyom* (black earth) regions.

Russia has only a small number of mountain ranges. The Urals serve as a dividing line between European and Asian parts of Russia, with the **Altai** range located deeper in Siberia. In the south, Russia shares the **Caucasus** mountain range with the other smaller countries of the region, while in the Far East, the **Kamchatka** mountains (on the peninsula of the same name) include some active volcanoes.

Climate

For many foreigners Russia conjures up an image of harsh, cold winter weather. And not without justification, as in parts of the north of Russia and Siberia temperatures can plummet to an almost unbearable minus 70° Celsius, with the effects of the cold compounded by the lack of daylight in the winter months. At the same time, however, other parts of the country enjoy a far more moderate climate, even subtropical in the case of the Black Sea coast, where you can find palm trees lining the seaside promenades.

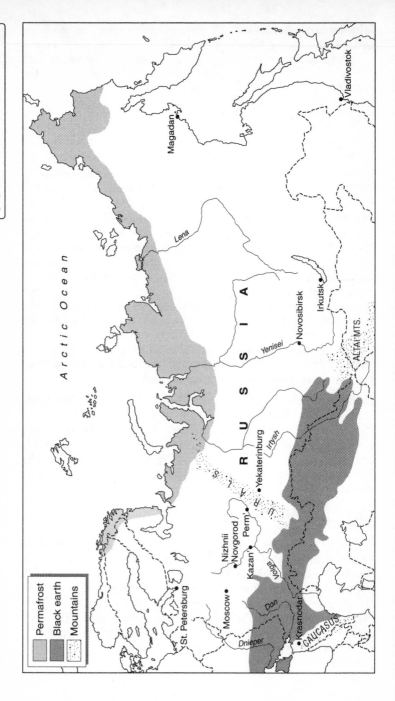

Rivers and lakes

There are some 120,000 rivers in Russia, all told. The most famous are the **Volga**, which flows from northwest Russia down to the Caspian Sea and the Ob', Irtysh, Yenisei and Lena, which traverse the icy territories of Siberia towards the Arctic Ocean. In the winter months many rivers, even the largest, are frozen up, covered with a thick layer of ice. Hardy souls come out and drill a hole in the ice, then sit next to it for hours waiting for fish to bite on their line – keeping themselves warm with the occasional (or maybe even frequent!) swig of vodka. During the thaw the river can become a dangerous place, with a good number of people losing their lives each year after they fall through the now thin ice.

There are also some two million fresh- and saltwater lakes, the largest of which are the Caspian Sea (home of the caviar-producing sturgeon) and **Lake Baikal**. Baikal is the largest freshwater lake in the world and is the focus of attention for Russia and foreign environmentalists, battling to preserve its ecosystem, which contains unique examples of certain species of marine life and fauna.

Minerals

Russia has an abundance of mineral resources, which have been the target of considerable domestic and international investment in recent years and which earn Russia a great deal of income through exports. Russia produces over 25 per cent of the world's natural gas, some 15 per cent of crude oil, as well as significant amounts of other minerals, with the largest deposits found in Siberia.

Origins of Russia

Russia has a fascinating, turbulent, often dark, yet at the same time inspiring, history. While accounts of its past have frequently been altered to suit the preferences of the rulers of the day, Russians have in more recent times been able to start to reclaim and reassess their own history – revealing in the process much about their present as well. In this brief overview of Russian history you can gain a sense of the major themes that have seemingly been ever present – invasion and suffering; suspicion mixed with fascination for the outside world; subjugation of the needs of the individual to the demands of the state; the cycles of reform and enlightenment, contrasted with reaction and repression. As Russia emerged from the collapse of the Soviet Union towards the end of the 20th century, would it be able to break free from the less appealing aspects of this legacy?

Early history

Russia has from the very start been a multicultural country. Indigenous peoples such as those in the north and Siberia, who had hunted and later herded deer across the frozen wastes for many thousands of years, were joined by migrants from various parts, combining to sow the seeds of the rich ethnic tapestry of what is now Russia. The more fertile south of Russia attracted successive waves of migrants, including the **Scythians**, who arrived at some time before the 5th century BC. They were followed by the **Sarmatians** in the 3rd century BC, the **Huns** in the 4th century AD, and the **Khazars**, who developed farming and trading communities between the 7th and 10th centuries.

The Slavs, the Varangians and Kievan Rus'

The migrants known as the Slavs, however, were to have a more extensive influence on the makeup of the population of Russia. Today's Russians (in common with Ukrainians and Belarussians) trace their ancestry back to the eastern Slavs, who moved into Russia from the west during the first millennium AD.

It was the Vikings (or **Varangians**, as the Slavs called them) who developed the first Russian state. According to the *Primary Chronicle*, which dates from **Kievan Rus'**, Novgorod was founded by Rurik in 862. Kievan Rus' itself was established in the city of Kiev – capital of modern-day Ukraine – by another Varangian in 880 and became a dominant centre for the next 200 years, expanding its sphere of influence, adopting Christianity in 988 under Vladimir I. The Cyrillic script was introduced at this time (see Unit 2).

Invasion and despotism

The Mongols and the rise of Moscow

Kiev's place as a centre of power was short lived, as other centres such as **Novgorod** and **Vladimir-Suzdal'** gained the upper hand through superior strength in battle and in commerce. The infighting among the principalities of Rus', however, made them an even easier target for the Mongols, who attacked in overwhelming numbers in 1237, rapidly overcoming their hapless opponents, many of whom were slaughtered. The Golden Horde of the **Tatars,** as the Slavs called them, ruled over the Russian principalities for the next two centuries, demanding that the princes pay them tributes. One of these princes, **Aleksandr Nevskii** of Novgorod achieved legendary status in Russia for his exploits in defeating the Swedes in 1240.

Among Russian cities the influence of Moscow grew during this time, with the church leadership relocating there in the early 14th century, and its princes retaining the title of grand prince (with Tatar approval). With time, Moscow's strength allowed it to act as the head of a campaign against the Tatars, defeating them at Kulikovo in 1380, although it would be another 100 years until the Golden Horde's dominance would finally be cast off.

Ivan the Terrible

Now free of foreign control, Russia's rulers could impose their own will more assuredly. **Ivan IV** – who acquired the nickname 'the Terrible' – became the Tsar of All Russia in 1547, some 13 years after coming to the throne at the tender age of three. His reputation comes from the reign of terror he imposed after his wife died of suspected poisoning. The nature and degree of destruction and torture that ensued – implemented by the ruthless *oprichnina* (a secret police force) – left a deep imprint on Russia, echoed in Stalin's own terror some 400 years later.

The time of troubles

Ivan died in 1584 and **Boris Godunov** – brother-in-law of Ivan's weak son – assumed control of the country. His tenure was later challenged by a pretender to the throne, who claimed to be Dmitrii, a son of Ivan the Terrible. This 'False Dmitrii' gained the backing of the **boyars,** the Russian nobles, and attained the throne. These events were followed by the *smuta,* or time of troubles, which saw Russia suffer bitter domestic political infighting and foreign invasions. As a result of one of these, Moscow was captured by the Poles. The *smuta* was finally put to an end in 1613, when the young **Mikhail Romanov** was elected tsar – thus starting the dynasty that would remain at the head of Russia until 1917. The early Romanov rulers put back into place a system of autocratic government, which included the enserfment of the peasants.

The Romanovs

Peter the Great

Under the reign of **Peter the Great** (1682–1725) – a giant of a man well over two metres in height – Russia was to take considerable steps towards modernization, moving closer to mainstream cultural developments in Europe and developing a more sizeable presence on the international stage. Soon after taking the reins of Russia, he set off on a prolonged visit to Europe, during which he observed at first hand how Western societies functioned – even working as a carpenter for some time.

On his return he vigorously set about introducing change in Russia – overriding the opposition of the church and the nobility in the process. Peter introduced a Table of Ranks, which rewarded good service with promotion and, in the higher grades, hereditary titles. He also oversaw an expansion of Russian military power and influence, defeating the Swedes, for instance, and gaining control of vital sea ports on the Baltic. On a marshy area on the Baltic coast he founded the city of Saint Petersburg, moving the capital there from Moscow as a symbol of his intent to bring European influence to bear on Russia.

Catherine the Great (1761–1796)

Catherine was not Russian, but German, the daughter of a prince who married the heir to the Russian throne, Peter, out of ambition. She quickly adapted to Russian culture, and swiftly, too, dispatched her husband in a coup after he had succeeded to the throne. (She was aided by one of what were to be many lovers.) Catherine then assumed the role of monarch herself and began a long reign that would be remembered for progress (her embracement of European enlightenment prompted reform in education and law and promotion of the arts) but also for repression and neglect of the lot of the serfs (the peasant rebellion of 1773–1774 led by the Cossack **Pugachov** was emphatically crushed, for example). The contradictions between the aspirations of the enlightenment and the abject poverty and suffering of the masses was highlighted in *Journey from Saint Petersburg to Moscow*, written by **Radishchev** in 1796, marking a new stage in Russian intellectual dissent.

Reform and reaction

Catherine was succeeded by her conservative son **Paul I**, who was soon to be killed in a coup in 1801. His son, **Aleksandr I** (1801–1825), was by nature a liberal reformer and the early years of his reign included further development of the education system. However, it was to be the series of conflicts with Napoleon that would dominate his period as tsar. Defeats by Napoleon led to the Treaty of Tilsit (1805), yet the uneasy alliance was broken in 1812, when Napoleon's huge army of some 600,000 invaded Russia. An inconclusive battle was fought at **Borodino** and the French subsequently entered Moscow – only to find that it was burning down around them.

When Aleksandr died heirless in 1825, his brother Konstantin declined the throne, and **Nikolai**, the youngest brother was due to become tsar. However, liberal-minded officers organized a rally in Saint Petersburg, calling for Konstantin – only to be put down by troops loyal to the new regent, who had ordered that they receive 'a whiff of grapeshot'. The *Dekabristy* (Decembrists), as those who had taken part in the protest were called, were exiled to Siberia and the reactionary reign of Nikolai I began, supported by the 'third section' (the tsarist secret police) and summed up by the slogan 'Orthodoxy, Autocracy and Nationality'.

THE COSSACKS

The Cossacks have a legendary status in Russia and abroad, gained from their fierce reputation as warriors and also from the way they sought to preserve their independence through the centuries. Cossack communities (found in the south of Russia as well as in Ukraine) attracted many who wanted to leave the restrictions of lives as serfs (or running away from problems of various kinds). Their fighting ability was used by the tsarist regime, with autonomy given in return for service in the army. The Cossack way of life was suppressed in the Soviet period, but there has been something of a revival of traditions since the demise of the USSR.

Although reform was stifled under Nikolai, the course that Russia should take was the subject of considerable – if suppressed – debate. The arguments of the 'Westernizers' and 'Slavophiles' clashed, the former wishing Russia to adopt European ideas, the latter promoting what they saw as traditional Russian values. This divide, which, as we have seen, was present before the 19th century, can still be detected in political and cultural discourse in the Russia of the early 21st century.

Before Nikolai died in 1855, he had overseen Russia's drift into the costly Crimean War against Turkey, France and Britain, which his son and heir, **Aleksandr II**, ended in 1856. Aleksandr (1855–1881) came to power determined to effect reforms that would ameliorate the problems that the Crimean War had highlighted. The most notable reform was the **abolition of serfdom** in 1861, the yoke that had held up the development of Russia's countryside for centuries. This was an essential step, if Russia were to begin to catch up with the process of industrialization seen in Western Europe. Indeed, during Aleksandr's reign the manufacturing sector grew, as did the railway network. But Russia still lagged far behind and social discontent increased – many peasants remained dissatisfied with the outcome of their emancipation, as they were still impoverished, while industrialization had itself caused new social problems in the towns. The expression of the desire to change the status quo assumed a violent character when, in 1881, the tsar was assassinated by a bomb thrown at his carriage. Under his son, **Aleksandr III** (1881–1894), reform was once again curtailed, and those seen to be threatening the existing political order were suppressed. Among those who were exiled to Siberia at this time was **Vladimir Ulyanov**, who would later adopt the name **Lenin**, and who left Russia for Europe after completing his sentence in 1899, to continue to work towards the goal of overthrowing the tsarist regime.

The 1905 revolution and the establishment of the *Duma*

Nikolai II (1894–1917) was a weak-willed ruler, but was at heart opposed to liberal reform and the reduction of the influence of the tsar. He faced mounting problems both at home and in Russia's foreign relations, however. The disastrous Russo–Japanese war culminated in the loss of the whole of the Baltic fleet off Japan in May 1905. This blow had been preceded by *Bloody Sunday* in January 1905, an event that had sent shockwaves through Russia, when tsarist troops had bloodily put down a peaceful demonstration in St Petersburg. Russia descended into chaos, with a general strike held in October 1905 (led by the St Petersburg *soviet*, or council), uprisings seen in the countryside and even mutinies seen in military units (including the battleship *Potyomkin*, immortalized in Eisenstein's film of the same name).

Against his instinct Nikolai had no option but to grant concessions, and opened the way to the election of a parliament (*Duma*) in 1906, although he dismissed the first two parliaments that were elected as he disliked their leftist composition. The introduction of a revised electoral system produced a *Duma* more to the tsar's taste. His appointment as prime minister, **Pyotr Stolypin**, proved an adept politician, and pushed forward long-overdue and much-needed reform in the countryside. However, Stolypin was assassinated in 1911 and the reform process lost momentum, while the tsar and his family succumbed to the mysterious influence of a monk named **Rasputin**, whose apparent ability to treat the tsar's son, who suffered from haemophilia, gave him a status in the court that aroused the envy and wrath of many in the Russian aristocracy and political elite. Rasputin was eventually murdered by members of the aristocracy in late 1916.

Towards revolution

Russia, meanwhile, had become embroiled in the bloody quagmire of World War I, which had proved ever more costly in lives, resources and territory – by 1916 Russia had lost control of Poland, as well as large stretches of Ukraine, Belarus' and the Baltic coast. In Russia itself, the deprivations of the peasants and the workers led to increasing tension, with strikes and riots taking place. Nikolai, meanwhile, assumed personal command of the army at the front, ignoring the looming crisis at home (which Tsarina Aleksandra played down in her letters to him): his response when pressed to take action was to dissolve the *Duma*.

In February the first of the Russian revolutions of that year took place, with the members of the *Duma* and the members of the Petersburg soviet (which attracted the support of workers and soldiers) combining forces to leave Nikolai with no option other than to abdicate. Power was assumed by a provisional government, first under Prince L'vov, then under Kerenskii. Notwithstanding the unpopularity of the war with Germany, the provisional government continued the military campaign – a factor that was to allow Lenin and his *Bolshevik* party to win over mass support, through their slogan 'peace, land and bread', a promise to take Russia out of the war.

The October Revolution

The Bolshevik faction of the Russian socialist movement had proved better organized and more appealing to the masses than the *Menshevik* faction. The former, meaning 'majority' in Russian, had called for violent means to be used to do away with the tsarist regime, while the Mensheviks (those in the minority) under Plekhanov had argued for a more peaceful transition. In April 1917 Lenin returned to Russia from Europe (with the help of the German government, which hoped he would succeed in taking Russia out of the war). The Bolsheviks' popularity increased after a failed attempt by General Kornilov to put down the soviets and by 25 October they felt ready to launch the revolution that was to have such a huge impact not only on Russian, but on world politics. After a swift success in taking over the seat of power in Petersburg (whose German-sounding name had been changed to the more Russian Petrograd), Lenin was named as head of the Council of People's Commissars, aided by a certain **Iosif Stalin** and **Leon Trotskii**. The Soviet era had begun.

The Soviet Union: 1917–1945

Vladimir Lenin

From civil war to New Economic Policy

The fledgling state was soon flung into chaos, despair and destruction, in a civil war that lasted from 1918 to 1921. The Soviet (Red) side faced a range of opponents collectively labelled as the 'Whites'. The disparate nature of the White forces, however (they included those loyal to the tsarist regime, social revolutionaries and foreign intervention forces, including US and British troops), as well as the fact that the communist authorities held Moscow, to which the capital had reverted, meant that the Reds finally emerged victorious. Yet in the process millions had died in a savage conflict that had divided communities and families and left the country on the verge of social and economic ruin (as depicted in Pasternak's novel *Dr Zhivago* and the film of the same name).

During the conflict the Soviet government had imposed 'War Communism', which had led to mass nationalization of industry and agriculture and the extension of strict centralized control over resources. Now, Lenin decided, a more lenient approach was required, namely the **New Economic Policy** (**NEP**), in which a certain amount of capitalism was allowed back into the economy, in a pragmatic attempt to revive the country. Private farmers were able to increase food production, and the *nepmen* (small-scale business people) were free to develop limited commercial activities.

Collectivization and industrialization

NEP remained in place until 1927 and helped the Union of Soviet Socialist Republics (USSR) to get back on its feet. The country still lay years behind the more advanced Western countries, however – a motivating factor behind the policies of collectivization and industrialization that were introduced and ruthlessly implemented under Stalin. Stalin had succeeded Lenin as General Secretary of the Communist party (the highest political office in the USSR), after the latter had died in 1924, his functions shattered by a series of strokes. Stalin had manipulated his succession with great skill, removing uncompromisingly those who stood in his way – including Trotskii, who was forced into exile and eventually killed by Soviet agents in Mexico in 1940.

Stalin's demands that the *kulaks*, or richer farmers and peasants, be liquidated, in order to facilitate the setting up of collective farms that would produce food according to state quotas, led to chaos and an enormous amount of suffering, including the mass starvation of millions of people. This contributed to the exodus to the towns, where they joined the industrialization programme, which aimed to bridge the gap with the West through five-year plans that squeezed the capacity of the workforce to its limits. By 1941, the Soviet Union had indeed begun to catch up – but it was to be at a huge price to its population.

The purges

Any hope that the Communists would do away with the more sinister trappings of the ancien regime, such as the use of secret police and policies of repression, had quickly been dispelled after the Bolsheviks came to power. The *Cheka*, set up after the revolution, had continued the tsarist tradition and begun that of the Soviet era, violently dealing with those who stood in the path of the new order. By the late 1930s the secret police went under the name NKVD (People's Commissariat for Internal Affairs), and they were prepared to take part in one of the greatest series of crimes against humanity seen in world history. The target had by now shifted from the kulaks to those closer to the seat of power – and the paranoid Stalin. The assassination of the popular Leningrad party boss Kirov – whom Stalin saw as a rival – in 1934, sparked the **purges**, a frenzy of arrests, torture, show trials, execution and exile to labour camps (the *GULAG* network) that led to the deaths of an estimated 8 million people, a scar whose imprint can still be seen in the face of Russia today.

The Great Patriotic War, 1941–1945

A more immediate consequence of the purges was their effect on the Red Army, with thousands of officers falling victim. While increased industrial output and a prioritization of the defence sector had raised the USSR's military potential considerably, in terms of key personnel the Soviet armed forces were weakened just at the time that World War II was descending on Europe. Although time was bought by the non-aggression pact signed by Molotov and Ribbentrop, foreign ministers of the USSR and Germany, in 1939, the Soviet army was still struggling to recover its strength by the time Hitler launched Operation Barbarossa – the invasion of the Soviet Union – in June 1941.

German forces made swift progress against the weaker Soviet opposition and soon occupied much of southern Russia, were within sight of Moscow, and laid siege to Leningrad. However, the advance was halted by the severity of the Russian winter and by the Red Army, which recovered from early defeats and began to receive more equipment. Bloody battles, in which no quarter was spared, were fought at Kursk and in the city of Stalingrad, with the Soviet side eventually proving too determined, skilful and numerous. A long campaign began to push the German army back to Berlin, which the Soviet forces eventually entered ahead of the other allies in April 1945. The relief of victory was mixed with a numbing realization of the scale of destruction in the USSR itself – the number of deaths among civilians and service personnel is estimated at a staggering 26 million. It is not surprising that even today, the Great Patriotic War is seen as a major defining moment in not just Soviet, but also in Russian history.

From superpower status to the end of the USSR

The start of the Cold War

The summits between the 'Big Three' leaders – Stalin, Roosevelt and Churchill – at Tehran and Yalta decided the nature of the political map in Europe for the next 45 years. In the period following victory over Germany, Soviet forces consolidated their position in East–Central Europe, ensuring that the USSR gained a cluster of satellite states with Communist governments. The superpower rivalry between the Soviet Union and the USA, and Communism and capitalism, quickly developed into the Cold War.

Meanwhile, the limited amount of contact that had developed between the Soviet Union and the Western allies during the war was clamped down upon during the 'anti-cosmopolitan' campaign, as Stalin re-established his authority in a new wave of purges.

Destalinization and the thaw under Khrushchov

Stalin's long and terrible tenure in office ended with his death in 1953. **Nikita Khrushchov** (1894–1971) emerged as the new leader and oversaw a process of **destalinization**, announced in his 'secret speech' to the 20th Party Congress, in which he spoke about the crimes that had been committed under Stalin's authority.

Indeed, under Khrushchov, the Soviet Union appeared, for a time at least, to be entering a new era. **Yurii Gagarin** blasted into space and the history books as the first cosmonaut, living standards were improving and a greater (if still limited and closely monitored) level of contact was permitted with the West through visits of foreign students, tourists and business people. A **thaw** also occurred in cultural affairs, with **Solzhenitsyn** able to publish his story *One Day in the Life of Ivan Denisovich*, describing life in the GULAG.

The uneasy relationship with the West worsened significantly, however, first over the Berlin Wall, which provided a physical support to the Iron Curtain, and then the **Cuban Missile Crisis** of 1962, in which the USA and USSR came close to fighting a nuclear war. This last event, in particular, undermined Khrushchov's authority in the Soviet hierarchy and he was deposed from office in 1964.

Brezhnev and stagnation

Leonid Brezhnev (1906–1982) was a more conservative and cautious politician than Khrushchov and turned around a good deal of the reform momentum that his predecessor had introduced. Brezhnev's watchword was stability and for a time this approach did allow for a deceptive level of relative economic prosperity, as the hardships of the wartime generation gave way to more comfortable lifestyles – in particular for those among the *nomenklatura*, or party elite. Yet the word which sums up the Brezhnev period more than any other is *zastoi* (stagnation) – the policy of stability was not accompanied by actions to develop the economy, with the result that by the early 1980s the Soviet Union was seen to be moving deeper into crisis. Domestic problems were matched by difficulties on the international scene: after a period of detente in the early 1970s, relations with the USA and the West had again taken a turn for the worse, over human rights, the Polish issue and the Soviet invasion of Afghanistan. The sense within the Soviet Union that change was desperately needed was already acute by the time Brezhnev died in 1982, yet the suspicion that the solutions would not come from the older generation of Communist leaders was reinforced emphatically when Brezhnev's two successors – **Yurii Andropov** and **Konstantin Chernenko** – died shortly after assuming office, in 1984 and 1985 respectively. The USSR's plight demanded a new approach.

Gorbachov's reforms and the collapse of the Soviet Union

This is what the new General Secretary, **Mikhail Gorbachov** (b. 1931), promised when he took office in 1985. Young and energetic, Gorbachov quickly showed that he was prepared to introduce radical change into Soviet political and economic life and to overcome resistance from powerful groups in the nomenklatura, the armed forces and elsewhere. His policy of *perestroika*, or restructuring, was intended to revitalize the faltering Soviet economy, while *glasnost'* (openness) was supposed to promote a more open and public debate in the Soviet media and society at large. Later, the goal of democratization was added, with a promise to extend greater political freedom and power to the population (a Congress of People's Deputies was elected in 1989, the first free elections in the Soviet Union's history).

In foreign policy, a dramatic improvement in relations with the West was achieved through arms reductions and other tangible aspects of a dialogue in which the mutual suspicions that had been in place for decades began to be cleared away. There was talk of 'Gorbymania' in the West, the style of the popular and media-friendly Soviet leader and his wife Raisa contrasting sharply with that of previous general secretaries.

At home, however, Gorbachov faced greater criticism and growing problems, as the policy of glasnost' allowed the public to criticize far more openly the range of concerns facing the country. The **Chernobyl'** nuclear power plant catastrophe in 1986 shook the nation; the waste of the war in Afghanistan was attacked by leading intellectuals such as Andrei Sakharov; and Gorbachov's economic reforms stalled. The country was ready for more than just cosmetic change – increasingly, the population came to demand sweeping reform, up to and including the breaking of the Communist party's monopoly of power.

The revolutions in East–Central Europe in 1989 spelled the end of Soviet domination, and Gorbachov's government acquiesced to the break-up of the Communist bloc peacefully (in contrast to the interventions in Hungary in 1956, Czechoslovakia in 1968 and Poland in 1980). Within the USSR, too, there were increasing demands for independence from Moscow heard in the republics, notably in the Baltic republics, while in the area of Nagorno–Karabakh civil war broke out between Armenians and Azeris. Gorbachov's apparent 'turn to the right' in the winter of 1990–1991, when special forces were used to break up independence demonstrations in Latvia and Lithuania, resulting in several deaths, symbolized the decline of Soviet power.

In August 1991, while Gorbachov was resting in his dacha on the Black Sea, a coup attempt was made in Moscow, led by the vice-president, Yanaev, the KGB chief and the Minister of Defence. The appeals of this 'State of Emergency Committee' to the armed forces to support them were met with caution, however, with the military unwilling to see itself split along political allegiances. The leader of the parliament of the Russian Federation, **Boris Yel'tsin** (b. 1931) (a popular and energetic politician, who had made his name as Moscow party boss), led the opposition to the coup, famously standing on an armoured personnel carrier to speak to the crowds gathered outside the 'White House', or parliament building. The coup attempt quickly fell apart after three days, with thankfully only a small number of casualties. Yet when Gorbachov, released from captivity, flew back into Moscow, he failed to appreciate how much his country had changed in that short time – the decline of the Soviet Union now seemed inevitable.

Boris Yel'tsin leading the opposition to the August 1991 attempted coup

In the autumn of that year, Gorbachov made desperate attempts to save the union, but in early December Yel'tsin met with the leaders of the Ukrainian and Belarussian republics to proclaim the establishment of a Commonwealth of Independent States. Gorbachov finally resigned on 25 December and the Soviet Union – born out of so much bloodshed and suffering – withered away with little more than a whimper.

The New Russia

The economy – from state control to free (and sometimes wild) market

Yel'tsin and his prime minister, Gaidar, lost no time in announcing radical reforms to kick-start a free economy in the newly independent Russian Federation, with price liberalization introduced (prices for many goods had hardly risen for decades in the USSR) and a mass privatization programme set in motion. The shock therapy approach of these reforms backfired, however, as many ordinary citizens saw their meagre savings wiped out through inflation and Yel'tsin was forced to put a brake on the pace of change.

The Russian economy struggled throughout the 1990s to adapt to the opportunities and the risks inherent in the free market. Industrial production declined, as outmoded factories producing unwanted goods found themselves competing with foreign imports that began to flood Russia. A tiny minority of people found that they could – legally or otherwise – make enormous amounts of money and these so-called 'New Russians' were quick to show off their wealth at home and abroad. However, organized crime (the '*Mafiya*') also grew rapidly. Meanwhile, a growing proportion of the population found itself hovering around the official poverty line, as unemployment (or the non-payment of wages to the employed) began to be more widespread; worryingly, a steady rise was seen in the number of people slipping below the poverty line into outright destitution. Sometimes with the state's safety nets eroded, there was no escape for such victims of the transition other than to look to criminal activities.

The state of socio-economic problems worsened in 1998, when the crisis in the Russian economy forced the government to devalue the rouble, thus undermining a great deal of the commercial development that had taken place to that point, forcing businesses and individuals to brace themselves to pick up the pieces and rebuild again.

Political turbulence

Despite the economic problems of the early 1990s, Yel'tsin continued to enjoy popular support, apparently confirmed in a referendum he called in April 1993 to ask for a vote of confidence in the direction of reform. Although the process of transformation was proving painful, it seemed that most people – especially the young – had no desire to turn the clock back and return to the Soviet system. However, Yel'tsin did face a number of political challenges from the opposition, which held the parliament. In October 1993 the executive–legislative rift came to a head when **Khasbulatov** and **Rutskoi** (Yel'tsin's former vice-president) faced a standoff with Yel'tsin, who blockaded the 'White House' where the parliament was sitting. The affair ended violently when Yel'tsin ordered tanks to fire on the building – ending the dispute, yet causing many to question how committed the Russian president was to the development of democratic norms.

RETHINKING AND REDISCOVERING HISTORY

The study of history has traditionally been a tricky and at times dangerous business in Russia, as official interpretations of the past have changed according to the outlook of the authorities or the whim of the ruler, with sanctions imposed on those who stray from the line of the day (some history teachers were sent to the GULAG under Stalin for 'misinterpreting' history, for example). In the late 1980s, it became possible (under glasnost') for Russians to begin to retrieve their history, and since the fall of the USSR more and more archives have been reopened and memoirs taken from the shelves where they have lain for decades, as the new Russia takes a step forward by looking back to see where it has actually come from.

The opposition to the government was subsequently provided by the Communists, under **Zyuganov**, and by the nationalist Liberal Democrats, under the neofascist **Zhirinovskii**. It was the sight of this 'hard-line' alternative to Yel'tsin that caused Western governments to continue to lend their support to the incumbent president, including the arrangement of considerable financial contributions and loans to the Russian economy and in spite of Yel'tsin's excesses and failings. As the 1990s went on, Yel'tsin's health worsened (a process hastened by alcohol consumption) and at times his ability to perform his duties was severely restricted.

Russia's democratic transformation has also been tested to the limits by the wars in Chechnya, a small republic in the south of the country, which has been attempting to gain independence from Moscow since the early 1990s. The decision to send the military into Chechnya in late 1994 led to tens of thousands of deaths among civilians and combatants and wide-scale destruction of the republic. Following the 1996 ceasefire brokered by former General Lebed', Chechnya descended into a state of violent anarchy, before federal forces again intervened in the autumn of 1999. The bloody conflict came to an uneasy end in 2003.

The rise of Putin

The launch of the second Chechen war was overseen by the new prime minister, the unknown **Vladimir Putin** (b. 1952), a former KGB officer from St Petersburg. By December 1999 Putin was backed by a new political faction, called Unity, which swept to success in the parliamentary elections. On 31 December, Yel'tsin ended speculation about whether or not he would break the rules and run for a third term in office by handing over the reins to Putin as acting president. In March 2000 Putin was elected president – the completion of an incredible rise from obscurity to power. His youthful, energetic image contrasted markedly with that of Yel'tsin and he continued to enjoy the popular support of a population who listened expectantly to his promises to restore Russia's status in the world and revive its economic and political fortunes (although some, at least, were concerned by his talk of the need for a strong state and his desire to impose controls over the media). However, as leaders throughout Russia's history have known, it is one thing to make proclamations from the capital, but to effect change throughout this vast territory is an enormous challenge. Meanwhile, the legendary patience of the Russian people continues, as they wait for the potential for prosperity and stability that their country has within it finally to be delivered.

GLOSSARY

большевики (pl.)	*Bolsheviks*
вечная мерзлота (f.)	*permafrost*
Великая Отечественная война	*the Great Patriotic war*
восстание (n.)	*uprising*
гражданская война (f.)	*civil war*
декабристы (pl.)	*Decembrists*
доисторический (adj.)	*prehistoric*
Западники (pl.)	*Westernizers*
застой (m.)	*stagnation*

индустриализация (f.)	*industrialization*
климат (m.)	*climate*
коллективизация (f.)	*collectivization*
кулак (m.)	*kulak*
крепостное право (n.)	*serfdom*
меньшевики (pl.)	*Mensheviks*
монголо–татарское иго (n.)	*Mongol-Tatar yoke*
опричнина (f.)	*oprichnina*
революция (f.)	*revolution*
Российская империя (f.)	*Russian empire*
Россия (f.)	*Russia*
славофилы (pl.)	*Slavophiles*
Советский Союз (m.)	*Soviet Union*
Союз Советских Социалисти-ческих Республик (m.)	*Union of Soviet Socialist Republics*
средневековье (n.)	*Middle Ages*
ссылка (f.)	*exile*
тайга (f.)	*taiga*
тундра (f.)	*tundra*
царь (m.)/царица (f.)	*tsar/tsarina*
электрификация (f.)	*electrification*

Taking it further

Books

This is just a tiny selection of the many thousands of books out there on Russian history!

Figes, Orlando, *A People's Tragedy* (London: Cape, 1996). A much-praised work on the Russian Revolution, looking at how the tumultuous events from the 1890s to the 1920s affected the people of Russia.

Fitzpatrick, Sheila, *Everyday Stalinism* (Oxford: Oxford University Press, 2000). An insight into the nature of life in Russia during the dark years of Stalin's reign.

Hosking, Geoffrey, *Russia and the Russians* (London: Penguin, 2001). An impressive survey of 1,000 years of Russian history.

Massie, Robert, *Nicholas and Alexandra* (New York: Ballantine Books, 2000). Takes you inside the lives and experiences of the last of the Romanovs.

Service, Robert, *The History of Twentieth Century Russia* (London: Penguin Books, 1998). A good introduction to Soviet history.

Films

Watching a movie can be a good way to get a feel for a country's history, as well as its culture. Apart from Russian-made films, such as the silent-era movie *Battleship Potyomkin* (on events in the 1905 revolution), or the 1994 film *Burnt by the Sun* (available with subtitles), there have been a good number of television adaptations of literary classics made in the West (such as the recent *Anna Karenina* by the UK's Channel 4), as well as feature films in English on Russian themes, such as *Doctor Zhivago* (for a taste of what it was like before, during and after the October Revolution and the civil war), and the more recent *Enemy at the Gates*, about love and the futility of war, set in the Battle of Stalingrad during World War II.

02

the Russian language

To the foreigner the path to understanding the Russian language might seem to be surrounded by barriers that are as imposing and impenetrable as the Iron Curtain used to be – the alphabet, the case system, aspects and myriad prefixes and suffixes. But don't despair! Russian isn't actually so difficult to learn, especially once you've mastered the basics. It won't infuriate you with exclusions to rules in the same way that English does and pronunciation is a lot more straightforward than for some other European languages. So, **поговорим по-русски!** (*pogovorim po-russki* – let's speak Russian).

The basics of the language

The alphabet

The **Cyrillic** script was devised by a monk called Cyril with help from his colleague Mefodii. It was based on the Greek alphabet, with some Latin letters used as well, and some additional letters were devised to reflect the sounds of Russian. The modern Russian alphabet has 33 letters, shown in the following table next to their transliterated version and a pronunciation guide. Hard and soft signs do not represent sounds themselves. The hard sign is used to separate the syllables in some words, but is not found that often. The soft sign is more ubiquitous and is used to 'soften' the sound of the preceding consonant, or sometimes to separate a consonant from such vowels as **я** [ya] and **ю** [yu].

а	[a]	a as in father	о	[o]	o as in bore
б	[b]	b as in box	п	[p]	p as in peach
в	[v]	v as in visit	р	[r]	r as in rat
г	[g]	g as in goat	с	[s]	s as in sip
д	[d]	d as in daughter	т	[t]	t as in tired
е	[ye]	ye as in yet (when stressed)	у	[u]	oo as in shoot
	[e]	e as in bet (when unstressed)	ф	[f]	f as in feather
			х	[kh]	ch as in loch
			ц	[ts]	ts as in quits
ё	[yo]	yo as in yonder	ч	[ch]	ch as in chick
ж	[zh]	s as in treasure	ш	[sh]	sh as in shift
з	[z]	z as in zoo	щ	[shch]	as in posh china
и	[i]	ee as in feet	ъ	["]	hard sign
й	[i]	y as in boy	ы	[y]	
к	[k]	k as in kit	ь	[']	soft sign
л	[l]	l as in bottle	э	[e]	e as in let
м	[m]	m as in motor	ю	[yu]	yu as in yule
н	[n]	n as in novel	я	[ya]	ya as in yak

Some practice at pronouncing Russian sounds

You'll need practice to get your tongue and mouth moving in a Russian way. One trick to achieve the «ы» sound, for example, is to put a pen between your teeth and say the English word 'tee' (which should come out something like the Russian «ты» – 'you')! The Russian «п» (English 'p') is not aspirated – in other words, if you hold your hand in front of your mouth when you say a word such as парк (park), you shouldn't feel any breath hitting your palm. The «т», «д» and «л» ('t', 'd' and 'l') sounds are made with the tongue against the back of your top front teeth (as opposed to putting your tongue against the ridge above the top teeth in English) – try saying такси (*taksi*), дача (*dacha*) and лампа (*lampa* – lamp).

And just for fun – have a go at these tongue-twisters!

«На дворе трава, на траве дрова» – *Na dvore trava, na trave drova*. (In the yard there is grass, on the grass there is firewood.)

«Шла Саша по шоссе и сосала сушки» – *Shla Sasha po shosse i sosala sushki*. (Keeping the alliteration: Sasha strolled along the street and sucked a sweet – literally, Sasha walked along the road and sucked crackers.)

A grammar lesson – Урок грамматики

Let's have a brief look at some of the basic characteristics of Russian grammar. Pay attention now!

Gender
Nouns come in three kinds – feminine, masculine and neuter. You can tell the gender of most nouns from their ending – usually masculine nouns end with a consonant, feminine nouns end in 'a' or 'я', and neuter nouns with 'o' or 'e'.

Cases
Russian nouns change their endings according to which of the six cases – nominative, genitive, dative, accusative, instrumental and prepositional (locative) – is being used. The cases indicate a particular function of a noun in a sentence (e.g. the subject of a sentence is always in the nominative case, the prepositional case is used when a word states where something is, the accusative is used for the direct object in a sentence and so on). The endings of all descriptive words (pronouns, adjectives, participles) associated with the noun have to change as well to match the noun's case. For example, the phrase «этот большой дом» (*etot bol'shoi dom* – this big house) will change to «Я живу в

этом большом доме» (*Ya zhivu v etom bol'shom dome*) when you want to say 'I live **in** this big house'.

This may seem complicated when you start off, but after a while you come to get a feel for the language and appreciate why Russia has proved to be such a rich source of poetry. The flexibility of Russian means that the order of words is less important than in English, because the case endings show where the subject and object of the sentence are. For example, 'Aleksei loves Yelena' can be put as «Алексей любит Елену» and also as «Елену любит Алексей» (*Aleksei lyubit Yelenu* and *Yelenu lyubit Aleksei*). Putting the subject after the object like this changes the emphasis in the sentence, but not the basic meaning – in both cases, it is Aleksei who is the subject (i.e. the person doing the action) and Yelena is the object.

Aspect and tense

Verbs have two **aspects** in the past and future. The **imperfective** is used to show a repeated, continuing or uncompleted action, while the **perfective** shows a single, completed action.

For example: Imperfective – «Он читал эту книгу всё лето» (*On chital etu knigu vsyo leto* – *He was reading / read this book all summer*).

Perfective – «Он прочитал это письмо сегодня утром» (*On prochital eto pis'mo segodnya utrom* – *He read this letter this morning*, i.e. and finished reading it).

This is tricky, of course – but you'll be pleased to know that it's compensated for by a relatively straightforward and simple tense system.

Stress in Russian

No, not what you get after struggling with all that you've just read! There is a set pattern of stress (which bit of a word is pronounced with more emphasis) for Russian words, with only one syllable in each word stressed, no matter how long the word is. This is different from English, where longer words have more than one stress – the word 'organization' in English has two stresses, for instance, while «организация» (*organizátsiya*) in Russian only has one.

In standard Russian, certain vowels are pronounced differently according to whether they are stressed or unstressed in a particular word. So, in the word «молоко» (*moloko* – milk), where the last syllable is stressed, the first two 'o's are pronounced more like 'a', while the last one is pronounced 'o', so the word actually sounds like 'malakó'.

Something missing?

A good starting point for understanding the difference between Russian and English is to listen to the common mistakes a Russian speaker will make in English. For example:

- The Russian verb 'to be' (быть) does not have a present tense, so you may hear a Russian say in English 'I – student', meaning I **am a** student.

- Russian has no **articles** ('the', 'a') and native Russian speakers can often be heard either mixing them ('I have the new job', meaning 'I have a new job') or leaving them out altogether ('He is good friend of mine').

Looks familiar

And some more good news. Once you've cracked the alphabet and begin to read some Russian (or take a look around if you're visiting Russia), you'll soon find that many words actually look pretty familiar. The Russian vocabulary includes many words originating from French, German, English and other European languages – see if you can decipher the following commonly found words! (Answers given in Taking it further on page 40.)

бизнесмен
кино
клуб
лидер
ресторан
такси
тротуар

Russian exports

English and other languages have also incorporated a number of Russian words over the years. It is said that the word bistro, or café, has its origins in the command given by victorious Russian soldiers when they were in Paris after the defeat of Napoleon in 1812, as they ordered drinks and told the waiters that they wanted to be served quickly – быстро (*bystro*). Bolshy comes from Bol'shevik and was used in English from 1917 to denote someone who is being difficult or rebellious. Спутник (Sputnik) became a generic term for satellite after the launch of the first satellite in 1957. And there are quite a lot more – see if you can remember them!

Dialects

For such a large country, the amount of variation in accent in Russian is surprisingly limited, perhaps a result of the practice of sending teachers trained in the major cities out into the countryside to educate the masses. This means more good news for the foreign student of Russian, who is – with few exceptions – likely to be able to understand Russian speakers no matter from which part of Russia they come (which is just not the case for those poor people who come to different regions of the UK after studying the Queen's English!).

There is an amount of variation, however, with a basic distinction existing between the so-called «оканье» (*okanye*) of northern regions and the «аканье» (*akanye*) of standard Russian. If you recall the piece on stress in the grammar lesson you had earlier in this chapter, you'll remember that in standard speech an unstressed 'o' is pronounced 'a'. Well, in *okanye*, an unstressed 'o' is often pronounced as a more open 'o' sound. Meanwhile, in the distinctive accent of Muscovites, the unstressed 'o' is elongated, producing something that is a little like the way a true Cockney will say the word 'London' (Lahn-don) or an American will say 'shahp' or 'bahx' for what is 'shop' or 'box' in standard UK English.

ПОГОВОРКИ И ПОСЛОВИЦЫ (*POGOVORKI I POSLOVITSY* – PROVERBS AND SAYINGS)

Russian is full of *pogovorki i poslovitsy*. Many Russians use them all the time. They are usually moralistic in tone, showing that such virtues as industriousness, patience, honesty and fidelity are rewarded. The optimistic sentiments they contain were used to help the long-suffering Russian people through the hardships of life under the tsars and the Communists (not to mention the current times as well…).

Examples include such wise offerings as:

Terpenie i trud vsyo peretrut (Patience and hard work will overcome everything)

Glaza boyatsya, a ruki delayut (Your eyes are frightened by the task but your hands get on with it)

Konchil delo, gulyai smelo (Once you've finished your work, then you can relax)

In the south of Russia, the intonation pattern is more musical and emotional (perhaps as a result of the additional sunlight they receive?) and the letter «г» is pronounced almost like an emphatic English 'h', rather than the standard Russian 'g' sound. People in different areas of the south can also use grammatical structure, vocabulary and stress patterns that differ from standard Russian. Mikhail Gorbachov, for example, who came from Stavropol region, was infamous for his idiosyncratic 'mistakes' in misplacing the stress in many words.

Regional accents tended not to be heard that much on Soviet TV and radio (apart from speeches by senior politicians, that is), with a stilted version of the standard accent predominating. Again, this is changing now, as the Russian media are able to present a more varied picture of the Russian language.

Other languages spoken in Russia

Russia's amazing ethnic tapestry is reflected in the abundance of languages spoken in the country, with over 100 languages still active at the start of the 21st century. They range from Russian's close Slavonic relations of Ukrainian and Belarussian, through Finno-Ugric languages as diverse as Veps and Karelian (found near the Finnish border) to Khanty and Komi-Zyrian, spoken by peoples in the far north of Russia. Then there are languages of the Turkic family, stretching from Bashkir to Yakut, as well as a variety of languages spoken by the peoples of the Caucasus region.

A good number of these languages find themselves, unfortunately, in a weak position, with fewer and fewer members of the community carrying on the tradition of using the language. This is the result both of attempts made by the Soviet regime to make Russian the dominant language (and, under Stalin, actively to suppress minority cultures) and of a general trend among the young to use Russian out of preference, seeing it as a route to better educational and employment opportunities. In recent years there have been attempts at the revival of these languages, driven from the grassroots as part of the overall tendency towards reasserting ethnic roots, and from Moscow, through the promotion of learning minority languages as part of education policy. Just how far such measures will prove successful in reversing the decline in usage remains to be seen – but it is to be hoped that this amazing collection of fascinating languages, and their cultures, will be maintained for future generations to admire and cherish.

Names and terms of address

Patronymics

Every Russian person has three names – as well as their first name (*imya*) and their last name (*familiya*), they also have a patronymic name (*otchestvo*). As you can guess, this is made from their father's name – for sons, an -ovich (or sometimes -evich, after certain letters) ending is added to the father's *imya*, for daughters the suffix -ovna (or -evna) is used. So, for example, Ol'ga and Andrei, the daughter and son of Ivan, will be known as Ol'ga Ivanovna and Andrei Ivanovich. The patronymic is used in formal circumstances and is the equivalent of saying Mr or Mrs in English. You are not usually addressed by your patronymic until you reach adulthood. Even for Russians, some patronymic combinations can be a bit of a mouthful, but sometimes a shortcut version is used, as in the case of Aleksandr Aleksandrovich, who becomes San Sanych!

Diminutives

In informal situations, and with children, Russians also use a wide and imaginative selection of variations on a person's *imya*. Here are some examples, but the list can be endless, as Russians use the large range of suffixes available to them to make ever more elaborate and affectionate names for their nearest and dearest.

Anna can become Anechka, Anyuta, Anyutka, Anyutochka, Annushka, Anyusechka, Nyura, Nyurochka, Nyeta, Nyetka, Nyetochka and so on! Vladimir can be called Volodya, Volod'ka, Volodechka, Voloden'ka, Vova, Vovka, Vovochka, Vovchik etc. etc.

So, if you happen to meet Vladimir Vladimirovich Putin, you could (if you knew him *really* well!) say '*Privet, Vovchik!*'.

ВЫ ИЛИ ТЫ? WAYS OF SAYING 'YOU'

As in many languages, Russian has a formal/plural and informal way of saying 'you'. Вы (*vy*) should be used for more than one person, or when you don't know someone that well (or want to show respect); ты (*ty*) is used with friends and family, and with children. There are interesting variations – in some parts of the south of Russia, a mother or father can still expect to be addressed as «вы» by their offspring, no matter how old the latter are.

Attracting someone's attention

If you walk around Russian streets, you'll soon hear that Russians use a variety of words for addressing people whom they do not know. In the old Soviet days, *tovarishch* (comrade) was used often and can still be heard today, although mainly by older people or in an ironic sense. In the later years of the USSR, as people became increasingly disillusioned with the regime, the word *tovarishch* was gradually discarded and people started to use other forms of address – which didn't always sound that polite! They went from the perfectly acceptable '*prostite*' or '*izvinite*' (excuse me) and '*devushka*' (Miss) or '*molodoi chelovek*' (young man), through the less cultured '*zhenshchina*' (woman) and '*muzhchina*' (man), to downright rude (but sometimes funny!) ways of grabbing someone's attention, such as '*Ei, Vy v krasnom palto!*' (Hey, you in the red coat!). You'll also find that even people who are well past the first flush of youth can still be called '*devushka*' or '*molodoi chelovek*'!

In the post-Soviet era the terms *gospodin* and *gospozha* (Mr and Mrs) that were used before 1917 are making a comeback in Russia (although they were used throughout the Soviet times for referring to foreigners) and there has also been a debate on whether *sudar'* and *sudarynya* (which roughly translate as 'sir' and 'madam') should come back as well.

Where Russian has come from and where it's going

The origins of the language

Russian is related to the other **Slavonic** languages, as you can hear if you visit Slovakia, Poland or Bulgaria, for example. By the 10th century three groups of Slavonic languages – Eastern, Southern and Western – had emerged. Russian's closest linguistic neighbours are the other descendants of Eastern Slavonic – Ukrainian and Belarussian – and native speakers of these languages will be able to understand quite a lot in each other's languages.

The similarities between the various groups made it possible to have a common written language, known as **Old Slavonic** or Old Church Slavonic, which kept its place as the written language of Russia until well into the 18th century, reflecting the influence of the church. Then, during the reign of Catherine the Great, the Russian language took over as the country's literary tradition developed, and the outstanding academic and man of letters **Mikhail Lomonosov** (1711–1765), suggested the use of three categories of language – High Style (Church Slavonic); Middle Style (for literature and science); and Low Style (for everyday usage). The Moscow dialect was used as the basis for Standard Russian.

Alongside the progress that the Russian language made in the 19th century, under the influence of such luminaries as Aleksandr Pushkin (see Unit 3), it should be noted that the upper classes in Russia from the 18th to the early 20th centuries tended to use French a great deal, which served as another divide between them and the increasingly discontented masses. (Even Lenin scribbled notes in other languages when working on his revolutionary texts!)

Revolutionizing the language

The October Revolution of 1917 sparked off enormous change in the Russian language as well as in society as a whole.

- The old-style alphabet was simplified in 1918, as the Bolsheviks began their ambitious programme of liquidating illiteracy. Some redundant letters were removed and the spelling and appearance of letters was rendered more straightforward. (Nowadays there is a fashion among some Russian shops and companies to use the old letters in the spelling of their name – sometimes not that authentically – the Russian equivalent of putting 'Ye olde taverne' in English.)

- Terms of address also changed a great deal, as 'bourgeois' words such as господин/госпожа (*gospodin/gospozha* – Mr and Mrs) gave way to the more egalitarian and proletarian товарищ (*tovarishch* – comrade) and гражданин/гражданка (*grazhdanin/grazhdanka* – citizen).

- Acronyms and abbreviations – some of them monstrously ugly, such as «ШКРАБ» (SHKRAB, short for *shkol'nyi rabotnik* – schoolworker or teacher) sprang up like mushrooms after 1917, reflecting the pace of change in official life at least (and leaving the person on the street scratching their head to work out what they all meant!). As time went on, the uglier abbreviations died out, while others changed to suit new policies and trends: the title of the secret police, for example, went from VChK (Cheka) through GPU, OGPU, NKVD, NKGB to James Bond's sparring partner, the KGB (*Komitet Gosudarstvennoi Bezopasnosti* – Committee of State Security), and finally to its current, post-Soviet title of FSB.

- The names of streets and towns were also changed to suit the times, with the most famous examples of the latter being Leningrad (formerly St Petersburg, which had already changed to the less German-sounding Petrograd during World War I) and Stalingrad (formerly Tsaritsyn), which later became Volgograd during the process of destalinization. During the later years of perestroika, a movement began to restore the original names of towns and streets, to symbolize the shattering of the Communist party's control. The citizens of Leningrad voted to have their city renamed St Petersburg (Sankt-Peterburg) in a referendum held in 1991 and a wave of other changes followed. In the city of Yaroslavl', the central streets carry signs that list all the previous names of that road – with sometimes as many as seven signs hanging one under another! And of course the name of the country itself changed, as people fell asleep one night in the Soviet Union and woke up the next day in the independent Russian Federation.

- There was also a penchant for giving children symbolic names connected with the revolution or with progress: Vladlen came from *Vlad*imir *Len*in, while Ninel' is Lenin backwards; Traktor (yes, some boys were called that!) marked the development of Soviet agriculture; while children called Raketa (rocket) had an explosive reputation to live up to... And there were cases of a brother and sister being called Rev and Lyutsiya – so when they were called to the dinner table, their parents would presumably shout out '*Rev-i-Lyutsiya*' (Revolution)! Later, during and after the cultural thaw of the 1960s, a rash of foreign names became popular (Rudol'f, Izabella, etc.), while the perestroika period unleashed a return of names that recalled those of the tsar's family and the nobility: Anna, Anastasiya, Nikolai, Pavel. In recent years, there's been a trend to use old Russian names that had been somewhat forgotten, such as Darya, Kseniya, Fyodor and Yegor, as well as more imports, like Karolina, Dzhonatan and Arnold.

Increasingly, the language of state officials and the mass media became stultified, as the USSR adopted something akin to Orwell's nightmare vision of 'newspeak', pilloried in the satirical stories of **Mikhail Bulgakov** and other writers. One of the low points of the Russian language's development (or perhaps more accurately stagnation) during the Soviet years was reached when **Leonid Brezhnev** was praised as a writer of extraordinary talent for the memoirs he had produced. In his later years Brezhnev's rambling, incoherent and mistake-ridden speeches were a source of amusement for the population and embarrassment for the authorities (there was even a special team employed by Soviet television to edit out the frequent slips of the tongue that Brezhnev made in his speeches before they could be broadcast!). One of the more hilarious examples comes from Brezhnev's inability to pronounce one of his favourite words, '*sistematicheski*' (systematically), which came out as '*siskimasiisski*', which sounds rude in a childish way.

The liberation of Russian? From held tongues to linguistic explosion

The language of real life continued to evolve outside the official domain, of course, despite the dominance of Soviet-style Russian in official discourse and Russians were adept at knowing which version of the vernacular to use in particular situations, as summed up in a line from the song '*Skovannye odnoi tsepyu*' (Tied by the same chain) by the rock group *Nautilus Pompilius*: *Odni slova dlya kukhon', drugie dlya ulits* (One set of words for the kitchen, another for the outside world). This self-monitoring process was especially important in the dark years under Stalin when a casual remark could lead to a spell in the camps. The population adopted ingenious methods of keeping their right to linguistic freedom alive, through Aesopian allusions, parody of official language and through the use of slang and swear words!

Ругательные слова (*rugatel'nye slova* – swearwords)

The puritanical character of the Soviet state meant that even mild swearwords and vulgar phrases were virtually banned from the public sphere (by way of illustration, there was really no need for a 'bleep' machine on Soviet TV, as programmes and films just didn't have any 'offensive' words in them). This didn't mean that people didn't swear in Soviet times – just the opposite! The prisons and the armed forces (as in most countries) proved fertile breeding grounds for crude yet imaginative innovations, while for some in the intelligentsia and the population at large the use of swearwords was a way of making a statement of rebellion. Nowadays, swearwords can be heard and read much more often in the media, in literature and in films. It's also not so much a male-dominated thing to swear now.

Слэнг (*sleng* – slang)

Non-vulgar slang words also entered mainstream speech from a variety of sources, with criminal subculture playing its part again, as well as other providers such as the Soviet hippy culture of the so-called *sistema* from the 1960s on. As we have already seen, the Russian language includes a large number of borrowings from other languages and current youth slang draws heavily on English in particular for its inspiration. In the 1980s, for example, young people could be heard saying «кул» (*kul* – cool), while other English words were given a Russian twist, as in «герла» (*gerla* – from 'girl').

Borrowings after 1991

The 1990s saw a veritable deluge of borrowings flooding the Russian language (principally from English), as the rapid marketization of Russia was accompanied by the jargon of advertising, the stock market, and other facets of the new economic order, with increased access to the internet adding further momentum. The Russian language simply did not include the words to describe Western business culture (or they had been long forgotten) and it would have struggled to produce them quickly enough to cope with demand – but in any case, many people were more than happy to use foreign words, as a way of showing how trendy they were, but also of demonstrating their commitment to the changes taking place in society. Such words as «маркетинг» (*marketing*), «рейтинг» (*reiting* – rating), «шейпинг» (*sheiping* – a form of aerobics) and «ток-шоу» (*tok-shou* – talk show) were adopted and sometimes adapted with new meanings added (the original use of the borrowed word *reiting*, for example, to refer to the popularity of movies and chart music (as in English) has been extended for use as a means of 'rating' potential boyfriends and girlfriends). At times the pace of borrowing has left ordinary people (especially of the older generation) reeling in its wake, as TV presenters, journalists and advertising agents have outdone each other with ever more subtle and incomprehensible innovations. Try decoding the following words (given only in Cyrillic!): «мониторинг»; «имидж-мэйкер»; «консалтинг»; «кофи-брейк». You probably wouldn't get, though, the more obscure «пиарщик» (a person working in public relations – from the English PR, Public Relations)!

Words of caution were uttered by some observers, including the writer and arch-conservative **Aleksandr Solzhenitsyn**, who warned of the potential corruption of the Russian language, while the Russian Orthodox Church has also been active in promoting what it sees as the need to defend the Russian language, and the topic of so-called *ekologiya yazyka* (linguistic ecology) has given rise to a number of studies. However, although there has been some mention of introducing limits on the amount of borrowings to be used in the media and in official discourse, this has not got very far and Russia is still a long way from seeing anything like the activities of the Academie Française in France. Moreover, history has shown that while Russian has, over the centuries, soaked up thousands of words from other languages, it tends to adapt them, sometimes change their meaning and Russify them, discarding those that are found to be not that useful in the end. The same is proving to be true in the post-Soviet era.

Russian today: under threat or flourishing?

It is clear that the transformation of Russian society has sparked off a wide-ranging and far-reaching revolution in the Russian language, which has left linguistic experts, politicians and the general public arguing over the merits and dangers that they perceive such changes to have brought. The features of this revolution, some of which have been touched on already, include:

• The liberalization of the language of the mass media, in which a much greater variety of registers is now used, in a style that is far closer to that used in everyday life.

- Politicians in Russia are often criticized for their low level of speech culture, but at least now they are seen to be speaking spontaneously, not in a sterile fashion reading out pre-prepared speeches.
- A huge amount of borrowings from foreign languages has been seen.
- Obscenities are now heard frequently in the street and on TV.
- Many people point to declining standards in linguistic competence in all areas of language use.

Of course, whether you see a particular trend as positive or negative depends on how you look at the issue. Linguistic norms are always being challenged in any language – this is how they develop, after all. Criticism of a 'drop' in linguistic culture, for instance, misses the point that nowadays many more people are able to have their say in the public arena than was the case in the Soviet times. It is important, of course, to make sure that certain basic standards are maintained and with this goal in mind the Russian government has introduced programmes to support the development of the Russian language, drawing on its rich traditions and reflecting the nature of life in the 21st century.

Russian in the world

According to studies made on language usage, some 170 million people worldwide regard Russian as their first language, with the overall total including second-language speakers set at 288 million. Russian comes seventh in the list of world languages by first-language speakers, after Chinese (Mandarin), Spanish, English, Bengali, Hindi and Portuguese.

On the official level, Russian's position as a lingua franca among the Soviet successor states and the countries of East–Central Europe has been eroded, as the political elites of many of these countries (justifiably) demand that their language is given equal status and as English is taking over more and more as the language for communicating with Western countries. On the ground level people are more pragmatic and Russian is still widely used in the former Soviet republics, where apart from local Russian populations there are also many people who have a fluent command of Russian. The level of knowledge of the language is likely to decline over time, however, now that it isn't promoted as the language of the state as it was during Soviet times.

Further afield, Russian is spoken among émigré communities in Israel, North America and Western Europe, although the number of opportunities for foreigners to study the language in their own country are often relatively limited. (In the UK, for instance, it is not offered in many schools and university-level provision is constantly under threat from budget cuts and a lack of government support.)

GLOSSARY

аканье (n.)	*akanye*
акцент (m.)	*accent*
вид глагола (m.)	*aspect of verb*
вокабуляр (m.)	*vocabulary*
время (n.)	*tense*
выражение (n.)	*expression*
глагол (m.)	*verb*
грамматика (f.)	*grammar*
грамотный (adj.)	*literate*
диалект (m.)	*dialect*
жаргон (m.)	*slang*
значение (n.)	*meaning*
мат (m.)	*swearwords*
местоимение (n.)	*pronoun*
наречие (n.)	*adverb*
неологизм (m.)	*neologism*
несовершенный вид (m.)	*imperfective aspect*
оканье (n.)	*okanye*
падеж (m.)	*case*
предложение (n.)	*sentence*
прилагательное (n.)	*adjective*
произношение (n.)	*pronunciation*
разговорная речь (f.)	*colloquial speech*
речь (f.)	*speech*
ругаться матом (vb.)	*to swear*
слэнг (m.)	*slang*
словарь (m.)	*dictionary, vocabulary*
слово (n.)	*word*
совершенный вид (m.)	*perfective aspect*
существительное (n.)	*noun*
числительное (n.)	*numeral*
язык (m.)	*language, tongue*

Taking it further

Answers to quiz on borrowed words used in Russian:

бизнесмен	*biznesmen*	businessman
кино	*kino*	cinema
клуб	*klub*	club
лидер	*lider*	leader
ресторан	*restoran*	restaurant
такси	*taksi*	taxi
тротуар	*trotuar*	pavement

Learning Russian

The best way to take Russian further, of course, is to study the language. Nowadays there are plenty of opportunities to study Russian in Russia, on intensive programmes – try an internet search for the latest offers. Alternatively, enrol on a language programme or have a go at studying the language by yourself (perhaps you're already doing so, with one of the *Teach Yourself Russian* courses?).

Books

If you want to explore the sociolinguistics of Russian further, try *The Russian Language Today* (London: Routledge, 1999) by Larisa Ryazanova-Clarke and Terence Wade, which gives a comprehensive review of the development of Russian in the 20th century. For a lively journey through some of the language that your language course might not cover, try Edward Topol's *Dermo!: The Real Russian Tolstoy Never Used* (New York: Dutton Plume, 1997).

Websites

Information on the many languages spoken by the peoples of Russia can be found on:

www.tooyoo.l.u-tokyo.ac.jp/Russia/bibl/index.html and
http://odur.let.rug.nl/~bergmann/russia.htm

Meanwhile, **www.gramota.ru** provides a rich source of information on a range of aspects relating to the Russian language.

03

literature and thought

In this unit you will learn
- about Russia's literary roots
- about 19th century Russian literature
- about Soviet literature
- about literature in the new Russia

From epic stories of battles against Tatar armies, through the exploits of dashing yet lonely heroes and tragic tales of love in the Caucasus mountains, to sumptuous balls whose serenity is contrasted with the waste of the battlefield, then grotesque worlds where noses can walk away from their owners, on to the soul-searching existential torments of a young murderer, divine poetry that describes the crushing inhumanity of the Terror and postmodern images of a crisis of identity in today's Russia – this is Russian literature!

It has produced some of the most important works of poetry, prose and drama in the world, but for Russians it has always been much more than an art form: it has helped to define what it is to be Russian, what Russia is – and, as in the title of the famous work by **Nikolai Chernyshevskii** – *What is to be Done?* (*chto delat'?*). The debate over social change has been one of the recurrent themes that have resonated in Russia's literary canon, with writers drawing their readers' attention to the problems they believed were afflicting the country – and often paying a high personal price for doing so. Some lost their lives as a result of their work and their involvement in politics: Pushkin's friend **Kondratii Ryleyev**, a poet, was hanged for his participation in the Decembrist protests in 1825; over a century later, the poet **Osip Mandel'shtam** died in one of Stalin's camps. Others escaped with lighter, yet still harsh, sentences: Pushkin himself was punished by internal exile, as was Dostoyevskii (after facing a mock execution). Others still (such as Gertsen, Bunin, Nabokov, Solzhenitsyn) left Russia, either 'voluntarily' or through expulsion and were forced to carry on their work abroad. The writer's fate in Russia has thus often been a tragic one and has reflected too the fate of the country as a whole. The social message contained in their works has often been perceived to be at least as important as the literary value, inspiring their own and subsequent generations.

The other eternal themes found in Russian literature, such as the debate over spirituality and the Russian soul (*russkaya dusha*), and the importance of the individual and his or her identity (*lichnost'*), have been echoed in Russia's philosophical traditions. It is often said that Russia has produced little in the way of original philosophical thought (although there have been a number of significant contributions to the world of philosophy, from such figures as Berdyaev and Solovyov). This stems at least in part from the same isolation that initially held up the development of Russian literature, with philosophical ideas taking some time to arrive in Russia, before being adapted by Russian thinkers to suit the local conditions. And being a philosopher in Russia has tended to be a risky business as well, courting suspicion and possibly persecution from the authorities (hence the importance of literature as a means of conducting philosophical debate through fiction – although the tsarist, and later Soviet, censors were often wise to this as well). At the same time, Russia has, perhaps more than any other country, seen its social and political life influenced by grand philosophical debates and dogmas: the Soviet state's violent imposition of Marxist–Leninist ideology being the starkest example of this.

Russia's literary roots

Kievan Rus' and Muscovy

It was not until the 18th century that literature in Russia began to use the Russian language, with Old Church Slavonic having been employed until that point. This fact meant that the Orthodox Church played a leading role in the early development of Russia's literary traditions. During the period of domination of Kievan Rus', a number of important works were produced, including the *Sermon on Law and Grace* (*Slovo o zakone i blagodati*), written in 1050 and seen as the first literary work produced in Russia; chronicles (*letopisi*), most famously the *Primary Chronicle* (also known as the *Tale of Bygone Years*) (c. 1113), which provides a history of the people of Russia and the other East Slav nations; and the *Tale of Igor'* (*Slovo o polku Igoreve*).

The Tatar yoke served to hold up the development of literature in Russia, although the theme of the struggle against this domination provided the inspiration for a good number of works, including the tale *The Battle Beyond the Don* (*Zadonshchina*) shortly after the battle itself was fought in 1380. Another key theme was that of putting Moscow forward as the 'Third Rome', the rightful inheritor of the leadership of Orthodoxy and the legacy of Rome and Constantinople; and the creation of numerous works recording the lives of saints. An interesting work from the early 16th century, *Domostroi*, provides a guideline to how heads of Russian households should conduct themselves.

> ### LANDMARKS OF RUSSIAN LITERATURE:
> ### *THE TALE OF IGOR'*
>
> *The Tale of Igor'* (**Slovo o polku Igoreve**) is the most astounding example of the literature of this period, written around 1185–1187, and recounts in lyrical prose the events leading to the defeat of Duke Igor' of Novgorod in 1185. The richness of the Tale's style has led some over the years to doubt its authenticity, with suggestions made that the manuscript was written much later than the 12th century, although the debate has tended to come down on the side of its being a genuine work.

Folklore

Alongside this written literature there was also a rich oral tradition, drawing inspiration from both pagan and Orthodox influences. The *byliny* were epic songs, based on historical and mythical subjects. The heroes of the *byliny* included *bogatyri*, or knights, fighting valiantly against the Mongols. Another form of the oral tradition, that was later collated in written form and which has retained its importance and popularity to this day, is the *skazka*, or folk tale, with a cast of characters that includes *Baba Yaga*, a witch who is said to inhabit the dark Russian forest.

The 18th century

As Russia began to enter into more contact with Western Europe, so its literature came to reflect these influences, as seen in the early Russian drama of **Polotskii** and nascent poetic traditions. Peter the Great's programme of modernization pushed such developments further, while Catherine the Great – herself a playwright – proved to be an avid patron of Russia's literary establishment. She corresponded at length with Voltaire and French literature and thought made a strong impact on the Russian scene, as the ideas of the Enlightenment were imported and Russian neoclassical style emerged.

As we saw in Unit 2, at this time Russian language finally replaced Old Church Slavonic as the literary vernacular, with Mikhail Lomonosov making a great contribution to the study of Russian and its usage. In poetry, **Gavrila Derzhavin** (1743–1816) took the art of writing odes to new heights, producing a style that drew on 'high' and 'low' styles and which were truly Russian, in contrast to the imitations of foreign poetry produced by less talented contemporaries. **Nikolai Karamzin** (1766–1826) relied more on French influences, but nevertheless made a huge contribution to the Russian literary style through such prose works as *Poor Liza* (*Bednaya Liza*) (1792).

The 19th Century

The Golden Age

The foundations laid by Derzhavin, Karamzin and others inspired young aspiring writers in Russia to join them in exploiting the intrinsic poetic qualities of the Russian language, with this outpouring of talent producing what became known as the Golden Age (*Zolotoi vek*) of Russian poetry, at the start of the 19th century. Their ranks included the romantic poet **Vasilii Zhukovskii** (1783–1852) and **Konstantin Batyushkov** (1787–

Aleksandr Pushkin

1855), but by far the most influential and famous of Russia's literary sons of this – and any other era, for that matter – was the great **Aleksandr Pushkin** (1799–1837). His genius began to sparkle even when he was just a pupil of the famous progressive lycée at Tsarskoe Selo. By the time of his death, he was already recognized as Russia's bard and has retained this status ever since, with his poetry regarded by most as the pinnacle of Russian literature. His poetic work includes the novels in verse *Yevgenii Onegin* (see p. 46), *Ruslan i Lyudmila* (1820), and *Mednyi vsadnik* (*The Bronze Horseman*) (1833). The following extract, from his poem *Ya pomnyu chudnoe mgnovenie* (1825) (I recall a wonderful moment) gives a good example of just how captivatingly beautiful his poetry could be:

Ya pomnyu chudnoe mgnovenie:	I recall a wonderful moment:
Peredo mnoi yavilas' ty,	You appeared in front of me,
Kak mimoletnoe videnie,	Like a fleeting glimpse,
Kak genii chistoi krasoty.	Like the genius of pure beauty.

Pushkin proved to be a master of genres, moving effortlessly between lyrical poetry, prose (e.g. *The Queen of Spades* (*Pikovaya dama*) (1834) and *The Captain's Daughter* (*Kapitanskaya dochka*) (1836)), verse drama (*Boris Godunov*) (1825), and historiography. He also mixed romantic style with influences from Russia's folk traditions, making a major contribution to the literary language. Pushkin himself was a dashing, attractive man, who lived a life every bit as romantic as that of his characters – and in the end he was killed in a duel that he had been lured into by his enemies, who forced him to defend his wife's honour. Pushkin's name lives on, however, and his mythical presence in Russian culture extends far beyond the literary realm, serving as a symbol of freedom and spiritual ascendancy over oppression.

A number of poets who were close to Pushkin, such as Yevgenii Baratynskii and Anton Delvig were dubbed the *Pushkinskaya pleyada* (Pushkin Pleiad). However, Pushkin's direct heir is usually considered to be **Mikhail Lermontov** (1814–1841), a Russian Byron who, by the time he too was killed in a duel at the tragically young age of 27, had managed to take Russian romanticism to its highest point. His work includes *Mtsyri*, (1840), whose narrative perfectly captures the emotions of its hero, a monk who briefly enjoys freedom among beautiful natural surroundings after escaping from his monastery, before dying from exhaustion; the popular but less impressive epic poem *Demon* (*Demon*) (1830–1841); and the novel *A Hero of Our Time* (*Geroi nashego vremeni*) (1840), this last giving a fine psychological portrait of its main character, Pechorin.

LANDMARKS IN RUSSIAN LITERATURE: *YEVGENII ONEGIN*

This novel in verse is Pushkin's most celebrated accomplishment, written between 1823 and 1831. A narrator recounts the story of unrequited love between Yevgenii, a Petersburg sophisticate, and the naive Tatyana, but along the way he also provides a vivid description of life among Russia's high society and the poet's own journey to find himself.

The age of the novel

After Pushkin and Lermontov had prematurely left the scene, the poetic tradition was carried on by two notable poets, **Fyodor Tyutchev** (1803–1873), famous for the philosophical content of his poems, and **Afanasii Fet** (1820–1892). By the 1840s, under the influence of such figures as the critic **Vissarion Belinskii**, Romanticism had given way to Naturalism, and subsequently Realism, and poetry had ceded its position to prose, as the era of the great Russian novels commenced. The comic, dark, at times semi-surreal works of **Nikolai Gogol'** (1809–1852) painted an absurd yet disturbingly accurate picture of Russian life. In *The Overcoat* (*Shinel'*) (1842) – one of the greatest examples of the short story genre in any language – the hero Akakii Akakievich is a poor clerk obsessed with acquiring a new coat. He uses various ridiculous means to scrimp and save in order to buy the coat, only to have it stolen from him. Akakii falls ill and dies, the prosaic nature of his death mirroring the lack of purpose and humanity in the mundane life he had led. We see more of the absurdity of life in *The Nose* (*Nos*) (1836), in which no one seems to think the disappearance (and eventual return) of a certain Kovalyov's nose to be anything out of the ordinary. Gogol''s most important work is the novel *Dead Souls* (*Myortvye dushi*) (1842), a stinging commentary on provincial Russian life and a masterpiece of style.

The works of **Ivan Turgenev** (1818–1883) reflect the preoccupations of the Russian educated classes, as they navigated the waves of reform and reaction in the mid-19th century. Turgenev was a master of style, yet there was increasingly a tension apparent in his work between his pursuit of literary form and his recognition that his writing should contain a strong political and social undertone. His *Hunter's Sketches* (*Zapiski okhotnika*) (1852) is an understated and elegantly written protest against the inhumanity of serfdom and is purported to have played a role in bringing about the emancipation of the serfs in 1861. Turgenev's most accomplished work is the novel *Fathers and Sons* (*Ottsy i deti*) (1862), in which he provides a telling account of the gulf that was apparent between the cautious liberal reformers of the 1840s and the more aggressive Nihilists of the 1860s, represented by the novel's hero, Bazarov.

The character of the lazy, overweight and politically indifferent landowner **Oblomov**, in the novel of the same name by **Ivan Goncharov** (1812–1891), published in 1859, contrasts greatly with that of Bazarov, highlighting the inertia and resistance to change that frustrated those committed to social reform. Both are examples of character types that were hotly debated in literary and philosophical analyses. One such type, the 'superfluous man' (*lishnii chelovek*), formulated by the leading intellectual **Aleksandr Gertsen** (often translated as Herzen) (1812–1870), refers to the plight of the Russian educated man who has lost his sense of moral purpose. These superfluous men have made frequent appearances on the pages of Russian literary works, from Pushkin's *Onegin*, to Pasternak's *Zhivago* and beyond.

Nikolai Leskov (1831–1895) displayed great mastery of language in his works, which included anti-nihilist novels and the melodrama *Lady Macbeth of Mtsensk District* (*Ledi Makbet Mtsenskogo uezda*) (1865). **Nikolai Nekrasov** (1821–1878) is remembered for his 'civic' poetry, in which he railed against the injustices of his time. **Mikhail Saltykov-Shchedrin** (1826–1889) wrote brilliant satire and the novel *The Golovlyovs* (*Gospoda Golovlyovy*) (1875–1880), a dark and pessimistic family saga.

RUSSIAN THOUGHT: SLAVOPHILES AND WESTERNIZERS

The failed Decembrist revolt of 1825 had underlined the differences between those who advocated radical change and those of more conservative leaning. From the 1830s the debate between the so-called Slavophiles and Westernizers added to the sense of discord. The Westernizers, through such influential voices as **Chaadaev**, **Gertsen** and **Belinskii**, argued that Russia's future depended on assimilating ideas and technology from Western Europe. The Slavophiles, whose number included **Ivan Kireyevskii** and **Konstantin Aksakov**, emphasized what they saw as Russia's distinctive qualities that set it aside from Europe. The major themes of this debate – on whether Russia is European or 'Eurasian'; on the role of the state and the nature of civic and individual rights – have been a feature of Russian life ever since.

Drama

Russian theatre was relatively little developed by the early 19th century, but the input of leading literary figures, including Pushkin and Gogol, served to begin to rectify this shortcoming. Pushkin's play in verse *Boris Godunov* (1825) has tended to be rarely performed, although a star-studded production of the play, with Russian stage and screen actors directed by the English producer Declan Donnellan was staged in Russia and in Europe and North America in 2001–2002. The satire on

Moscow society *Woe from Wit* (**Gore ot uma**) (1833) by **Aleksandr Griboyedov** (1795–1829) is better known and is regarded as a classic of Russian theatre. In the play *The Inspector General* (**Revizor**) (1836), Gogol provides a characteristic indictment of the absurdities of Russian provincial life. The best-known works of drama of the mid-19th century, however, belong to **Aleksandr Ostrovskii** (1823–1886), who wrote some 50 plays, including *The Thunderstorm* (**Groza**) (1860), the story of an adulterous affair set in a conservative provincial town. (See also pages 122–5.)

Dostoyevskii and Tolstoi

Fyodor Dostoyevskii (1821–1881) stands tall among the world's literary giants, and his major works – written after the exile to Siberia that had such a haunting impression on him – are well known to many foreign readers, who often see him as the quintessentially Russian author. His novels explore a wide range of complex philosophical and moral issues and serve as a vehicle for the discussion of trends of thought that would follow him. *Notes from the Underground* (1864) (**Zapiski iz podpolya**), for instance, predicts the development of existentialist ideas in the 20th century, with its study of the nature of free will. Dostoyevskii also made a major contribution to the development of the novel as an art form, with the critic Mikhail Bakhtin identifying, for example, the importance of 'polyphonic' style (use of several narrative voices) in Dostoyevskii's work.

The novel *Crime and Punishment* (**Prestuplenie i nakazanie**) (1866) is a study of morality and religion and tells the story of the torturous repentance undergone by Raskol'nikov, a young student who commits a premeditated murder. In *The Idiot* (**Idiot**) (1869), the hero Prince Myshkin, who resembles Christ, loses his sanity among the greed and passion of Petersburg society and is complicit in the murder of the woman he loves. *The Devils* (or *The Possessed* in some translations) (1872) (**Besy**) deals with political themes and includes stinging criticism of Turgenev and the ideas of the Nihilists. (Dostoyevskii was a conservative.) In his last novel, *The Brothers Karamazov* (**Bratya Karamazovy**) (1880), Dostoyevskii reaches the height of his literary powers, in a work that embeds far-reaching metaphysical ideas in a story that delves, at times, into burlesque style. The novel deals with the very different reactions of three brothers (Ivan, Dmitrii and Alyosha) to the murder of their father and explores issues concerning justice, faith and God:

> Imagine that it's you who are constructing the building of human fate, with the eventual aim of making people happy and giving them peace and rest, but in order to do this it would be necessary and unavoidable to torture to death just one tiny creature... Would you agree to be the architect under such conditions, and put up this building on the foundation of unavenged tears?

LANDMARKS IN RUSSIAN LITERATURE: *WAR AND PEACE*

This huge work was originally intended as a family novel, with an anti-war message, yet by the time it was published as a complete work it had been turned into a historical novel with a strong patriotic sentiment. It is rightly regarded as a classic of world literature. The story follows the fortunes of four families from 1805–1820, from the opulence of St Petersburg ballrooms to the bloody waste of battlefields. The accuracy of Tolstoi's depiction of historic events can be questioned and the great length of the novel calls its cohesion into doubt for some critics. However, Tolstoi's principal characters shine out and it is clear with whom the author's sympathies lie: the natural qualities of Natasha Rostova and the simple honesty of the peasants are set against the futile reflections of the more intellectually inclined characters.

The work of **Lev (Leo) Tolstoi** (1828–1910) stands in contrast to that of Dostoyevskii. Tolstoi was from a noble family, and began his literary career with a short novel, *Childhood* (*Detstvo*) (1852), followed by his *Sevastopol Stories (Sevastopol'skie rasskazy)* (1855–1856), based on his experiences as an artillery officer during the Crimean War. From these early works the reader gained a taste of what was to become Tolstoi's trademark style, of realist prose imbued with a strong, moralizing tone together with in-depth psychological portraits. Alongside his work as a novelist Tolstoi also threw his energies into pedagogical work, running a school for local peasant children on his estate at Yasnaya Polyana and writing textbooks.

Tolstoi is best remembered for his two giant masterpieces, *War and Peace* (*Voina i mir*) (1865–1869) and *Anna Karenina* (1875–1877). In the latter, Tolstoi explores and pronounces judgement on the morals of Russian society, through his depiction of the descent of the novel's tragic heroine, Anna. Her adulterous affair with a young officer, Vronskii, her subsequent neglect of her son and her vain attempts to retain Vronskii's attentions are contrasted sharply with the 'good' example of the marriage of Konstantin Levin and Kitty Shcherbatskii. Anna eventually commits suicide by jumping under a train, one of the many negative symbols of modernization found in the novel. This extract is taken from the point in the novel where her death occurs:

> The candle by which she had been reading this book so full of troubles, deceit, grief and evil, flared brighter than ever and lit up for her everything that had previously been in darkness, flickered, faded and then went out for ever.

In the later stages of *Anna Karenina* some signs can be detected of the personal crisis that Tolstoi was to undergo in the late 1870s, after which he turned away from writing novels and began to develop his philosophical ideas, which included a rejection of the church, the promotion of non-violent protest and a harshly puritanical view of women and sex. The fiction of these years, such as *The Death of Ivan Il'ich* (*Smert' Ivana Il'icha*) (1886), *The Kreutzer Sonata* (*Kreitserova sonata*) (1889) and the novel *Resurrection* (*Voskresenie*) (1899) reflects these obsessions.

Three giants of Russian literature: Dostoyevskii, Tolstoi and Chekhov

The Silver Age

The short stories and plays of **Anton Chekhov** (1860–1904) represent a break with the moralizing of Dostoyevskii and Tolstoi. In his short stories, which include *Chameleon* (*Khameleon*) (1884) *A Horsey Name* (*Loshadinaya familiya*) (1885) and *Lady with a Lapdog* (*Dama s sobachkoi*) (1899), he takes us inside the lives of his characters, whom he often presents in a less than flattering light, drawing attention to their human frailties and shortcomings. He is also master of conveying the humorous side of everyday situations in a succinct style. In Chekhov's plays, which at the time they were first staged were seen as innovative, plot is secondary to details of everyday life, while the use of mood, produced often by sounds from offstage, is much in evidence. These features allow considerable scope for directors to choose how to interpret his plays. (Chekhov himself worked closely with the legendary Russian producer **Stanislavskii** and the Moscow Art Theatre.) In the West it his for his plays that Chekhov is best known: *The Seagull* (*Chaika*) (1896), *Uncle Vanya* (*Dyadya Vanya*) (1899), *Three Sisters* (*Tri sestry*) (1901) and *The Cherry Orchard* (*Vishnyovii sad*) (1904) are still performed regularly in theatres in Russia and abroad.

RUSSIAN THOUGHT:
VLADIMIR SOLOVYOV (1853–1900)

Solovyov is one of Russia's most prominent philosophers, who proposed the unification of Eastern and Western forms of Christianity according to his concept of 'Godmanhood'. Through his work on Sophia (Divine Wisdom) he influenced the Symbolist school of poets in Russia.

As the turn of century approached, the novel's supremacy ended, replaced by a new focus on the short story and on poetry. In the latter, the movements of Symbolism, Acmeism and Futurism dominated. **Symbolist** writers rejected the notion that literature could imitate reality, stressing instead the symbolic nature of art. There is a persistent theme of impending doom apparent in much of their work, reflecting the looming crises and revolutions in Russia. The most outstanding representatives of the movement are **Aleksandr Blok** (1880—1921) and **Andrei Belyi** (1880–1934), whose symbolist novel 'Petersburg' (*Peterburg*) (1913–1914) presents a nightmarish portrayal of the Russian capital through a complex stream of consciousness.

The **Acmeist** movement, led by the poet **Nikolai Gumilyov**, called for a focus on the essence of beauty, rather than on searching for symbols. This movement includes in its ranks the great poets **Anna Akhmatova** and **Osip Mandel'shtam**.

> ### LANDMARKS IN RUSSIAN LITERATURE:
> ### AKHMATOVA'S REQUIEM (*REKVIEM*) (1935–1940)
>
> *Requiem* is a cycle of poems on the theme of the purges and the arrest of Akhmatova's son. The power of the verse is overshadowed by the terrifying subject matter. The work holds a place deep in the emotions of Russians, keeping the chilling memory of those terrible years alive for each new generation.

The loose-knit groupings of avant-garde poets who contributed to the development of Futurist writing included the young poet **Vladimir Mayakovskii**. They experimented with linguistic innovation and drew inspiration from abstract painters such as Vasilii Kandinskii. Other outstanding poets of this era include **Marina Tsvetayeva** and **Boris Pasternak**.

Alongside the Modernist approaches adopted by some of their illustrious contemporaries, the writers of the so-called *Znanie* (knowledge) group, associated with the publishing house of the same name, stuck to more traditional literary genres. Well-known names from the group include **Ivan Bunin** (1870–1953), who wrote impressionist short stories, such as *The Gentleman from San Francisco* (*Gospodin iz San-Frantsisko*) (1916), with passion and nature key elements in his work; and **Aleksandr Kuprin** (1870–1938) the author of sentimental and colourful

Anna Akhmatova

stories on topical issues. The most significant member of the group is probably **Maksim Gorkii** (1868–1936), whose works (such as *Mother* (*Mat'*), published in 1907 and *The Lower Depths* (*Na dne*) (1902)) deal with the conditions endured by the working class (from which he had himself come) and the basis for revolutionary activity. Gorkii was to be one of the leading voices on literary matters of the Bolshevik party following the October Revolution of 1917.

The Soviet Period

Proletarian writers and fellow travellers

The social turmoil caused by the revolution and the civil war created an unstable cultural atmosphere. Writers who supported the new regime grouped into organizations such as *Proletkult* and the Russian Association of Proletarian Writers (RAPP), with the aim of developing a distinctive proletarian culture in keeping with the nature of the new Soviet state. Initially, however, the authorities were tolerant of writers who took a less fervently positive line (or even an openly critical one). Among these so-called 'fellow travellers' (*poputchiki*) were Mandelshtam, Leonov, Babel' and **Erenburg**. Writers who went further in their criticism of the new regime include the brilliant satirist **Mikhail Zoshchenko; Il'f and Petrov**, who jointly wrote comedies; **Yevgenii Zamyatin,** author of the anti-utopian novel *We* (*My*) (1924); and **Yurii Olesha,** whose novel *Envy* (*Zavist'*) (1927) challenges the brazen certainties of Soviet life through its absurd and hilarious attack on bureaucracy. Others, meanwhile, such as Bunin and Tsvetayeva, left Russia and joined Russian émigrés in Western Europe and North America. Among those to leave was

---

RUSSIAN THOUGHT: VLADIMIR LENIN (1870–1924)

Lenin added to and amended the works of Karl Marx, the resulting melange termed Marxism–Leninism and used as the ideological cornerstone of the Soviet state until its collapse. Practical considerations outweighed adherence to doctrine, with Lenin impatient to seize power in Russia ahead of the time prescribed according to Marx's dialectic framework. The Communist ideology that developed in the USSR became a veil behind which the Soviet state sought to justify and legitimate its actions, including its excesses of violence.

Vladimir Nabokov, who later produced the novel *The Gift* (*Dar*) (1938) and other works in Russian while in Berlin, before commencing his English-language literary career after moving to the USA. Of those who committed themselves to the Communist cause, the name of Mayakovskii stands out. His considerable poetic output mixed propaganda with witty and moving verse that continued in the innovative vein of his early years.

Socialist Realism

The willingness of the Soviet state to allow literary experiment and criticism of the regime ended in the late 1920s and an increasingly severe system of censorship was employed (continuing the tsarist tradition). The officially sanctioned style was to be Socialist Realism (using Gorkii's *Mother* as a model), in which positive treatment of Soviet life and achievements was to be used. For the most part, the straitjacket this imposed on creativity led to stilted, uninspiring work. The more accomplished examples of the 'genre' include the novel *Cement* (*Tsement*) by **Gladkov** and **Mikhail Sholokhov**'s epic novel *Tikhii Don* (1928–1940), known to English-language readers as *And Quiet Flows the Don* and *The Don Flows Home to the Sea*, which manages to convey the brutality of the civil war.

LANDMARKS IN RUSSIAN LITERATURE:
THE MASTER AND MARGARITA

Bulgakov's dark and comical novel intertwines plots set in Moscow of the 1930s (which the Devil is visiting) and Jerusalem at the time of Jesus Christ. Moving between witty satire and references to Goethe's *Faust*, it delivers a damning verdict on Soviet life and touches too upon eternal themes of mortality and religion. A famous line from the novel asserts that 'Manuscripts do not burn' (*rukopisi ne goryat*), a defiant gesture to the attempts of the Soviet state to smother literature.

The state's grip over the visible literary scene tightened in the 1930s, with the setting up of the Union of Writers, which came to offer considerable material benefits to officially endorsed writers, but which served as a tool to sanction those who strayed from, or refused even to approach, the 'correct' line. Among the long list of writers who endured such intimidation was the gifted novelist, short-story writer and dramatist, **Mikhail Bulgakov** (1891–1940), whose powerful plays such as *White Guard* (*Belaya gvardiya*) and satirical stories including

The Heart of the Dog (*Sobachee serdtse*) provided stinging and poignant commentary on the early years of Soviet rule. His greatest work, the novel *The Master and Margarita* (*Master i Margarita*), lay unpublished for some 27 years, but has since been recognized as a masterpiece. Another writer whose work suffered the same fate was **Andrei Platonov** (1899–1951), who was a committed communist, but in such works as the novel *Chevengur* (1928–1930) he skilfully portrays and condemns the conditions of life in the Soviet countryside.

RUSSIAN THOUGHT: NIKOLAI BERDYAEV (1874–1948)

Berdyaev was a Marxist and a religious philosopher, who was appointed as professor of philosophy at Moscow University in 1920. After being exiled from the USSR in 1922, he became a leading émigré figure in France, where he developed his work on Christian existentialism.

Thaws, stagnation and samizdat

After Stalin's death the cultural 'thaw' overseen by Khrushchov allowed the Russian literary community to begin to breathe again, at least for a short time, and the brash young poets **Yevgenii Yevtushenko**, **Andrei Vosnesenskii** and **Iosif Brodskii** (who was to become poet laureate of the USA and Nobel Prize winner for literature in 1987) enjoyed considerable popular appeal, later giving readings to packed stadia. The limits of tolerance were short, however. **Boris Pasternak** (1890–1960) a talented poet, saw his novel *Doktor Zhivago* published in the West in 1957, giving him instant fame abroad among those who read it and who saw the feature film that was soon made (directed by the British director, David Lean). The novel, which concludes with a cycle of poems, deals with the fate of a middle class family before and after the Bolshevik revolution. While not the most outstanding example of literature, the political contexts of the day contributed to Pasternak being awarded the Nobel Prize for literature in 1958, but the Soviet authorities did not allow him to receive the award.

The publication of **Aleksandr Solzhenitsyn's** (b. 1918) short novel *One Day in the Life of Ivan Denisovich* (*Odin den' Ivana Denisovicha*) (1962) in the leading literary journal *New World* (*Novyi mir*) stunned its readers with its account of life in the GULAG camps (in which Solzhenitsyn himself had been incarcerated). Solzhenitsyn went on to produce a huge body of work, dealing with aspects of Soviet and Russian history and contemporary life, including the novels *Cancer Ward* (*Rakovyi korpus*) (1968) and *The First Circle* (*V kruge pervom*) (1968). Solzhenitsyn's work attracted considerable criticism, however, and he was eventually exiled, spending over 20 years in the USA, before returning to live in Russia in the mid-1990s. Like Pasternak, Solzhenitsyn was awarded the Nobel Prize for literature in 1970.

The period of thaw did not last for long and under Brezhnev literary life suffered the same atmosphere of stagnation that pervaded life in the country as a whole. The most notable literary events were the scandals surrounding the arrest of Brodskii and the trial of the authors **Daniel** and **Sinyavskii**. Pushed underground by the censors, some writers took advantage of opportunities to print work clandestinely (*samizdat* or self-publishing) or even abroad (*tamizdat*, from the word *tam*, 'over there'). Others still kept their manuscripts in their desk drawers, ready to be taken out should the oppressive conditions ever be removed.

The confines of Socialist Realism were less and less adhered to, however. The writers of the 'Village Prose' school, such as **Vasilii Shukshin** (1929–1974) and **Valentin Rasputin** (b. 1937) produced a considerable amount of work in the 1960s and 1970s on the nature of life in rural Russia, where traditional patterns of culture were compared favourably with the problems of urban dwellers. Meanwhile, **Yurii Trifonov** (1925–1981), **Chingiz Aitmatov** (b. 1928) and others critically explored aspects of contemporary life.

Literature under glasnost', 1985–1991

The restrictions on writers withered away quickly under Gorbachov, leaving writers free – should they so wish – to engage in ever more open and far-reaching criticism of the Soviet regime in their works. Meanwhile, previously banned or repressed writers were 'rehabilitated', mostly posthumously, and their works started to emerge from the obscurity that the Soviet censor had imposed in the USSR (with Russians thus able, for instance, to read for themselves the works of Pasternak, Solzhenitsyn and others that foreigners had enjoyed access to for many years). The works of writers who lived in the West, such as **Eduard Limonov** (b. 1944) and **Aleksandr Zinovyev** (author of the satirical novel *Katastroika*), were also published. Other authors of note are **Andrei Bitov** (b. 1937) and **Viktor Yerofeyev** (b. 1947), whose striking novel *Russian Beauty* (*Russkaya krasavitsa*) (1990) sought to shake up prevailing literary conventions.

Literature in the new Russia: freedom or new restrictions?

The literary scene was still adapting to the consequences of glasnost' when the Soviet Union collapsed in 1991. In the years since then, the process of rediscovering the Russian literary heritage has continued, while a number of new writers of considerable talent have emerged. Meanwhile, concerns have been expressed that literature is now prey to commercial values, with problems in getting work published associated now not with censorship but with limited availability of financial resources. The spread of the internet has offset this, however, and Russian writers have been slowly getting used to the new freedoms that they and their profession have finally been granted.

RUSSIANS' READING HABITS: FROM *LIKBEZ* TO PULP FICTION

In 1918, the vast majority of the Russian population was unable to read and write, a problem tackled in the Soviet government's *likbez* (*likvidatsiya bezgramotnosti* or liquidation of illiteracy campaign). Later, the proud boast was that the Soviet peoples were the most avid readers in the world, who devoured both Russian works and any foreign literature in translation that was available. Since the end of the Soviet Union some disquiet has been expressed that standards are fallling: pulp fiction, often translations of trash literature, is popular, while in general people seem to be reading less. These worries would seem to be exaggerated, though – educated Russians are more often than not still able to put their Western friends to shame when it comes to knowledge about literature!

One positive development of recent years has been the rise to prominence of a number of female writers, in what has tended to be very much a male-dominated literary environment. They include the playwright **Lyudmila Petrushevskaya** (b. 1938), prose writer **Tatyana Tolstaya,** (b. 1951) and the poets **Yelena Shvarts** (b. 1948) and **Ol'ga Sedakova** (b. 1949).

Among male writers, the talent of **Mark Kharitonov** (b. 1937) was finally recognized when he became the first winner of the Russian Booker Prize in 1992, while the work of **Vladimir Makanin** (b. 1937) also belatedly caught the limelight. The postmodernist author **Viktor Pelevin** (b. 1962) has received widespread critical acclaim at home and abroad for his innovative and challenging works such as the novel *Omon Ra* (1991).

GLOSSARY

абзац (m.)	*paragraph*
автор (m.)	*author*
акмеизм (m.)	*Acmeism*
аллитерация (f.)	*alliteration*
глава (f.)	*chapter*
драматург (m.)	*dramatist, playwright*
жанр (m.)	*genre, style*
издательство (n.)	*publishing house*
комедия (f.)	*comedy*
лишний человек (m.)	*'superfluous man'*
мелодрама (f.)	*melodrama*
метафора (f.)	*metaphor*
нигилизм (m.)	*Nihilism*
образ (m.)	*character*
отрывок (m.)	*extract*
писатель (m.)	*writer*
писать (vb.)	*to write*
повесть (f.)	*novella*
поэзия (f.)	*poetry*
поэт (m.)	*poet*
произведение (n.)	*work (of literature)*
пьеса (f.)	*play*
рассказ (m.)	*story*
рифма (f.)	*rhythm*
роман (m.)	*novel*
романтизм (m.)	*Romanticism*
самиздат (m.)	*samizdat (underground publishing during Soviet times)*
символ (m.)	*symbol*
символизм (m.)	*Symbolism*
социалистический реализм (m.)	*Socialist Realism*
Союз Писателей (m.)	*Union of Writers*
сравнение (n.)	*simile*
стихотворение (n.)	*poem*
сюжет (m.)	*plot*
цензура (f.)	*censorship*
цитата (f.)	*quotation*
эпитет (m.)	*epithet*

Taking it further

To delve deeper into the history of Russian literature, try one or more of the following works:

Cornwell, Neil (ed.) *The Routledge Companion to Russian Literature* (London: Routledge, 2001).

Kelly, Catriona, *A History of Russian Women's Writing 1820–1992* (Oxford: Clarendon Press, 1994).

Moser, Charles (ed.) *The Cambridge History of Russian Literature* (Cambridge: Cambridge University Press, 1992).

Terras, Victor, *A History of Russian Literature* (New Haven: Yale University Press, 1996).

Wachtel, Andrew Baruch, *An Obsession with History: Russian Writers Confront the Past* (Stanford: Stanford University Press, 1994).

For a collection of some of the very best pieces of work from Russian literature, see Rzhevsky, Nicholas, *An Anthology of Russian Literature from Earliest Writings to Modern Fiction* (Armonk, NY: M.E. Sharpe, 1996).

There are translations available of many of the more popular works of 19th and 20th century authors, with contemporary writers covered by the popular GLAS New Russian Writing series of translations, based at the University of Birmingham (England). For those who are learning Russian, try short readers, which include glossaries and helpful notes (the Bristol Classical Press series can be recommended).

Bookshops

The internet has opened up possibilities to order books from stores in Russia or elsewhere in the world. In the UK, Russian books can be found at Thorntons booksellers in Oxford and Grant and Cutler in London, among others, while in the USA, Viktor Kamkin's bookstore stocks a large range of Russian-language books.

Websites

Try out some of the many websites dedicated to Russian literature, such as:

www.litera.ru/

which includes a wide range of resources on literature (in Russian), or

www.az.com/~katrinat/np/ruscol.htm

which provides a set of links to Russian- and English-language sites on Russian literature. To chat with other lovers of Russian literature and rub shoulders with some famous contemporary writers, drop in for a virtual coffee at the *Literaturnoe kafe v internete* –

www.tema.ru/rrr/litcafe/

04

art and architecture

In this unit you will learn
- about the origins of art in Russia
- about the influence of the church
- about Westernization and national style
- about the Soviet period
- about art and architecture in the new Russia

If we try to imagine Russia, a kaleidoscope of images comes to mind: majestic palaces, beautiful churches, simple peasant houses, but also imposing buildings and uninspiring apartment blocks. Russia's architectural heritage has much to admire in it, yet the tribulations of the country have left their mark on its buildings as well, with destruction and dilapidation all too evident in town and country. In the 'new' Russia efforts are being made to tackle the legacy of neglect – but will it be possible to save Russia's past?

In the world of art, too, Russia has much to boast about, from captivating folk art, through spiritually powerful icons, to the challenging and breathtaking contributions of avant-garde artists. It is clear that Russian art has had a major impact on the world stage – just look at the number of Kandinskii prints hanging in living rooms across the world! But how much do we know of the background to this art, the inspiration that lay behind its creation and the difficulties faced by Russian artists? In both art and architecture, as with so much in Russian life, the story has been one of foreign influences, the expression of national talent and ideas and of periods of repression and insularity followed by periods of enormous creativity and experiment.

Origins

Prehistoric art

The origins of Russia's artistic traditions stretch back to prehistoric times and fascinating examples of prehistoric art from Siberia and other parts of Russia are to be found in the **Hermitage** museum in St Petersburg, and in other museums across the country. An intriguing part of this heritage that dates from the Palaeolithic period (some 14,500 years ago) is a set of cave paintings that was discovered only in 1959 in the **Kapova** cave in the Ural Mountains. Further examples of the creativity and beliefs of the ancestors of today's Russians include megaliths in the north Caucasus mountains.

Folk art and crafts

Russia's rich folk art tradition includes *Palekh* wooden boxes, produced in the village of the same name, which are intricately painted and lacquered on a black background; from the town of **Gzhel'**, blue and white porcelain objects; *finift'* jewellery, produced in Rostov-Velikii; and *khokhloma* lacquered wooden bowls, spoons and other tableware and decorative pieces, traditionally black, red and gold in colour, and which can be used for dining as well as for decoration. The skills used to produce such items have not been lost and examples are available in their thousands for sale in Russia today – although buyers need to take care that they are buying the genuine thing!

Other examples of folk art include *vyatka* toys, which are said to be based on pagan idols; samovars from the city of **Tula**, which are sometimes decorated with *khokhloma*-style patterns, sometimes left as plain metal; painted metal trays from the village of **Zhostovo**; lace from the northern city of **Vologda**; shawls and headscarves from the town of **Pavlovo-Posad** with the distinctive designs that have made them recognizable as 'Russian scarves'; brightly coloured humorous

A Dymkovo toy

clay toys from **Dymkovo** which depict scenes from village life and folk traditions; glass and crystal objects from the town of **Gus'-Khrustal'nyi**. And, of course, the ubiquitous *matryoshka*, sets of nesting figures that fit inside one another. In recent years sets with the faces of Russian and Soviet leaders have proved popular with tourists! A distinctive feature of much of Russian folk art are the bright colours employed, which add to their charm and lift the spirits. Most Russian homes will have at least a number of such items on display or in use and interest in the folk art heritage has revived in recent years.

Traditional architecture

The indigenous peoples of Siberia and the Russian north were both sedentary and nomadic, with traditional dwellings including *chumy*, wigwam-like tents, as well as underground houses during the harsh winter. Although this way of life has almost disappeared now, some examples of communities living according to age-old custom can still be found.

An *izba*

The traditional Russian abode in the villages was the *izba*, a wooden cottage that is still found in abundance in the Russian countryside today. Features of the *izba* include the *pechka*, or stove, which might be ornately decorated and on which some members of the family would sleep during the cold months; and carved window frames, whose designs reflected regional variation across the country.

The construction of wooden buildings demanded a good degree of craftsmanship and some stunning examples of churches and houses have been preserved, including the famous collection of buildings on the island of **Kizhi** in northwest Russia, museums in **Kostroma**, northeast of Moscow, and **Malye Karely** near Archangel (**Arkhangel'sk**). In the **Kolomenskoe** museum in Moscow the wooden cabin that Peter the Great lived in during his time in Archangel can be found.

There are, as you might expect, a great many superstitions and traditions associated with life in the village. In some areas, for example, tossing a biscuit or loaf of bread is used to decide whether a plot of land is suitable for building on or not (if it lands the right way up, then the land is good, if the wrong way up, then bad luck will ensue if a house is built there). Another feature of Russian folklore is a mischievous but benign house spirit called the *domovoi*, which is supposed to look like a small animal and which lives with families – even going with them if they move house. It is a good thing to keep the *domovoi* on your side – and if the master of the house displays any bad attitudes to his family, work or house, then the *domovoi* will come to share these characteristics as well (woe betide the poor family!).

Influence of the Church

The decision by Kievan Rus to embrace Christianity in 988 opened the way to Byzantine influence on Russian art and architecture, with the principalities of Novgorod and Vladimir-Suzdal' soon following Kiev's lead.

Churches

The 'cross in square' design was duly adopted in the design of churches, along with the distinctive cupolas or domes. An example of architecture of this period can be seen in the **Cathedral of St Sofiya** in Kiev, Ukraine, built in 1037, although the exterior in particular has been heavily modified. With time, church styles were adapted to reflect their Russian surroundings, roofs made steeper to avoid the build-up of snow and windows narrowed. Novgorod and Pskov both made important contributions to the development of Russian architecture through their innovations in church design, with the latter producing the *kokoshniki*, gables that were used to support domes. **Vladimir-Suzdal'** (part of Russia's amazing *Zolotoe kol'tso* (Golden Ring) of ancient towns) also made significant advances, drawing on Romanesque and Caucasian styles and blending them with the Byzantine. The achievements of their architects can still be marvelled at, with the beautiful setting of such towns as Suzdal', Rostov Velikii and Yaroslavl' providing a breathtaking backdrop to these masterpieces.

Church of Ilya the Prophet, 17th Century, Yaroslavl'

SIGHTS OF RUSSIA: THE MOSCOW KREMLIN

The Moscow Kremlin, the adjoining Red Square and St Basil's cathedral with its colourful domes must be one of the most evocative sights in the world. Legend has it that Ivan the Terrible ordered the architect of St Basil's to be blinded, so that he couldn't produce anything of equal beauty anywhere else – a high price to pay for talent!

Moscow's claim to be the Third Rome led to a drive to establish its importance in architectural terms from the 15th century. Italian architects played a leading part in this work, transforming the **Kremlin,** for instance, into its current appearance. Other notable landmarks from this period that can still be seen in Moscow today include the **Novodevichii Convent.**

Icons

The practice of painting icons (*ikona,* pl. *ikony*) came to Russia from Byzantium and remained the dominant art form until the time of Peter the Great. A strict set of guidelines dictated what was and what was not permissible with regard to style and content, a factor that explains the common features of icons produced across the centuries (although shifts in style did occur). Unlike the aesthetic conventions of Western European art of this time, the emphasis was not on achieving a realistic likeness in the image, but on conveying a sense of spiritual presence, presenting the audience (the worshippers) with a window to the source of their faith. In the *izba* the icon would be kept in the *krasnyi ugol* (red corner) of the main living area. (The word *krasnyi* in Russian means red, but the original meaning of the word was 'beautiful' – hence *Krasnaya ploshchad'* in Moscow, while usually translated as 'Red Square', actually means 'Beautiful Square'.)

Icons traditionally were painted on wood and when they faded they were painted over, with the result that an old icon's original image will often have been obscured under several layers of more recent work. It was not until the early 20th century that a concerted effort was made to clean and restore Russia's icons – and the bold colours and fine artistry that emerged proved an unexpected and exciting revelation.

The most famous icon in Russia is **The Virgin of Vladimir,** which was brought to Russia from Constantinople in the 12th century, having originally been painted in Jerusalem. It has been present at various important events in Russian history, supposedly bringing good luck to Russian forces fighting the Mongols and Poles. It can now be seen in the **Tretyakov** gallery in Moscow.

Among the painters of icons, the most notable include **Theophanes** (the Greek), **Andrei Rublyov** and **Dionysius** and several influential schools (those of Vladimir-Suzdal', Novgorod, Pskov and Moscow), whose periods of dominance reflected the status of their cities at the time. The art of icon painting went into decline after the mid-16th century, when the church imposed stricter controls on the design of icons, although the end of the century saw the emergence of the Stroganov school, famous for the intricate detail of the paintings.

RUSSIA'S ARTISTS: ANDREI RUBLYOV

Andrei Rublyov (c.1360/70–1430) was a monk and assistant of Theophanes. His stylistic innovations had a profound influence on subsequent icon painting and his life is depicted in the memorable film *Andrei Rublyov* (1965), directed by Andrei Tarkovskii. Rublyov's most well-known masterpiece is the 'Old Testament Trinity', another of the Tretyakov's superb collection of icons.

Westernization

As in other areas of life, under Peter the Great's reign the fields of art and architecture were exposed to Western European influences and Baroque style came to Russia. Secular painting came to dislodge religious art from its dominant position, with foreign artists visiting Russia in increasing numbers and Russian artists sent abroad to be exposed to contemporary styles. In architecture, Peter's enormous project of building his grandiose capital of St Petersburg gave an ideal opportunity to adopt and adapt Baroque and Rococo styles to Russian conditions. Again, the Italian influence was strong, with **Gaetano Chiaveri** working under Peter and **Bartolomeo Rastrelli** employed during Elizabeth's reign, with the **Winter Palace** and the **Smol'nyi Convent** in his portfolio of achievements.

Under Catherine the Great, the more restrained nature of neoclassical designs in architecture were preferred to the exuberance of Rococo and Russia now found that it was actually leading the development of architectural tastes in Europe. Architects of note include **Charles Cameron** of Scotland

SIGHTS OF RUSSIA: THE WINTER PALACE AND THE HERMITAGE

Like the Moscow Kremlin, Petersburg's Winter Palace (*Zimnii dvorets*) is much more than an object of architectural fascination, having been the location of such important turning points in Russian history.

The Hermitage museum shares the palace's buildings, and has an enormous and awe-inspiring art collection, including masterpieces by foreign painters, as well as stunning examples of Russian work.

and the Russians **Matvei Kazakov** and **Vasilii Bazhenov**. Aleksandr I, in the early 19th century, oversaw the use of a more assertive classical style, seen as befitting the status of the Russian empire and as seen in the **Kazan Cathedral** in Petersburg, and **St Isaac's Cathedral**, also in the northern capital, which was built during Nikolai I's reign.

The Academy of Fine Arts was established in St Petersburg in 1757 and the skills of Russian artists were developed by foreign tutors. Among the few Russian names of note from this period is the portrait artist **Dmitrii Levitskii**. Early in the 19th century **Aleksei Venetsyanov** broke away from the contemporary trend of neoclassical painting and looked instead to Russian country life for inspiration. **Karl Bryullov** gained fame across Europe for his huge work 'Last Day of Pompeii', which he painted while in Italy in the 1830s and which now hangs in the Russian Museum.

Development of national styles

Later in the 19th century, there was a turn in architecture and art towards 'traditional' Russian styles and themes. A good number of buildings sprang up displaying influences from the Muscovite period including the Historical Museum in Moscow. In art, the focus on Russian motives was often intertwined with reflection of the social issues of the day, as artists, like writers, shook off romantic, neoclassical approaches and adopted realism. The writer Nikolai Chernyshevskii's influential article on the relationship between art and life was a catalyst for the type of change signified by the resignation of a group of students from the Russian Academy of Art in 1863, in protest against what they saw as the conservative nature of the academy and its failure to address the role of art as a medium for discussing the problems of society. In 1870, some members of this group came together to form the so-called Wanderers (*Peredvizhniki*), named after the series of travelling art exhibitions that they put on. The leading figures of the group included **Ivan Kramskoi** (1837–1887), **Vasilii Perov** (1833–1882), **Vasilii Surikov** (1848–1916), who painted scenes from Russian history and **Ilya Repin** (1844–1930), the most famous of Russian realists and one of Russia's best-loved artists, whose work includes the powerful 'The Volga Bargemen' and 'Zaporozhye Cossacks Writing a Mocking Letter to the Turkish Sultan'. The Wanderers received financial support from the middle-class entrepreneurs **Savva Mamontov** and **Pavel Tretyakov**. The estate of the former at Abramtsevo was turned into an artists' colony, while Tretyakov established the world-famous art gallery in Moscow that bears his name. Another name from this period is that of **Ivan Shishkin** (1832–1898), who remains extremely popular in Russia, where his evocative paintings of the Russian countryside, with sun-drenched forest scenes and depictions of balmy days in wheat fields, are felt to capture the vigour of life itself. **Isaak Levitan** (1861–1900) is held in similar regard, although his landscapes tended to be more serene, sometimes melancholic in nature.

Experimentation and revolution

The emphasis placed by realist artists on content over form came increasingly to be challenged in the turn of century period. The highly talented **Mikhail Vrubel'** (1856–1910), whose obsession with demons is reflected in many of his works, displayed Symbolist inspirations. **Valentin Serov** (1865–1911) is best remembered for his amazing portrait of the dancer Ida Rubinshtein.

In 1898, the *World of Art* (*Mir iskusstva*) magazine was launched by **Aleksandr Benois** and **Sergei Dyagilev** and signified a shift towards 'art for art's sake' that mirrored the trend in the literature of the Silver Age poetry of the Symbolists and others. The work of Russian artists was displayed across Europe and Dyagilev's role as an impresario with the **Ballets Russes** allowed **Leon Bakst** to showcase his striking costume designs. Other members of the group include **Konstantin Somov**, famous for paintings of harlequins and **Boris Kustodiev**, who depicted the lifestyle of the merchant class in an exuberant, sometimes outlandish fashion.

The emergence of avant-garde art in Russia coincided both with the period of social and political turbulence in the country in the first two decades of the 20th century and with the developments in Western European art circles taking place at that time. Russian artists interacted a great deal with their contemporaries in the rest of Europe and came to make a remarkable contribution to the world of art. Realism was decisively rejected in favour of Primitivism, Symbolism and abstract art. Among the myriad groupings to spring up was the important **Blue Rose** movement of Symbolists, founded by **Pavel Kuznetsov** (1878–1968), **Natalya Goncharova** (1881–1962) and her husband **Mikhail Larionov** (1881–1964) in 1907, and the **Knave of Diamonds** (*bubnovyi valet*) group, set up in 1910. Goncharova, who included motives from folk art and icon painting in her work, and Larionov began as neo-primitivist artists. By 1912 their work had evolved into Rayonism (*luchizm*), which was similar to the Futurist and Cubist work taking place in the West at the time and in which the emphasis was on painting the rays that the artists saw as emanating from objects.

RUSSIA'S ARTISTS: VASILII KANDINSKII (1866–1944)

Kandinskii was one of the pioneers of abstract art and his evocative and captivating paintings have proved timelessly popular with art lovers around the world. In Berlin in the years before World War I he co-founded the influential Blaue Reiter (Blue Rider) group of artists, before returning to Russia and becoming a leading art authority in the new Soviet state. He then left again for Germany, to the Bauhaus school, before emigrating again, this time to France.

The Knave of Diamonds group included in its ranks the great **Vasilii Kandinskii** (1866–1944) (who had previously also been associated with the Mir Iskusstva group), **Kazimir Malevich** and **Vladimir Tatlin**. Malevich developed the style of **Suprematism**, employing geometrical abstraction in painting, his work including 'White on White' (held in the Museum of Modern Art in New York). Tatlin began the **Constructivist** movement, in which machines, technology and modern materials were a central feature.

The works produced by the Belarussian-born **Mark Shagal** (usually transliterated as Chagall) (1887–1985) before leaving for France in 1910 already displayed the dreamlike quality that he would become famous for. **Kuzma Petrov-Vodkin** (1878–1939) drew inspiration from icon painting in his works, including the striking image of the 'Bathing of the Red Horse,' which he painted in 1912.

The Soviet period

Despite – or perhaps as a result of – the turmoil that ensued following the Bolshevik Revolution in 1917, avant-garde art continued to develop in the 1920s, as the Soviet authorities were prepared, for a time, to tolerate experimentation and diversity. The Constructivists built on the work of Malevich and Tatlin and emphasized an 'agitational' approach to art in support of the creation of a new society. The work of **Aleksandr Rodchenko**, **El Lissitskii** and others would later have an influence over the Bauhaus movement in Germany. Painting on canvas declined as artists of all schools took to other forms of expression, including set designs for the theatre and poster art, which became an important art medium throughout the Soviet period, used for propaganda purposes by the state. Some posters achieved recognition as classic designs and their influences have been seen in Western culture as well (see the 'Losing my religion' video of the US rock group REM, for example).

In architecture, meanwhile, **Konstantin Mel'nikov** (1890–1974), **Moisei Ginzburg** (1892–1946) and others sought to put Constructivist principles to work in the design of buildings (although their plans were, on the whole, not put into action).

Art and architecture in service of the Soviet state

The outburst of creativity of the 1920s was uncompromisingly squashed with the imposition in 1934 of Socialist Realism as the only acceptable style to be used by Soviet artists. The realism of the 19th century returned in the service of the people (i.e. the state) and talented artists emigrated, suppressed their talents or found themselves repressed by the authorities. Meanwhile, art galleries were cleared of items that were felt to exhibit negative values, unsuitable for Soviet society. Little art of value came out of the Soviet period, at least any that was officially endorsed.

In architecture, too, the experimentation of the 1920s gave way to austere, neoclassical designs of a grandiose scale, echoing the style seen in Nazi Germany at this time. The building projects of the Stalin era that can still be seen in Moscow today include the metro and seven 'wedding cake' gothic skyscrapers (a building of the same type was given as a 'present' to the city of Warsaw after World War II). Stalin's terrifying reputation produced a bizarre result in the Hotel Moscow, when he signed his authorization for the building in the middle of the two possible designs, one modern, the other in keeping with Stalin's preferred neoclassical style. The architects were so afraid to ask Stalin to clarify his decision that they decided to use both designs – and the building therefore has two non-matching façades.

SIGHTS OF RUSSIA: THE MOSCOW METRO

Moscow's underground railway was built in the 1930s as one of Stalin's great projects. Those who worked on it (including forced labourers) did so in harsh conditions and many died in the process, a human toll that hangs over the striking effect of the design of many of the metro's stations. The opulence on show – marble was used in about half of the stations – also resonates uncomfortably with the memory of the poverty and famine of that time.

As an architectural landmark, however, it is truly impressive. Perhaps the most famous station is Mayakovskaya (named after the poet), replete with marble of various colours and mosaics to designs by the artist Aleksandr Deineka.

The early Soviet period also saw an incredible amount of destruction by the authorities of symbols of the old order and of religion. Many country estates and churches were demolished or taken over for use as offices, sanatoria or as warehouses (the former estates of artistic figures escaped relatively lightly, however). This destruction was compounded during the years of World War II, as huge parts of western and southern Russia suffered under German occupation. During the war a good deal of art theft was carried out unofficially and officially by both sides, with the tracking down and return of the stolen items proving a contentious issue in the 1990s.

The Soviet state oversaw the erection of thousands of statues (adding to those left over from the tsarist period). There were those of Lenin, showing him deep in thought or rallying the crowd – or seeming to point to the nearest bus stop! These stayed until the end of the Soviet period, although those of Stalin were mostly removed after 1956. In addition, there were also many honouring a range of Soviet heroes. One of the most famous is that by the sculptress Vera Mukhina (1889-1953), of *Rabochii i kolkhoznitsa* ('The Worker and the Farm Girl') (1937), which stands near the VDNKh exhibition centre in Moscow and which is shown at the start of films made by the Mosfilm studio. Another striking statue is the *Rodina Mat'* ('Motherland') statue at Mamaev Kurgan, the site of one of the fierce battles around

Stalingrad during the Great Patriotic War. The towering 52-metre monument can be seen for miles around, as a lasting testament to the huge loss of life seen there.

After Stalin's death, the cultural thaw allowed for some degree of artistic revival and the dust covers were removed from a select number of previously banned works as they were put back into galleries. In architecture, the grandiose designs of the Stalin

---

THE UBIQUITOUS LENIN

While the censors saw to it that certain subjects were off limits to Soviet artists, one remained an outright favourite until the end: Lenin. Thousands upon thousands of busts, statues and portraits of the Communist deity were produced and Lenin would gaze down on the offices of everybody who was anybody.

---

era were discarded in favour of more modest designs. As part of an effort to rebuild the country after the ravages of war and the neglect of the population's needs under Stalin, apartment blocks built to a common design began to spring up across the USSR, allowing many who had previously lived in communal flats to move into their own flat. Many Russians today still live in flats of the so-called *khrushchovka* type: first built during Khrushchov's time, and unofficially named after him, and in which maximum use is made of a limited amount of space. However, later designs that use huge prefabricated concrete blocks are now more prevalent. The numbing impersonal sameness of Soviet buildings throughout the country forms a key part of the plot of the popular Soviet-era comedy film by the director **El'dar Ryazanov**, *Irony of Fate, or Hope You've Had a Nice Sauna* (*Ironiya sud'by, ili s lyogkim parom*) (1975), in which the tipsy hero goes to what he thinks is his flat, only to find out that it not his at all, but one that looks just like it, on a street just like his, but in another city altogether!

Underground art and architecture

While innovative artists were still frowned upon, at best, and punished at worst by the authorities, the more relaxed atmosphere of the Khrushchov and (to a lesser extent) Brezhnev years did allow non-official art to develop in the underground. Artists such as **Ernst Neizvestnyi, Ilya Kabakov** and **Mikhail Shemyakin** experimented with abstract, primitivist, hyperrealist and grotesque forms of art, but they had to take great care with regard to displaying their work, for fear of sanctions (the phrase *Apt art* refers to the fact that many underground artists held exhibitions in the small space of flats, with a strictly limited list of invited guests). Venturing into the open was far more risky, as the bulldozing of an unofficial outdoor art exhibition in Moscow in 1974 showed. As a result of such intimidation and constraints, a number of artists (such as Neizvestnyi) emigrated.

Sotsart was an approach developed by **Vitalii Komar** and **Aleksandr Melamid** in the mid-1970s. Echoing the Pop Art of Andy Warhol and other American artists, Sots art displayed images designed to mock and neutralize the stagnant ideological symbols of Soviet society. **Conceptual art**, led by **Ilya Klebakov** and **Andrei Monastyrskii**, grew from Sots art and aimed to reflect the nature of Russian life in the 1970s and 1980s.

New freedoms?

In the late 1980s art was able to begin to shake off the effects of decades of suppression, as state control was relaxed, then abandoned and the population was finally given the opportunity openly to decide for itself the merits of the art (such as that of the avant-garde of the early 20th century) that they could now gain access to. Dissident artists emerged from the underground and gained more widespread recognition, although some seemed to lose their sense of purpose and direction in the absence of control and restriction. Among the best-known artists of the perestroika period are **Sergei Bugaev** (known as 'Afrika'), **Konstantin Zvezdochetov**, who produced provocative postmodern style work, and **Ilya Glazunov**, who continued to enjoy considerable popularity in the New Russia on account of his distinctive style. Meanwhile, the *Mit'ki* group attracted attention as much for their eccentric lifestyle as for their work.

As Russia moved away from its Communist past, so some of the symbols of the Soviet era were removed. The statue of Dzerzhinskii, the first head of the Soviet secret police, was torn down from the spot opposite the KGB headquarters on *Lubyanka* square in Moscow, where it had kept an evil eye on events for so long; now it, and other relics of the ancien regime, were left to rot in one of Moscow's parks.

The 1990s saw a move away from the Conceptualism of the previous decade towards work in which meanings of the subject are emphasized more fully. Some artists have been able to take advantage of the new commercial opportunities to sell their works for considerable sums and there are frequent exhibitions and auctions of Russian art. Other artists have not adapted so well, of course, with some losing out because of the loose copyright legislation in Russia, seeing their work exploited by others but receiving next to nothing in return.

In architecture, the perestroika years and beyond have seen some efforts on the part of the authorities and civic associations to save and restore Russia's heritage, through attempts to renovate buildings that were either part-destroyed in the Soviet time or left in a dilapidated condition through neglect. The size of this task is a huge one and there are far from enough funds to save so many historic buildings. However, it is a positive sign that in some cities, at least, when old buildings do have to be demolished the building that replaces them has to conform in style and size to the surrounding buildings, in an attempt to retain a sense of harmony.

There is a great deal of new building taking place in Russia, some (especially in the larger cities) funded by foreign investment. While the design of some buildings can be seen to make an aesthetically pleasing contribution to the local environment (as in the case of the new British Embassy in Moscow, made out of glass and steel), other buildings have proved more controversial. Moscow's outspoken mayor, Yurii Luzhkov, has employed the architect **Zurab Tsereteli** to bring to life his ambitious and grandiose projects such as the enormously expensive reconstruction of the Cathedral of Christ the Saviour (which had been torn down under Stalin), the underground shopping complex on *Okhotnyi ryad* (Hunter's Row) and a large and very ugly statue of Peter the Great (although Tsereteli did also design the *Tragediya narodov* ('Tragedy of the Peoples') monument on *Poklonnaya gora* in Moscow). Despite the lively disagreements over taste that surround such developments, this is an exciting period of building and creativity in architecture, unfettered by the desire for the destruction of the old and the smothering of innovation seen not so long ago in Russia.

GLOSSARY

арка (f.)	*arch*
архитектор (m.)	*architect*
архитектура (f.)	*architecture*
бревенчатая изба (f.)	*village house made of logs*
выставка (f.)	*exhibition*
дворец (m.)	*palace*
домовой (m.)	*domovoi* (house spirit)
живопись (f.)	*painting*
икона (f.)	*icon*
иконопись (f.)	*icon painting*
искусство (n.)	*art*
колонна (f.)	*column*
купол (m.)	*dome* (onion-shaped, found on churches)
многоэтажка (f.) (colloq.)	*high-rise apartment block*
наличники (pl.)	*decorative window frames found on an* izba
натюрморт (m.)	*still life*
памятник (m.)	*statue*
пейзаж (m.)	*landscape*
Передвижники (pl.)	*'Wanderers'*
портрет (m.)	*portrait*
реставрация (f.)	*restoration*
скульптура (f.)	*sculpture*
стиль (m.)	*style*
строить (vb.)	*to build*
Третьяковская галерея (f.)	*Tretyakov Gallery*
хрущёвка (f.) (colloq.)	*khrushchovka* – popular term for apartment blocks built to a design first seen in Khrushchov's time
художник (m.)	*artist*
Эрмитаж (m.)	*The Hermitage* (art museum in St Petersburg)

Taking it further

The best way to sample the delights of Russian art, of course, is to take a look at the original thing. If you are lucky enough to be able to visit Russia, then a trip to the Hermitage in St Petersburg, or the Tretyakov Gallery in Moscow, will surely be on your itinerary. But many Western cities also have permanent or temporary exhibitions of Russian works of art (and the Hermitage has taken to sending substantial temporary exhibitions to London and elsewhere), while a number of commercial galleries have the works of contemporary Russian artists for sale.

Books

Bowlt, John (ed.) *Painting Revolution: Kandinsky, Malevich and the Russian Avant-Garde* (Bethesda, Maryland: Foundation for International Arts and Education, 2000).

Brumfield, William, *A History of Russian Architecture* (Cambridge: Cambridge University Press, 1993).

Hilton, Alison, *Russian Folk Art* (Bloomington, IN: Indiana University Press, 1995).

Leek, Peter, *Russian Painting* (Bournemouth: Parkstone Press, 1999).

Websites

You can find many examples of Russian art on the internet, as well as background information on painters. Try these:

www.rollins.edu/Foreign_Lang/Russian/ruspaint.html

(covers development of Russian art from icon painting to the present day)

www.funet.fi/pub/culture/russian/html_pages/posters1.html

(for examples of and commentaries on Soviet-era posters)

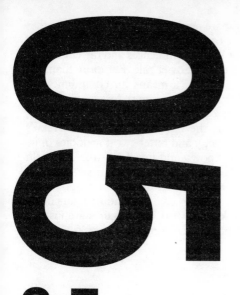

05

music and dance

In this unit you will learn
- about church music in Russia
- about folk music and dance
- about classical music
- about ballet
- about popular music and dance culture

Russia's musical traditions share many of the features of the other arts – a period of dominance of the church, the enduring appeal of folk customs, the mixture of Western influences and the emergence of Russian styles and the effects of Soviet rule. But more than any other art form, music has provided a means for communicating with the wider world, allowing Russian and foreigner alike to share the delight of listening to Russian music and watching Russian performers. From the elegance of Chaikovskii's symphonies to the passion, energy and bitter-sweet melodies of its folk songs, Russian music is known and loved the world over. In dance, too, Russia's contribution is enormous – Russian dancers from Nizhinskii to Nureyev have been at the forefront of the process of popularizing ballet, becoming international superstars as they did so. But the well-known works and figures are just the tip of a huge retinue of talent and achievement.

Church music

The Byzantine culture that brought icons to Russia also gave its tradition of church music, whose features were to play a key role in shaping the future development of Russian musical styles. Instruments were not to be used in Orthodox churches, a factor that held up the development of formal musical skills in Russia until the time of Peter the Great. Instead, music was produced by a unison chant, by male choirs. In the 12th century, the *znamennyi raspev* (*znamennyi* chant) was introduced, whose solemn tones were designed to glorify the words of liturgy they accompanied. From the 14th century, Russian features began to creep into the style, with the use of major and minor keys as well as polyphony seen in the 16th century and choirs came to include female voices. The *znamennyi* chant has a complex structure, whose composition and interpretation was mastered by only a few musicians and singers.

The art of church bell ringing developed from the 16th century and became a sophisticated art form in its own right, with bell ringers acquiring a high level of proficiency in their musical skills and producing a range of exquisite compositions, often unique to an individual church.

The traditions of church music were kept alive even during the darkest days of the Soviet regime and have been revived as the Orthodox church has gathered strength after the fall of Communism. For believers and non-believers alike, the sound of an Orthodox choir has a captivating, mesmerizing effect, especially if witnessed in the atmospheric surroundings of a church, as the priest swings the *kadilo* (incense lantern).

Folk music and dance

Alongside the church music tradition is the heritage of folk music and dance, a rich treasure trove of creativity stretching back to the times of the *Primary Chronicle* and beyond. The musical heritage ranges from the singing of *byliny* (epic stories), *protyazhnye pesni* (long, mournful songs) to joyful and lively ballads about love and life in the village. Female singers play an important role in folk songs, often performing as soloists or in a capella format of two or more voices. One of the distinctive sounds of this music is the practice of each member of the choir singing a variant (*podgolosok*) of the melody, producing a beautiful harmony, which is especially powerful in more melancholic pieces. The *chastushka* is a particular form of folk singing, which always uses the same melody and which presents a kind of banter between villagers. Some of the four-line songs have lyrics that have been passed down from generation to generation, while others are improvised on the spot. Famous folk songs to listen out for are '*Ei, ukhnem*' (known in English as the 'Volga boatmen song'), '*Oi, moroz, moroz!*' ('Oh, frost, frost!') and '*Vo pole beryoza*' ('In the field there is a birch tree').

THE BALALAIKA

A string instrument of the lute family, for many the balalaika is the 'sound' of Russia – the gentle yet powerful music produced by soloists and orchestras evoking the eternal qualities of Russia and its people, the endless steppe stretching into the horizon, the sadness and the joy of life.

The principal features of Russian folk dancing are well known in the West, where audiences have been amazed time and again by the agility and grace displayed by visiting Russian dance troupes. The male roles are generally extremely active and physically demanding, with the more acrobatic moves including the famous *vprisyadku*, for which the man has to kick out his legs while in a squatting position that is held for what seems an age and the *raznozhka*, in which the dancer performs the splits while jumping high in the air – not for the faint-hearted! Female parts are less acrobatic but no less challenging, with moves such as the *vrashchenie*, consisting of very fast rotations performed with various steps that take the dancers flying across the stage. In slower dances, female dancers make use of their long floor-length dresses to conceal the small steps being taken to give the impression that they are gliding over the floor. Throughout the dance repertoire, however, there is an exuberance and energy that is spellbinding and uplifting. Many of the dances tell a tale of village life, with courtship rituals a popular theme. The complicated technique takes years to perfect and the artists of professional troupes usually receive training in classical dance.

The energy and passion of Russian folk dancing

The knowledge of folk traditions was passed down orally from generation to generation and it is amazing that so much survived. For various reasons, some of the characteristic traits of the music and dance of particular regions were lost in this process. In the 19th and early 20th centuries, Russia's educated classes took a keener interest in the folk traditions of their country and enthusiasts set off around the countryside in search of authentic folk culture. While this brought greater attention to such traditions, it did lead to a blurring of the origins and distinctive styles that were to be found. Under Soviet government, a more negative and proactive effort was made to alter the nature of folk culture. As we have already seen, during the Soviet period folk traditions came under some threat at certain periods, as some in the Communist leadership regarded them as backward and as having too many ties to the 'national' Russian character. Although folk traditions were allowed to continue, there was an attempt to merge the various styles from around the country to produce a homogenized 'Soviet' version and this formed the repertoire that was most usually seen by Soviet and foreign audiences during ensuing decades.

In recent times, there has been a new wave of interest among ethnographers, musicians and others to seek out the roots of folk music and dance, bringing out the local and regional flavour that had previously been blurred. This process of uncovering the past has led to some fascinating and exciting developments in the revival and continuation of folk culture.

Classical music

The church's dominance over things musical at the level of the court held up Russia's exposure to the musical trends seen in Western Europe (Ivan the Terrible even composed and sang chants in church choirs himself). Peter the Great swept this isolation aside, bringing foreign musicians to his court and new capital city. But it was not until the 19th century that Russian composers began to make their mark – and what a mark it turned out to be.

The Russian tradition and the 'Mighty Five'

The founding father of Russian classical music was **Mikhail Glinka** (1804–1857), whose work included the operas 'Ivan Susanin' (1836) and 'Ruslan and Lyudmila' (1842), which drew on Italian influences, but signified at the same time the development of a truly Russian tradition. This was pushed forward in the middle of the century by the setting up of music conservatories in St Petersburg and Moscow by the Rubinshtein brothers.

Meanwhile, five young composers from St Petersburg came together in a group that was to be labelled the *moguchaya kuchka* (literally 'mighty group', more often called 'Mighty Five' or 'The Five'), which was to have a powerful impact in the world of music in Russia and abroad. The impulse for the group's creation was the feeling of its members – **Milyi**

Balakirev (1837–1910), **Aleksandr Borodin** (1834–1887), **Nikolai Rimskii-Korsakov** (1844–1908), **Modest Musorgskii** (1839–1881) and **Cesar Cui** (1835–1918) – that they needed to counterbalance what they saw as the over-reliance of the new conservatories on Western musical traditions. Instead, they called for music to reflect the Russian character and Russian traditions, echoing the sentiments of realist writers of the time. The five had only limited musical training and most carried on other careers, composing in their spare time (Rimskii-Korsakov was a naval officer, for instance, while Borodin was a chemist of some renown and Musorgskii worked in the bureaucracy).

Despite these apparent restrictions, the works of this group helped to forge the identity of Russian music, in which Russian folk music, the music of the church and influences drawn from across the Russian empire and its connections with the orient, were to be heard. Balakirev's work 'Tamara' (1882) draws on Eastern musical themes in its depiction of romance in the Caucasus mountains, while in one of Rimskii-Korsakov's most popular pieces, the symphony 'Scheherazade' (1888), the composer also uses oriental motifs skilfully in his portrayal of stories from 'Tales of 1001 Nights'. Rimskii-Korsakov's output also included the symphony 'Capriccio Espagnol' (1887) and the opera 'Sadko' (1898).

Musorgskii, arguably the most talented of the group, strove to reflect the lives of the ordinary people, something that shone through in his operatic masterpieces '*Boris Godunov*' (1868) and '*Khovanshchina*' (1872), while something of Musorgskii's personal unhappiness is reflected in the soaring drama of '*Ivanova noch' na lysoi gore*' ('Night on a Bald Mountain') (1867), well known to listeners at home and abroad. Alcoholism contributed to his early death, with Ilya Repin, the artist, producing a haunting picture of him in hospital just days before he passed away. Borodin, who was the son of a prince from the Caucasus, is best known for his opera '*Knyaz' Igor*' ('Prince Igor'), from which the popular '*Polovetskie tantsy*' ('Polovtsian dances') are taken and the work 'In the Steppes of Central Asia'.

The timeless beauty of the melodies in the music of **Pyotr Chaikovskii** (*or* Tchaikovskii) (1840–1893) have ensured that he has remained the best loved of Russia's composers at home and abroad, continuing his brilliant international reputation that was built up during his lifetime. He kept some distance between himself and the 'five', both in terms of music and in geography – many of his major works were composed in Moscow, forever the rival city of the other capital of St Petersburg where the 'five' gained their fame. Chaikovskii did not share the nationalist outlook displayed by the five to the same degree and in his music the influence of European styles is clear, although Chaikovskii also touched on patriotic themes, as in the glorious *'Torzhestvennaya uvertyura 1812'* ('1812 Overture') (1880) and made great use of Russian folk and church music in his compositions. He was chided by the nationalist composers of the *kuchka* for being over-sentimental – but generations of music lovers have begged to differ, as they were swept away by the emotional power of such works as the *'Pateticheskaya simfoniya'* ('Pathetique' Symphony No. 6) (1893), and *'Lebedinoe ozero'* ('Swan Lake') (1876) and *'Shchelkunchik'* ('The Nutcracker') (1892), two of Chaikovskii's three ballets. The composer's personal life was troubled, however, as he sought to hide his homosexuality through a disastrous marriage, before entering into a relationship with the widow of a wealthy businessman, who acted as his patron.

GREAT PERFORMERS: FYODOR SHALYAPIN
(1873–1938)

The great Russian bass Shalyapin is a legendary figure, who conquered the leading opera houses of the world with his breathtaking performances. His masterful portrayals of his characters were unrivalled, combining great psychological insight with his incredible voice and impressive physical presence.

Aleksandr Skryabin (or Scriabin) (1872–1915) managed, in his short life, to produce an impressive range of works, with an emphasis on piano compositions, which increasingly reflected the composer's mystical outlook on life. His *'Poema ekstaza'* ('Poem of Ecstasy') (1907) is an incredible piece, but Skryabin planned to surpass it with what was intended to be his masterpiece, 'The Mystery', which would have been a monumental work performed in the Himalayas, with the goal of purifying humankind through art! Unfortunately, Skryabin died before he was able to achieve this lofty goal. **Sergei Rakhmaninov** (or Rachmaninov) (1873–1943) was a more conventional composer, who produced the vast majority of his output of piano concerti (including the ever popular numbers 2 and 3), songs and symphonies before leaving Russia after the Bolshevik Revolution.

Innovation and revolution

The impact of the innovative music of **Igor' Stravinskii** (1882–1971) can be seen from the reaction to his world premiere of '*Vesna svyashchyennaya*' ('The Rite of Spring') in Paris in 1913: the French composer Saint-Saëns walked out in protest and fights even broke out in the audience! Stravinskii had studied under Rimskii-Korsakov and the latter's influence is shown in Stravinskii's use of motifs from Russian folk music. But Stravinskii soon developed a unique style that was brought to the attention of the wider world through his association with Dyagilev's Ballet Russes, for which he wrote the scores for the ballets '*Zhar-ptitsa*' ('The Firebird') (1910) and 'Petrushka' (1911). He carried on experimenting throughout his long career, which he continued abroad after leaving Russia in 1917.

As in the other art forms, the 1920s saw a good deal of tolerance of musical experimentation in the Soviet Union, with the Modernist themes developed by some composers before the revolution allowed to continue for some time at least. Two rival groupings were formed: the Association of Contemporary Music and the more politicized Russian Association of Proletarian Musicians. The former included the Ukrainian composer **Nikolai Roslavets** (1881–1944); **Aleksandr Mosolov** (1900–1971), who is famous for his '*Zavod. Muzyka mashin*' (literally 'Factory. The Music of Machinery', but usually translated as the 'Iron Foundry') (1928), in which the orchestra recreates the grinding sounds of industrialized progress; and **Dmitrii Shostakovich** (1906–1975). Shostakovich gained fame at an early age, with the premiere of his First Symphony performed in 1926 and his opera '*Nos*' ('The Nose') (1928) (from Gogol''s short story of the same name) following soon after in 1928. However, Shostakovich's spirit of experimentation was almost crushed by Stalin himself, when the Soviet leader saw the composer's opera '*Ledi Makbet Mtsenskogo uezda*' ('Lady Macbeth of Mtsensk District') in 1936 – the very next day an article appeared in the Communist party's newspaper *Pravda* denouncing the opera (Stalin had apparently not been pleased by the use of sexual themes and the dissonant sound of the music). The intimidation caused Shostakovich to draw back from the degree of artistic expression he had shown until now, although his genius still shows through in later works, notably in his Seventh Symphony, known as the 'Leningrad Symphony', written during the blockade of that city during World War II.

The clamp-down on music by the Soviet authorities also affected the output of another great Russian composer of this period, **Sergei Prokofyev** (1891–1953), who had returned to the Soviet Union in the early 1930s after spending some time abroad after the revolution. Some of his most popular works, including 'Romeo and Juliet' (1935), were written after his return, but the strain of censorship and criticism would tell on him. In 1948, both Prokofyev and Shostakovich found their work condemned as part of the 'anti-cosmopolitan' drive against foreign influences. While Shostakovich was able to breathe again as an artist after the death of Stalin, Prokofyev did not get that chance – he died on the same day as the infamous dictator.

The second half of the 20th century saw a new generation of Russian composers, whose works include some of the most radical pieces of music seen in the world during this period, notwithstanding (or perhaps inspired by?) the restrictions that these musicians faced in the more free, but still closely monitored cultural sphere in the USSR from the 1950s on. They include **Galina Ustvol'skaya** (b. 1919), a pupil of Shostakovich, with whom she had an initially close but later controversial and acrimonious relationship; **Edison Denisov** (1929–1996); **Sofiya Gubaidulina** (b. 1931); **Nikolai Karetnikov** (1930–1994); and **Alfred Shnittke** (1934–1998). Shnittke (or Schnittke) in particular attracted international acclaim for his works, which draw on a range of influences to produce complex, ambiguous images.

In the years before Gorbachov's glasnost' a number of leading and highly talented Russian musicians, such as the cellist and conductor **Mstislav Rostropovich** (b. 1927) and the pianist **Vladimir Ashkenazi** (b. 1937) left the USSR to continue their work in exile, gaining huge worldwide fame in the process. From the late 1980s on many of these émigrés returned to Russia, either permanently or on a frequent basis, ensuring that Russian audiences are able to savour the delights of their talents as much as concert-goers in the West. Meanwhile, the strong traditions of Russia's musical academies, now free from the ideological straitjacket that stifled them for so long, continue to produce musicians of world class, such as the young opera singer **Dmitrii Khvorostovskii** (or Hvorostovskii) (b. 1962), hailed as the baritone of his era, the pianist **Yevgenii Kisin** and the violinist **Maksim Vengerov**, while the work of young Russian composers is also heard at music festivals around the world.

Ballet

For many in the West, ballet is something that is synonymous with Russia: from the grace of such great ballerinas as Anna Pavlova and Natalya Makarova, to the power of its legendary male dancers, Russian ballet companies and dancers trained in Russian ballet schools have long been at the forefront of the development of this art form. Ballet has tended to be more accessible to the mass public in Russia than in the rather more elitist culture of, say, Britain. The admiring comments of English Socialist trade union worker Fred Kite (Peter Sellers) in the film *I'm all right, Jack*, when he states that Russia is a place where workers can look forward to ballet in the evening after a hard day in the field or factory, is not such a great exaggeration, as Russians of all backgrounds tend to be proud of their country's achievements in dance.

CULTURE FOR THE MASSES

One aspect of Russian life that foreigners often comment on is the high level of interest in and understanding of culture among the population. This can be attributed at least in part to the implementation of Lenin's famous dictum '*iskusstvo prinadlezhit narodu*' (art belongs to the people), in accordance with which ballet, opera and theatre companies took their work to the masses, through touring the country and selling tickets at very reasonable prices. In the education system, furthermore, 'high' culture was and is promoted as something to be appreciated.

Ballet first came to Russia with the wave of other foreign imports in the 17th century and its early development was pushed on by the personal involvement of Peter the Great's daughter, **Yelizaveta**, who later became tsarina (empress). She was, apparently, a skilful dancer who helped to fuse the Western ballet style with Russia's own folk traditions. Under her patronage, Russian ballet began to find its feet, with the help of successive choreographers from Italy and France, including **Charles-Louis Didelot** (1767–1837), seen as the father of Russian ballet. During the 19th century Russian ballet came to be seen as a model to follow by foreign companies, but by the end of the century its momentum was flagging. It was another Frenchman, **Marius Petipa** (1818–1910), who injected a fresh dynamism into Russian ballet after his appointment as First Ballet Master of the Imperial Ballet in 1869, introducing a greater theatrical element, as seen in his choreography of 'The Sleeping Beauty', to Chaikovskii's music, 'La Bayadère' and more than 50 other works. Moscow's Bol'shoi Company (the word *bol'shoi* means 'big' or 'grand') was noted for the spontaneity of its style and the inclusion of Russian folk influences, in contrast to the more refined approach of the Mariinskii ballet in St Petersburg.

The leading dancers of the Imperial Ballet became stars in Russia and abroad and were feted in high society: **Mathilde Kshesinskaya** (Kschessinska) (1872–1971) was a close acquaintance of Nikolai II, for example. **Anna Pavlova** (1881–1931), who possessed a fragile beauty and an extraordinary talent as a dancer, became Prima Ballerina with the Imperial Ballet at the age of 25. Later, after a spell with the 'Ballet Russes' she toured the world with her own company, tirelessly promoting the art of ballet and inspiring countless young people to take up dance, including Britain's celebrated choreographer, Frederick Ashton. The Pavlova dessert is named after her, created either in Australia or New Zealand (this is disputed!) when she was there on a tour.

Anna Pavlova as 'The Dying Swan'

The impresario **Sergei Dyagilev** formed the original 'Ballet Russes' company in 1909 and it quickly established a reputation as the leading force in world ballet, a mantle that it would hold until his death in 1929. He brought together the finest dancers from St Petersburg and Moscow, later recruiting foreign stars as well (including the English dancer Alice Marks, who 'russianized' her name to become Alicia Markova). The 'Ballet Russes' provided an exhilarating setting for experimentation in dance, led by the brilliant choreographer **Mikhail Fokin** (or Fokine) (1880–1942), who rebelled against the formal style of the Imperial Ballet, looking for new forms of expression and dramatic interpretation. Dyagilev's emphasis on achieving a synthesis of art forms, previously seen in his 'World of Art' movement, led to contributions to the company's work from leading artists, such as Natalya Goncharova and from Igor' Stravinskii who provided stunning scores for several of its innovative ballets. The company's most famous dancer was **Vatslav Nizhinskii** (or Nijinskii) (1890–1950), who mesmerized audiences with his fantastic leaps and his spellbinding character interpretation. Although the company was dissolved after Dyagilev's death, its legacy lived on, not least through the Georgian émigré **George Balanchine**'s (originally Georgy Balanchivadze) (1904–1983) work in developing the New York City Ballet.

Daring choreographic innovation was also seen in the USSR during the 1920s. notably in the work of **Fyodor Lopukhov** (1886–1973). Later, ballet came under attack from Marxist theorists, who dismissed it as a bourgeois art form. There were also attempts to introduce Socialist Realism into ballet, with uplifting themes emphasized and even tractors appearing on stage! The traditions of Russian ballet were preserved, however, through the efforts of such figures as **Agrippina Vaganova** (1879–1951), who drew on the classical legacy of the Imperial Ballet and merged it with the more acrobatic, physical style associated with the new Soviet approach to dance. Her pupils included **Galina Ulanova** (1910–1998) seen as one of the greatest dancers of all time.

During the rest of the Soviet period Russian dance companies stuck to the classical repertoire, for the most part, and innovation tended to be suppressed, a fact that held up the development of 'modern' dance in Russia. Aesthetic restrictions were a factor in the 'defections' of a number of leading Russian dance stars, following the introduction of frequent foreign tours by the Bolshoi and the Kirov (as the Mariinskii had been renamed). After Rudol'f Nureyev's 'leap' to the West in 1961, further defections included that of the great **Natalya Makarova** (b. 1940) in 1970 and **Mikhail Baryshnikov** (b. 1948) in 1974. Although such incidents were embarrassing as an indictment of the Soviet system, the ballet companies soon managed to replace their lost stars with new ones trained in their exacting ballet schools.

GREAT PERFORMERS: RUDOL'F NUREYEV
(1938–1993)

A larger than life character, as a dancer Nureyev drew comparison with Nizhinskii for his fabulous leaps and athleticism. After his defection he danced with various companies around the world, becoming a regular performer with the Royal Ballet in London, with the English ballerina **Margot Fonteyn** his frequent partner. Nureyev's flamboyant lifestyle ensured that he was never far from the headlines, but this never eclipsed his achievements on the stage, where he did much to develop the role of the male lead in classical ballet.

Since the collapse of the Soviet Union and the system of subsidies for the arts, the main challenge for Russia's ballet companies has been to adapt to the harsh commercial realities of the New Russia, which have entailed a demanding itinerary of overseas tours in order to bring in hard currency. The need to move on in artistic terms from the rather conservative stance of the Soviet era has led to a certain amount of turmoil as well, with the long-standing director of the Bol'shoi, **Yurii Grigorovich** forced out in 1995 after over 30 years in charge. In the 1990s it was the Mariinskii (the Kirov had now reverted to its original name) that seemed to have the upper hand in terms of artistic accomplishment, although by the turn of the millennium the Bol'shoi had pulled itself together once more and both companies were receiving enthusiastic reviews at home and abroad. In the sphere of contemporary dance new companies, such as the 'Kinetic' dance company in Moscow and the Iguana theatre in Petersburg, are making up for lost time.

Popular music and dance culture

Urban songs

Around the turn of the 19th century, the genre of urban song acquired enormous popularity, with songs sung in a gypsy style (*tsyganshchina*) at the forefront. The spirit of freedom evoked in the sensual, lively songs accompanied often by breathtaking performances by violin soloists captivated audiences, with performers like **Anastasiya Vyal'tseva** (1871–1913) and **Vera Panina** (1872–1911) becoming huge stars across Russia, with songs such as '*Ochi chyornye*' ('Dark Eyes'), their fame helped on its way by the spread of gramophones throughout the country. The so-called town or cruel romance (*gorodskoi romans* or *zhestokii romans*) was more Russian and refined in character. The songs of that era are still well loved in Russia today and **Aleksandr Malinin** and **Valentina Ponomaryova** are among the many artists to include them in their repertoires.

Revolutionary music and 'mass songs'

After the Bolshevik Revolution, popular songs were quickly adopted for use in boosting morale and for propaganda during the civil war. In the 1920s, the communist-oriented musicians' associations sought to promote songs with 'proletarian' themes, yet the public still preferred the *romansy* that it had grown used to listening to, with their focus on themes of relationships and the plight of individuals. The more tolerant atmosphere of the 20s also saw dances such as the foxtrot hitting dance halls across Russia and jazz was able to flourish for a time. Even an onslaught against such 'decadent' styles mounted by leading Communists in the late 1920s, that led to the arrest of some musicians, failed to convince the public to change their musical taste and by the early 1930s the authorities appeared to have given up, allowing the urban songs, folk music and jazz to stay out in the open, with stars of 'red jazz' such as **Leonid Utyosov** (1895–1982) and **Aleksandr Tsfasman** (1906–1971) gaining a huge following (Utyosov's music pleased Stalin, no less).

By the mid-1930s, though, Soviet Puritanism was gaining the upper hand and the 'mass song' (*massovaya pesnya*) boomed out of loudspeakers in the factories and in films, with uplifting lyrics that jarred with the misery and terror of the darkest times of the Stalinist era. Now musicians could not rely on the public to save them and they were forced to make their music more 'acceptable' or face persecution. The onset of war in 1941 and the enormity of the struggle and suffering that ensued, created an urgent need for morale-boosting songs, with one of them – '*Katyusha*' – becoming a favourite not just in the USSR but in other Allied countries as well. During the war jazz again enjoyed something of a revival and Western hits (such as those of Glenn Miller) were heard in dance halls, but the end of the war and the paranoia that accompanied the start of the Cold War once more forced jazz and other musicians to calm down their music or be quiet altogether.

Stilyagi, bards and *sovetskaya estrada*

In the 1950s, the staid conservatism that the Communists tried to impose on young people came under increasing pressure, with the quaint innocence of the 'mass song' doing little to excite Soviet youth, who were beginning to hear more about the rock and roll revolution taking place in the West (despite the best efforts of the Soviet government to stop them gaining access to it). In larger cities, the more daring young people flouted Soviet conventions by dressing up in distinctive clothes (such as tight trousers and brightly coloured ties), a trend that earned them the name *stilyagi*, from the word *stil'* (style). In 1957, the staging of the World Youth Festival in Moscow brought Western rock and pop music to the USSR (allowed in by the unwitting Soviet government), giving Soviet youth a further taste of what they were missing and thus serving to create an even bigger demand for home-grown rock and pop music.

SPREADING THE SOUND

A combination of resourcefulness and technology helped to ensure that Western music, as well as that of Soviet musicians not supported (or even suppressed) by the Soviet state could still reach the hands of an eager audience. X-ray plates were bought for a cheap price, then used to record music. And through the use of tape recorders, *magnitizdat* did for music what *samizdat* did for literature, allowing fans to pass copies of recordings across the country.

Around this time, the so-called *bardy* (bards) started to attract a growing audience, first among the urban intelligentsia of Moscow, Leningrad and a few other large cities, but soon spreading among a large section of the population. In this genre of *avtorskaya pesnya* (author's song), the performer would sing his or her poetry usually to a solo guitar. The most famous bards were **Bulat Okudzhava** (1924–1997), whose songs such as '*Poslednii trolleibus*' ('The last trolley bus') struck a chord with his listeners with their honest and moving portrayal of life; **Aleksandr Galich** (1918–1977), who sang about the darker side of Soviet life – the terror of the purges, criminals, the hard life of ordinary people; and **Vladimir Vysotskii** (1938–1980).

Vysotskii was a film and stage actor (based at the famous Taganka Theatre in Mosow), but his incredible superstar status in Russia came as a result of his performances and recordings as a bard artist. His distinctive, gruff voice bellowed out over his guitar as he touched on just about every aspect of Soviet life, including taboo subjects of alcohol, sex and crime. His image as a man of the people endeared him to fans from all walks of life and his extravagant (for the Soviet Union) lifestyle, with his long-distance marriage to French actress Marina Vlady and his alcohol problem, made him a cult figure in Russian culture – and the whole nation seemed to mourn his tragically early death.

The far tamer scene of the so-called *sovetskaya estrada*, or Soviet pop, was much more acceptable to the authorities, with artists such as **Iosif Kobzon** (b. 1937) appearing on stage, television and radio for years with a mixture of sentimental songs and politically correct pieces dedicated to Soviet achievements (such as the building of the BAM railway). Folk music, too, was promoted in preference to the subversive sound of rock, although in the 1960s **Zhanna Bichevskaya** brought a individual 'folk bard' style that was compared with the work of Joan Baez.

GREAT PERFORMERS: ALLA PUGACHOVA (b. 1949)

The charismatic Pugachova broke into the limelight in 1975, and soon acquired superstar status, with a limousine, foreign travel and a turbulent private life. She gained a place in the hearts of the people with her feisty character, powerful voice and her looks and is one of the biggest selling artists in the world (although hardly known outside the former Socialist bloc). Now married to her fourth husband, the singer **Filip Kirkorov**, Allochka – or Alla Borisovna, denoting more senior status – is still an ever present figure in the world of Russian music.

The *estrada* scene was livened up, though, by the emergence of stars such as **Alla Pugachova** and **Valerii Leontyev**, who were able to stretch the priggish norms of officially accepted culture while still remaining within its bounds. Later in the 1970s, disco music from Europe and North America made inroads into the USSR, with discotheques springing up in the major cities, and groups like Abba and Boney-M acquiring a huge following among fans for whom their music represented a taste of life in the West.

Rock and the underground

Rock musicians had to spend much of their time underground. The first rock groups had emerged in Russia in the 1960s and by the 70s there was a thriving rock scene, with groups such as *Mashina vremeni* (Time Machine), led by **Andrei Makarevich** (b. 1953) and *Akvarium*, led by **Boris Grebenshchikov** (b. 1953) developing a considerable fan base with the help of *magnitizdat*, as well as through *kvartirniki*, unofficial concerts held in apartments.

In contrast to the more commercially driven Western rock music scene, leading figures in Russian rock have tended to place at least as much emphasis on words as on music, with rock legends such as **Aleksandr Bashlachov** producing powerful poetry that earned him a reputation as the conscience of Russian rock. Some artists saw their music as a form of social protest, a counter to the official culture and made strong political statements with their songs (e.g. DDT's song '*Revolyutsiya*'). Others, such as the 'supergroup' *Nautilus Pompilius*, led by **Vyacheslav Butusov** and **Ilya Kormil'tsev**, sang about love but also wrote songs that provided a telling social commentary on life in the USSR. Others, such as **Yurii Naumov**, merely wanted to be free to express their creativity without censorship and control. This was not that easy to achieve, however, as the Soviet authorities regarded rock music with some alarm, seeing it as a subversive influence on the young and clamping down on the activities of rock groups: by way of example, **Yurii Shevchuk** and his group *DDT* (originally from Ufa) were labelled 'agents of the Vatican'! They can laugh about this now, but it stands as an example of the sinister paranoia of the KGB back in the early 1980s, which also resulted in the singer **Zhanna Aguzarova** spending some time in prison as punishment for her work. The pressure arising from such intimidation could have serious consequences – Naumov eventually emigrated to the USA, to find greater artistic freedom there, and Bashlachov committed suicide at the age of just 28, the strain of carrying the burden of his talent perhaps proving too much to bear.

Rock musicians, therefore, had to be careful, leading double lives, in which they pretended to be 'ordinary' Soviet citizens on the surface, while carrying on their rock careers in the underground. **Viktor Tsoi**, leader of the group *KINO*, for example, officially worked as a heating attendant in a block of flats – an easy job that left him plenty of time for composing songs and making unofficial tours and concerts. Despite official sanctions and the lack of open media coverage, these groups built up a huge following, becoming cult figures among the young – the hallway outside Boris Grebenshchikov's very humble apartment in Leningrad was forever crowded with worshipping admirers, eager to share the spirit of aesthetic freedom that 'BG' was seen to represent. The 1980s were a time of great creativity among the Russian rock community, with other important contributions coming from **Kostya Kinchev** and *Alisa* (Moscow), and the experimental avant-garde work of **Sergei Kuryokhin** and his 'Pop Mechanics' (the subject of a BBC documentary in the 'Comrades' series in the early 1980s).

The music and dance scene post-1991

The opening up of the country signalled by glasnost' allowed musicians to play a more prominent part in cultural life, with large-scale concerts now allowed and rock groups able to begin to reap the financial rewards of their talents. But the fall of Communism in 1991 and the political and social flux that followed, seemed to cause a crisis in Russian rock, as it adjusted to the absence of the ideological structures that had been in place before and as new commercial opportunities and constraints emerged.

The Russian public were perhaps less interested now in the music of protest and conscience, more keen to listen to the Western music that they could now get access to (not least through illegally produced CDs) or to the less challenging sound and lyrics of home-grown pop music, some of which shows a strong influence from Western trends, but with a discernible Russian style present too in the songs of many bands. Russian pop music has benefited from a growing amount of investment from newly set up record companies, allowing groups to produce videos that soon reached a high standard. Dance music also began to assume a leading position: following the first experiments with house music and rave parties in the late 1980s and early 1990s, Russia followed the patterns seen around the world, with DJs in clubs first in Moscow and Petersburg introducing the latest sounds to the Russian scene, with provincial cities quickly catching up.

At the start of the new millennium, Russian popular music was in a more or less healthy state, then, with veteran stars such as Pugachova, Grebenshchikov and Butusov still performing, alongside established groups such as *Agata Kristi* and newcomers like the group *Mummii Troll'* (influenced by

Britpop), the singer **Zemfira**, boy band *Ivanushki-International*, as well as leading DJs such as **DJ Groove** and **DJ Fonar'**, all taking advantage of the freedoms that so recently had been denied.

Very few of those with an eye on the rock and pop music scene would have failed to notice the controversial duo **TATU** who made their debut in UK charts in 2002, staying at no.1 for several weeks with 'All The Things She Said'. Lena Katina (psychology student at Moscow Humanitarian College) and Julia Volkova (a student at the State Musical Variety and Jazz Arts School) went on to gain 3rd place in the Eurovision song contest in 2003 with *'Ne ver', ne boysya, ne prosi'* (Don't believe, don't be afraid and don't ask). By 2003 **TATU** had already sold more than one million albums around the world.

GLOSSARY

авторская песня (f.)	'author's song'
андеграунд (m.)	the underground
артист балета (m.)	ballet dancer (male)
балалайка (f.)	balalaika
балерина (f.)	ballerina
балет (m.)	ballet
на гастролях (pl.)	on tour
знаменный распев (m.)	znamennyi chant
классическая музыка (f.)	classical music
колокольный звон (m.)	bell ringing
композитор (m.)	composer
концертный зал (m.)	concert hall
магнитиздат (m.)	magnitizdat
меломан (m.)	music lover
могучая кучка (f.)	mighty group
опера (f.)	opera
оркестр (m.)	orchestra
песня (f.)	song
романс (m.)	lyrical song, usually accompanied by guitar
советская эстрада (f.)	Soviet pop
танец (m.)	dance
танцор/танцовщица (m./f.)	dancer (male/female)
хор (m.)	choir
хореограф (m.)	choreographer

Taking it further

Books

Cushman, Thomas, *Notes from the Underground: Rock Music Counterculture in Russia* (Albany: State University of New York Press, 1994).

Latham, A. (ed.) *The Oxford Companion to Music* (Oxford: OUP, 2002).

Maes, Francis, *A History of Russian Music* (Berkeley: University of California Press, 2001).

Minor, William, *Unzipped Souls: A Jazz Journey Through the Soviet Union* (Philadelphia: Temple University Press, 1995).

Mundy, Simon, *Tchaikovskii* (London: Omnibus Press, 1998).

Solway, Diane, *Nureyev* (New York: William Morrow, 1998).

Websites

The 'Sounds' site at **www.zvuki.ru** has a huge collection of music files that you can download. Or you can search by style of music (e.g. Russian folk songs) or artist in English and Russian – and you'll come up with thousands of sites to choose from.

Concerts

If you visit Russia, look for listings of music and dance events in the local newspapers or check for tickets in newspaper kiosks in the town. Some major venues for music and dance are (in Moscow) the **Chaikovskii Concert Hall**, the **Moscow Chaikovskii Conservatoire** and the **Bol'shoi Theatre** and (in St Petersburg) the **Philharmonic Symphony Hall** and the **Mariinskii Theatre**.

Watch out for concerts by visiting Russian artistes as well – classical orchestras, ballet companies, folk troupes and rock groups all make frequent tours to Western Europe, North America and elsewhere.

06 festivals and traditions

In this unit you will learn
- about the Russian calendar
- about Russian traditions
- about food and drink
- about Russian superstitions

As those who know Russia well can confirm, the Russians like to celebrate hard and often! Over the centuries, they have accumulated a huge itinerary of festivals, holidays and merrymaking traditions and it is only a slight exaggeration to suggest that if Russians were to celebrate every single one of these, they would be able to spend almost the whole year in one long party!

These traditions stem from separate roots – old Russian celebrations, many of which had their origins in pagan rites and rituals; the traditions of the many ethnic groups that make up the Russian population; festivals connected with the Russian Orthodox Church; and Soviet-period holidays. During Communist rule, there were attempts to suppress the traditions of pre-revolutionary times, but their memory was kept alive and many have been revived in recent years. Meanwhile, in the New (post-Soviet) Russia, holidays to mark the coming of a new era – such as Russian Independence Day – have been added to the calendar, as have Hallowe'en and other dates, thus packing the year even more fully than ever before! Some of the best known and most important of these days follow.

Russia's year of celebration

Yanvar' – January

Novyi god – New Year's Day
Staryi novyi god (Old New Year) 14 January

The celebration of the coming of the New Year has moved about quite a lot over the course of Russian history – in Russian

---

OLD AND NEW CALENDARS

Until 1918, Russia continued to use the Julian calendar (set up by Julius Caesar), in contrast to the Gregorian calendar that had become the standard in Western Europe some time before. By 1900, the difference between the calendars had reached 13 days – so the Great October Revolution was actually celebrated in the USSR on 7 November (new – Gregorian – calendar), although it had taken place on 25 October according to the old calendar. For the same reason, Russian Orthodox Christmas takes place on 7 January, and the 'old' New Year on 14 January – giving children (and their parents) a crafty opportunity to have both Christmas and New Year twice!

folk tradition, it was at the start of March, while for the Orthodox Church it was 1 September. As usual, it was Peter the Great who changed everything, placing New Year on 1 January.

It has always been one of the most important days of the year, a time for giving presents and holding parties. During the Soviet period, when Christmas was not officially recognized, the significance of the New Year celebrations increased.

Russians decorate a fir tree (*yolka*) (another of Peter the Great's imports) and have a Santa Claus-like figure in *Ded moroz* (Grandfather Frost), who is helped by *Snegurochka* (the Snow Maiden). At midnight on 31 December, the president appears on television to give a New Year's speech, families toast one another with champagne and enjoy a festive meal and then will often go out on the street to join outdoor dances, fireworks and other festivities – no matter how cold it is!

7 January

Rozhdestvo – Christmas

Before the change to the new calendar, Christmas was celebrated on 24–25 December. It was always a time for much celebrating, eating and drinking in old Russia. Traditionally, people would fast on Christmas Eve, breaking this with a meal

---

SVYATKI

During the time of **Svyatki**, from Christmas to New Year, fortune telling (**gadanie**) would take place, with girls and sometimes boys eager to find out anything they could about their future husband or wife!

---

after the evening service, with *kutya*, a kind of porridge, served as the main dish. It was also associated, as in the West, with giving presents and distributing charity to the needy. This holiday has had something of a revival in Russia since the late 1980s, although mainly for Orthodox believers, with New Year continuing to be the main festive day. Despite some ongoing restrictions, other faiths also enjoy much greater freedom now and are able to celebrate their festivals and holidays openly.

25 January

Tatyanin den' / Den' studentov
Tatyana's Day / Students' Day

The lives of saints are remembered in *imeniny* ('name days') such as Tatyana's day – and anyone else who has that name can also celebrate on that day. This is a favourite day for Russian students, as Tatyana is their patron saint – and her day marks the end of the winter exam session.

Fevral' – February

14 February

Den' Svyatogo Valentina – St Valentine's Day

This has gained huge popularity in recent years – with the romantic streak of Russians shown by the other name for this holiday – *Den' vlyublyonnykh* (Lovers' Day).

DAYS DEDICATED TO PROFESSIONS

In accordance with the Communists' glorification of the world of work, just about every single profession was awarded a day in the calendar to honour its achievements. This tradition has continued in the New Russia, with an ever expanding range of days dedicated to spheres of work from the medical profession to the post office, aviation and even customs workers. However, the notorious figure of the **vakhtyor** (doorman), an ever present feature of Russian anecdotes (the famous comedian **Mikhail Zadornov** called Russia **strana vakhtyorov** – a country of doormen), doesn't seem to have been given his own day just yet!

---

23 February

Den' zashchitnika Rodiny / Otechestva
Defender of the Motherland/Fatherland Day

This day was originally dedicated to the armed forces, but has increasingly come to be regarded as the day to honour Russian men (who felt left out at the attention given to women on 8 March!)

End of February / early March

Maslyanitsa – Shrovetide

In pre-revolutionary times, *Maslyanitsa* (from the Russian word *maslo* – butter) was a joyous period of festivities, with much eating and drinking and the strength of its tradition survived the Soviet period (when it was known as the 'Farewell to Russian Winter'). The weeklong activities would include making *bliny* (pancakes); tobogganing (the descent was supposed to signify travelling between the two worlds); rides on *troikas*; and burning a straw person to mark the end of winter.

The legendary Russian *troika*

Mart – March

8 March

Mezhdunarodnyi zhenskii den' – International Women's Day

A day when Russian women can expect compliments, gifts and privileged treatment from men – perhaps to try to make up for the rest of the year! This holiday was promoted actively by the authorities in the Soviet period, keen to show that women enjoyed equality in the USSR.

THE *TROIKA*

The *troika*, from the Russian word *tri* (three) was a sleigh or carriage pulled by three horses side by side. In folklore the troika was seen to symbolize the spirit of Russia, as the writer Nikolai Gogol' showed in his novel *Dead Souls*, when he compared Russia to a speeding troika that no one could overtake, flying who knows where.

Aprel' – April

1 April

Den' smekha – Day of Laughter

Russians enjoy April Fool's Day as much as anyone. In the late 1980s one of the national newspapers took advantage of the more open atmosphere of glasnost' to play a huge prank, placing a mock advertisement asking for members of the public to write in for a chance to join the cosmonaut training programme – and received sackloads of applications!

Paskha – Orthodox Easter

Easter was the most important holiday of the year in tsarist Russia, marked by fasting, which is broken after the church service by eating eggs that have been painted (usually a shade of red), a bread called *paskha* and *kulich*, a traditional dessert. The famous **Fabergé eggs**, made of gold and covered by an intricately decorated enamel shell, date from the time when Tsar Aleksandr III ordered one from the St Petersburg jeweller Karl Fabergé as a present for his wife, the tsarina. It is a time when families pay a special visit to the graves of their loved ones, leaving food and other gifts.

Mai – May

1 May

Den' mira i truda – Day of Peace and Labour

May Day was until recently officially celebrated as *Den' mezhdunarodnoi solidarnosti trudyashchikhsya* (International Workers' Solidarity Day). Soviet leaders and their guests would watch the parades on Red Square, while the population would join in similar events across the country.

9 May

Den' pobedy – Victory Day

The commemoration of the ending of the Great Patriotic War (World War II) is still a major event in Russia, not surprisingly, given the enormous losses suffered by the USSR. Veterans don their medals and the war years are remembered in parades, in schools and by the media.

Iyun' – June

12 June

Den' nezavisimosti – Independence Day

To mark the announcement made by Boris Yel'tsin of the independence of the Russian republic from the USSR in 1990. The republic of Tatarstan (part of the Russian Federation) has also taken to marking its own 'day of independence' (on 30 August).

Belye nochi – White Nights

For over a month in midsummer, when the twilight extends well into the night in the northern latitudes of Russia, the majestic backdrop of St Petersburg provides a dramatic and romantic setting for the White Nights season, during which concerts and other cultural activities take place.

DEN' GORODA – TOWN FESTIVAL

In recent years it has become fashionable to commemorate the founding of Russian towns and cities with a day of festivities. St Petersburg's day, for instance, is at the start of White Nights on 29 May.

Sentyabr' – September

1 September

Den' znanii – Day of Knowledge

The academic year starts on this day and the work of teachers, and the importance of learning, is honoured. Pupils bring huge bouquets of flowers for their teachers and in the media education is the issue of the day.

Noyabr' – November

7 November

Great October Socialist Revolution Day

The most important day in the Soviet calendar, but nowadays commemorated by an ever shrinking number of devotees to the Communist cause and those nostalgic for the old days of the USSR. Some readers may remember the dramatic television pictures that would be shown on Western TV each year, of missile launchers and tanks rumbling across Red Square in Moscow, in front of the Soviet politburo watching on top of Lenin's mausoleum.

POSIDELKI – EVENING PARTIES

In pre-revolutionary Russia the autumn and winter months saw *posidelki* held frequently. They included work-related gatherings (with women and girls engaged in various tasks) and more light-hearted parties to which the girls would invite the local young men – and the singing, dancing and games that ensued certainly staved off the boredom of the long winter nights!

Traditions of Russian life

Weddings

Traditional church weddings have made something of a return to fashion since the end of Communism, although marriage at the local registry office (known usually by its acronym ZAGS) is still required. A church wedding is a fascinating occasion, with one of the traditions revolving around *ventsy* (crowns) decorated with precious stones, that are held above the heads of the bride and groom throughout the service by their 'witnesses' (best man and bridesmaid). By the end of the ceremony, the witnesses' arms will be ready to drop off!

After a Russian wedding it is the custom for the couple to be driven around the town to visit important sites, such as historical monuments and the eternal flame commemorating those lost in war. The wedding banquet and party that follows is a marathon of high spirits and pranks that lasts for two days. The bride and groom are posed various challenges and tasks, ranging from having to sweep up coins thrown on the floor by the guests, to the groom having to 'buy' back his wife (usually with vodka). During the feast the newlyweds will frequently hear the persistent cry of *Gor'ko!* (bitter!) from all present, a sign that they should kiss in order to make the bitter wine sweeter. They will also be asked to take a bite of a loaf of bread – whoever takes the larger bite is set to be the head of the household!

KEEPING FOLK TRADITIONS ALIVE

Russia's folk traditions have long had to endure attempts to smother them – from the Orthodox Church (which regarded them as dangerous for their pagan overtones) and by the Soviet authorities, which dismissed their 'backwardness'. Despite – or perhaps because of – such problems, Russia has managed to hold on to a surprising amount of its folk culture, although there are concerns as to whether this heritage will be passed on to the current young generation.

The traditions of non-Russian peoples have faced similar threats over the ages, their plight all the more precarious because of the smaller population sizes of the ethnic groups concerned (some northern peoples may comprise only a few hundred people today).

In post-Soviet Russia efforts are being made to preserve both Russian and non-Russian folk traditions, through education programmes, the establishment of museums and the work of historical societies. Those visiting Russia should try to get to events where traditional costumes are worn, folk crafts are demonstrated and historical scenes re-enacted. In the **Kolomenskoe Museum** in Moscow, for example, visitors can get 'married' after dressing up in medieval Russian clothes.

Birth traditions

In the old days, the choice of name for a newborn baby would often be dictated by the name of the saint's day closest to which she or he was born. The local priest may not even have consulted the parents, deciding for himself how to name the child.

In Soviet times, baptism was actively discouraged by the atheist government – although this did not stop a growing number of party officials (*apparatchiki*) having their children christened from the 1970s on.

Death rituals

After a death in a family, the family covers the mirrors in the house for some time. Wakes (*pominki*) are also held on certain dates (e.g. 40 days after the death).

Banya – the Russian bath

An unmissable experience for those who travel to Russia is a visit to a *banya*, the Russian version of the sauna. The *banya* has played an important role in Russian life for centuries, with birth, marriage and death rituals associated with it.

Traditional costume

For a real visual treat, the visitor to Russia should take a look at the beautiful traditional clothes worn by Russian women (the men's attire was much plainer!). In the northern parts of Russia, women wore an ankle-length shirt (*rubakha*), with a sleeveless *sarafan* on top. In the south, a part-embroidered long shirt was covered with a wraparound skirt called a *ponyova*. Married women wore a headdress known as a *kokoshnik*. The elaborately decorated garments took many hours of skilled handicraft to make and would be passed down from generation to generation.

Food and drink

For special occasions, Russian dining tables will threaten to collapse under the weight of the many sumptuous delights of Russian cuisine! To start off with, there will be a range of mouth-watering *zakuski* (hors d'oeuvres), such as *ikra* (caviar), salted cucumbers (sometimes topped with honey), salted or pickled mushrooms, smoked or marinaded fish, *baklazhannaya ikra* (a 'caviar' made from aubergines), *salat Olivye* (Salat Olivier, named after a French chef resident in Russia in the 18th century), *pirozhki* (little pies) with various fillings, along with *chyornyi khleb* (black bread) and, perhaps no surprise here, vodka.

VODKA

Vodka is consumed neat in Russia (no watering down of the 40% (or more) proof allowed with orange juice here!), although apart from the standard variety of vodka there are a number of flavoured vodkas, using fruit, herbs, pepper or other ingredients.

While the origins of vodka are the subject of debate, Russians have been drinking the potent transparent liquid for centuries. The ability of Russian men (in particular) to consume copious amounts of vodka is legendary – but the impact of excessive drinking and alcoholism can be devastating for the individual and those around them.

It makes the ideal accompaniment to *zakuski*, however, and on special occasions those present are expected to down a shot each time a toast is called (and Russians know many, many forms of toast!).

For the main course, goose (for a really special celebration) or duck might be cooked with apples, or chicken *tabaka* (a Georgian dish – Russians use many recipes from former Soviet republics) might be prepared, or perhaps a fish recipe, such as *kulebyaka* (a layered pie, traditionally made with salmon).

And then for dessert, you might be offered *tort Napoleon* or *vareniki*, a Ukrainian dish, comprising dumplings filled with fruit or sweet cottage cheese. This will usually be accompanied

A samovar

by *chai* (tea), which is just about the antithesis of the potent vodka, but which is also drunk in large amounts by Russians. Traditionally made with a *samovar*, tea first came to Russia with the Tatars. Apart from imported varieties, the Krasnodar region in the south of Russia also produces tea.

Everyday food is simpler, of course, but also extremely tasty. Russians tend to eat a lot of soup and not just during the cold winter months, when it can really help to warm you up. *Borshch* (beetroot soup) came originally from Ukraine and the south of Russia, but it is made across the whole country. It comes in several varieties, using different combinations of ingredients. *Shchi* (cabbage soup) is also popular, as is *okroshka*, a cold and extremely refreshing summer soup. The main ingredient is *kvas*, a non-alcoholic cold drink made from rye bread.

Or you might have *pel'meny*, a ravioli-like dish from Siberia made with slightly spicy meat, *golubtsy*, parcels made from cabbage and stuffed with meat and rice or *solyanka*, a thick stew made with meat, fish or just vegetables.

Russians still like to buy their vegetables in the market (*rynok*), preferring fresh produce to pre-packed meals and frozen food. In winter months, families will usually have a stock of carefully preserved fruit and vegetables, often grown on their dacha.

Bread (**khleb**) is a powerful symbol in Russian culture and is ever present in the traditions of country life in particular. A **karavai** of bread is still used to bless those who have just been married, for instance, or to welcome a stranger, who is offered bread which she or he then has to dip into salt before tasting.

Superstitions

Russian culture is full of superstitions and even urban sophisticates will often religiously adhere to the patterns of behaviour and beliefs that have been passed down for countless generations before them. So, whatever you do, when you are in Russia make sure you do not:

* Shake hands across the threshold.
* Go back into a flat or a house if you have forgotten something – ask someone else to get it for you.
* If you are single, do not sit on the corner of a table (otherwise you won't get married for 7 years!).

And make sure you:

* Sit down for a couple of minutes before heading off on a journey.
* Spit over your left shoulder three times to avoid bad luck (luckily for bystanders, this has only got to be a 'symbolic', rather than actual act of spitting!).
* Buy only odd numbers of flowers – an even number is used only for funerals.

There are many, many more dos and don'ts. But as we don't have space to put them here, you'll just have to find them out for yourselves. (Your Russian friends will be quick to point them out to you!)

GLOSSARY

баня (f.)	*steam bath*
белые ночи (pl.)	*'White Nights'*
блюдо (n.)	*dish/course*
Дед Мороз (m.)	*Grandfather Frost*
день города (m.)	(lit. town day) *town festival*
День международной солидарности трудящихся (m.)	*International Workers' Solidarity Day*

день рождения (m.)	*birthday*
ёлка (f.)	*New Year tree*
закуски (pl.)	*hors d'oeuvres*
именины (pl.)	*name day*
каравай (m.)	*traditional round loaf of bread*
кухня (f.)	*cuisine/kitchen*
Масляница (f.)	*Shrovetide*
Международный женский день (m.)	*International Women's Day*
Новый год (m.)	*New Year*
отмечать (vb.)	*to celebrate, to mark (an occasion)*
Пасха (f.)	*Easter*
праздник (m.)	*festival, celebration*
предрассудки (pl.)	*superstitions*
Рождество (n.)	*Christmas*
самовар (m.)	*samovar*
свадьба (f.)	*wedding*
Снегурочка (f.)	*the Snow Maiden*
Старый новый год (m.)	*old New Year*
тост (m.)	*toast*
тройка (f.)	*troika*
традиция (f.)	*tradition*

Taking it further

If you are able to travel to Russia for a vacation, check out the listing of events for the time that you are there and try to attend any celebrations or special occasions that you can, to get a first-hand taste of Russia's traditions. Or make contact with the nearest Russian community to where you live and ask if you can join in as they carry on these traditions abroad – you're sure to be more than welcome!

The website **http://ru.narod.ru/** contains a wealth of information on all aspects of Russian culture (in Russian), with seasonal recipes, materials on traditional crafts, songs, Russian names and so on.

Why not try your hand at making some Russian food? We've included a couple of recipes at the end of this book on pages 231–3, but there are many books on Russian food available in English – two that we have found extremely useful are *The Cooking of Russia*, by Karen Craig and Seva Novgorodtsev

(London: Martin Books, 1990) and Susan Ward's *Russian Regional Recipes* (London: Apple Press, 1993). This book is somewhat inappropriately named, as it includes details of the culinary traditions of all former Soviet republics – but the recipes really work! There is also a very handy online guide to Russian food at

www.russianfoods.com

Or you might try out any Russian restaurants located near you. The degree of authenticity of the contents of the menu can vary quite a lot, but you'll often get a good impression of the nature of Russian cuisine. Our favourite experience of tasting Russian food outside of Russia was in Helsinki, where there is an impressive collection of Russian restaurants – so, if you are ever passing through Finland...!

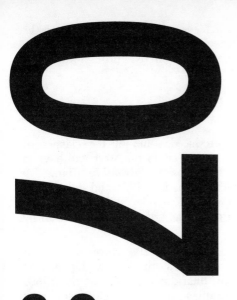

07

creativity in other spheres

In this unit you will learn
- about cinema and theatre in Russia
- about the Russian media
- about science and technology
- about Russia's space programme

Here we look at the many achievements of Russians – and the obstacles they found in their way – in a variety of spheres ranging from cinema, theatre and circus, through the mass media, to science and technology.

Cinema

Russian filmmakers have produced some of the classics of cinematic history. Just about everyone in the West will have at least seen excerpts from *Bronenosets Potyomkin* (*Battleship Potyomkin*) by **Sergei Eisenshtein**, made in 1926 and still rated as one of the greatest films ever made – do you know the scene where the crowd is fleeing down the Odessa steps, fired on by tsarist troops?

From the avant-garde films of the 1920s, through Socialist Realism movies of the Stalinist era, the challenging artistic pieces of **Andrei Tarkovskii**, hilarious comedies of the 1960s and 70s, gritty urban dramas and the uncompromising treatment of historical subjects of the 1980s, to the ideologically unrestricted and more commercialized films of today, Russia's cinematic heritage offers the outsider a valuable insight into a society that was closed off from us for so long, that seemed so strange and distant – yet which, as we can see through its films, is full of people living ordinary lives in extraordinary circumstances.

Early years of film

The art of film-making came to Russia soon after the screening of the first film – footage of the coronation of Tsar Nikolai II (1898) can often be seen in documentaries of that period – while the first domestic Russian production came in 1908. Before World War I, several studios sprang up, with those of **Aleksandr Drankov** and **Aleksandr Khanzhonkov** in particular vying to woo audiences, as the avid cinema-going habit of Russians was born. The stars of the pre-revolutionary cinema included **Ivan Mozzhukhin** (1889–1939) and **Vera Kholodnaya** (1893–1919), whose sad eyes grabbed the hearts of the country. A principal feature of Russian films of this time, as shown in the work of director **Yevgenii Bauer** (1865–1917), is the slow pace of the action and the focus on the characters' emotional expression. Apart from home-made productions, foreign stars such as Charlie Chaplin and Max Linder were also big hits (aided by the

fact that this was still the silent era, of course) and big names of
Hollywood, such as Douglas Fairbanks, would remain popular
into the 1920s and 30s.

Cinema and the revolution

The power of film as a medium not just for entertainment but
also for propaganda was recognized by the Bolsheviks, with
Lenin famously stating: 'Of all the arts, film is the most
important for us.' Especially important at a time when the
majority of the population was still illiterate, films provided an
effective weapon in the consolidation of Soviet rule, with special
trains carrying agitprop cinemas to the far-flung corners of the
country.

Meanwhile, the leading directors in the young Soviet state, such
as Eisenshtein and **Lev Kuleshov** (1899–1970) experimented
with all aspects of the film-making art, with the technique of
montage becoming a hallmark of their work. In this, the
psychological effect of the film and the underlying message
would be enhanced through placing symbolic images into the
body of the action through intricate editing. In Eisenshtein's
Strike, for example, an image of cattle being slaughtered is used
to intensify the impact in the plot itself, in which workers were
being killed. The use of the 'Kuleshov effect' can also be seen in
the two most famous films of that director, *Neobychainye
priklyucheniya mistera Vesta v strane bol'shevikov* (*The
Extraordinary Adventures of Mr West in the Land of the
Bolsheviks*) (1925) and **Po zakonu** (*By the Law*) (1926).

FILM-MAKING LEGENDS: SERGEI EISENSHTEIN
(1898–1948)

Eisenshtein was a genius in the world of cinema, both as a director
and as a theorist who wrote extensively on the art of directing.
Skilfully employing the montage effect (see main text), Eisenshtein
packed his films with complex symbols. He completed only seven
films (the Soviet authorities halted production of several projects),
but his body of work is outstanding. It includes the films **Stachka**
(*Strike*) (1925), his first feature movie; *Battleship Potyomkin* (1926),
which recounts part of the story of the 1905 revolution; **Oktyabr'**
(*October*) (1928); **Aleksandr Nevskii** (1938); and perhaps his
greatest films, **Ivan Groznyi** (*Ivan the Terrible*), Parts I and II (1944
and 1946), which drew criticism from Stalin that stopped work on
the planned third film in the trilogy.

Vsevolod Pudovkin (1983–1953) also experimented with the editing process, with *Mat'* (*Mother*) his best-known work. In the field of documentary film, the work of **Dziga Vertov** (1896–1954) offers a revealing and fascinating insight into the development of Soviet society. **Yakov Protazanov** (1881-1945) who had made his name as a director before the revolution, made *Aelita* (1924), set on Mars and *Sorok pervyi* (*The Forty-First*) (1926), about a female Bolshevik sniper who falls in love with the White officer prisoner whom she is guarding, but then shoots him when he tries to escape.

Stalinism and the cinema

Experimentation and ambiguity were squeezed out in favour of positive, clear-cut storylines under Socialist Realism. The decline of the avant-garde film that this brought about suited the Communist authorities, of course, but the cinema-going public too, for the most part, preferred the easier-to-follow plots of uplifting comedies and musicals to more intellectual films. The ideological message contained in Socialist Realist films could be ignored, to some extent at least – people (like the average film watcher anywhere) were more interested in entertainment and a chance to escape from the harsh realities of everyday life. One of the major films of this period was *Chapaev* (1934), directed by the unrelated **Vasilyev** 'brothers,' **Sergei** (1900–1959) and **Georgii** (1899–1946). It told the story of a Bolshevik hero from the civil war, and it is a mixture of heroic exploits, action and comic subplots.

From thaw to stagnation: film under Khrushchov and Brezhnev

The suffocation of cinematic creativity under Stalin had led to a slump in film production by the early 1950s, but it soon picked up in the more relaxed and less threatening atmosphere of Khrushchov's thaw. The human side to storylines could now be emphasized more fully, as in *Ballada o soldate* (*Ballad of a Soldier*) (1959), directed by **Grigorii Chukhrai** (b. 1921), the moving story of a young Russian soldier in World War II. It was also a time to reflect on the legacy of ideological devotion and introduce greater ambiguity into the underlying message of films. In 1961 **Mikhail Romm**, a director who had been involved in film-making since the 1930s, and had made several films covering the life and work of Lenin, released the film

Devyat' Dnei Odnogo Goda (*Nine Days of One Year*) about the nuclear age, without offering a clear good/bad judgement on the film's main characters.

FILM-MAKING LEGENDS: ANDREI TARKOVSKII
(1932–1986)

Tarkovskii was a master of composing thought-provoking images that called upon the viewer to come to their own interpretation of the 'poetic reasoning' of the film. The themes of memory, of the role of art and the artist and a sense of loss pervade his films.

With highly unconventional and complex plots, his work often seems confusing, especially to audiences in the West used to Hollywood-style patterns, but his work was widely appreciated by discerning audiences at home and abroad, where his films picked up many festival prizes. The Soviet authorities responded to his films by delaying their release and by putting obstacles in Tarkovskii's way – with the result that he made only seven films in his career.

Highlights include **Andrei Rublyov** (1966), a portrait of the 15th-century icon painter that raises eternal questions about art and life; **Solyaris** (*Solaris*) (1972), set in a futuristic setting in outer space; and **Zerkalo** (*Mirror*) (1975), a beautiful and complicated autobiography of Tarkovskii. Frustrated by the restrictions of the USSR, he defected to the West after his film **Nostal'giya** (*Nostalgia*) was completed in Italy.

Directors of considerable talent emerged in the 1960s, exploring new boundaries of the cinematic art or raising questions about the nature of Soviet society and thus testing the limits of the Soviet censor's tolerance. In 1962, Andrei Tarkovskii's first film, *Ivanovo detstvo* (*Ivan's Childhood*) appeared, signifying the arrival of a cinematic genius, but the ambiguities inherent in his work aroused considerable suspicion among the ideological watchdogs.

For some directors, the commitment to their art led to the 'shelving' of their films, as the censor decided they could not be shown to the Soviet public. **Andrei Konchalovskii** (b. 1937) completed his realistic portrayal of country life *Istoriya Asi Klyachinoi, kotoraya lyubila, da ne vyshla zamuzh* (*The Story of Asya Klyachina, Who Loved but Who Did Not Get Married*) in 1967, yet it was shown for the first time only in 1987. The films of the talented director **Kira Muratova** (b. 1934) received the same treatment. Often the reason for shelving could be based more on the fact that it starred an actor who had fallen out of favour (such as the comedian **Savelii Kramarov**, who emigrated to the USA in 1984, and later starred alongside Arnold Schwarzenegger in the film *Red Heat*).

During the pre-glasnost' years Soviet Russian cinema also produced some hilarious comedies, with those directed by **Leonid Gaidai** (1923–1993) among the most successful. His enormously popular film *Brilliantovaya ruka* (*Diamond Arm*) (1968), featuring the legendary actors **Yurii Nikulin** and **Andrei Mironov**, is repeated frequently on Russian TV today and contains a host of what are called *krylatye frazy*, expressions uttered by characters in the film that have since become part of the everyday language. '*Shol, upal, prosnulsya – gips!*' ('I was walking along, fell down, came around – and there was this plaster!'), the unconvincing explanation that Nikulin's naive character gives as to why his arm is covered in a plaster (and, unbeknown to him, hiding a set of diamonds that a smuggling gang has hidden there), is often used, for example.

The 1970s and 1980s saw a number of films dealing with historical subjects, the classics of literature, and *byt*, or aspects of daily life. The well-loved adventure film *Beloe solntse pustyni* (*White Sun of the Desert*), directed by **Vladimir Motyl'** in 1970, is ritually watched by Russian cosmonauts before take-off. **Aleksei German**'s innovative films incurred the wrath of the censor, delaying their release until the perestroika period, when his *Moi drug Ivan Lapshin* (*My Friend, Ivan Lapshin*) (1983, shown 1985) made a considerable impact with its gritty portrayal of life in the 1930s. Konchalovskii's brother, **Nikita Mikhalkov** (b. 1945) further enhanced his reputation as a director of merit through his films based loosely on Chekhov's story *Platonov*, and Goncharov's novel *Oblomov*.

The *byt* film genre touched upon issues of contemporary life, human values, relationships. **El'dar Ryazanov**'s (b. 1927) prolific work includes the fairy-tale like comedy *Ironiya sud'by ili s lyogkim parom* (*The Irony of Fate, or Hope you've Had a Nice Sauna*) (1975), shown on Russian TV every New Year's night. Other notable films include **Georgii Daneliya**'s (b. 1930) *Osennii marafon* (*Autumn Marathon*) (1979), as well as *Moskva slezam ne verit* (*Moscow Does Not Believe in Tears*) (1979) directed by **Vladimir Men'shov** (b. 1939). This was a huge success among the Russian public – the snooty dismissal of the film by some in the intelligentsia notwithstanding. A sentimental comedy-drama about the lives of three women, it broke box office records in the USSR and was awarded a Hollywood Oscar.

Cinema post-1985

After Gorbachov's arrival on the scene as General Secretary, the film industry started to shake itself free from the shackles that had constrained it for so long. Most of the previously 'shelved' films were dusted off and shown publicly for the first time. Directors were able to be much bolder in their treatment of subjects, ranging from the demythologizing of history, as in **Elem Klimov**'s horrifying and graphic depiction in *Idi i smotri* (*Come and See*) (1985) of the German occupation of a Belarussian village during World War II, to piercing social criticism that expressed the depths of discontent in Soviet society, as in **Vasilii Pichul**''s *Malen'kaya Vera* (*Little Vera*) (1988) an exploration of sex, violence and social problems in the working-class surroundings of a provincial town. Sergei Solovyov's atmospheric *Assa* (1987), filmed in a wintry Yalta, explores intergenerational conflict and the pressing need for change through an innovative storyline.

Alongside domestic success, there was also recognition abroad for Russian film-making, with **Pavel Lungin**'s *Taksi-blyuz* (*Taxi Blues*) winning him the Best Director award at the 1990 Cannes Film Festival. Although some in the film intelligentsia mouthed lofty concerns for the artistic integrity of the industry (admittedly, there were some films of dubious quality produced), the appearance of freedom meant that films – both good and bad – could afford to dispense with subtleties and ambiguities and confront their topic and their audience head on, reaching out to the wider public and serving as a kind of safety valve for releasing the tensions and frustrations that had been mounting in the USSR for so long. In documentaries, too, the work of the great Latvian director **Juris Podnieks** (1950–1992) exposed the myths and lies surrounding previously taboo subjects such as the Afghanistan War, while his innovative *Legko li byt' molodym?* (*Is it Easy to be Young?*) (1987) touched a chord with the increasingly alienated Soviet youth.

Mention must also be made of the fine tradition of animated film-making in Russia. Among the top names in this field are **Yurii Norshtein** creator of the film *Skazka skazok* (1979) and **Aleksandr Petrov** (who has won an Oscar for one of his cartoons).

The early 1990s were seen as dark times by many in the Russian film industry. Cinema attendance fell, as a result of increased ticket prices, greater availability of videos for hire and the worsening quality of many of the films being shown. Increasing numbers of cinemas were being turned to other uses (as nightclubs, for instance). Filmmakers, meanwhile, were having to learn the lessons of the market, with costs increasing dramatically. As with the other arts, Russian cinema was also affected by the trauma of the end of Soviet rule (that many in its ranks had desired) and the flux of the transition period. This, and the absence of the stifling, puritanical censorship of old, was reflected in the trend for *chernukha* (from the word 'black'), with films dealing with extremes of violence and depravity, and sex being portrayed ever more explicitly.

While audiences may have been interested in watching life at its worst for some time, the tribulations of everyday life in the New Russia led people to seek a form of escape in cinema once more. This explains the ongoing attachment to 'feel-good' movies from the Soviet period and the popularity of Hollywood films with simple storylines and predictable endings. By the turn of the new millennium, cinemas were filling up again (although ticket prices remained a problem) but most films on offer were foreign imports.

Russian films are, however, still being produced. The directors of artistic, avant-garde films still have difficulties in making their films in Russia, but now it is down to money, not ideological restrictions – thus leaving them in a position familiar to many directors of such films across the world. However, several – such as Lungin and Konchalovskii – have been successful in gaining sponsorship abroad and their films can be seen in international film festivals, even if they receive little attention at home.

The best-known post-Soviet Russian films in the West have been Nikita Mikhalkov's **Utomlyonnye solntsem** (literally 'weary of the sun', translated as *Burnt By the Sun*) (1994) and **Sibirskii tsiryul'nik** (*The Barber of Siberia*) (1999). *Burnt by the Sun* looked at the impending persecution under Stalin's purges faced by a civil war hero (played by Mikhalkov himself) and his family. The film enjoyed a substantial budget and was made in a glossier style more akin to Hollywood movies than the Russian tradition, a fact that helped it to pick up an Oscar for best foreign film.

Two films in particular have played a role in asking the audience – and society at large – to reflect on the consequences of recent conflicts and the nature of Russian society. In *Musul'manin* (*The Muslim*) (1995), directed by **Vladimir Khotinenko**, Yevgenii Mironov plays a Russian soldier who has been held captive for years in Afghanistan, where he converted to Islam and who now returns home to his native village to face hostility, alienation and rejection from family and former friends. **Sergei Bodrov**'s 1996 film *Kavkazskii plennik* (*Prisoner of the Caucasus*) dealt with the open wound of the first Chechen war, which was only drawn to a close in the summer of that year.

Meanwhile, a new generation of directors has shown a willingness to adapt to the new conditions and the new tastes of the viewing public. The popularity of the film *Brat* (*Brother*) (1996), directed by **Aleksei Balabanov**, shows the penchant for *boeviki* or combat/action movies. The enormous success of the comedy *Osobennosti natsional'noi okhoty* (*Peculiarities of the National Hunt*) (1995), directed by **Aleksandr Rogozhkin**, stems from the appeal of its zany humour and its exploration of what it means to be Russian, as seen from both inside and outside.

Theatre

Early restrictions

Theatregoing established itself as an important part of Russian life in the 20th century and Russian theatre exerted a considerable influence on the international level, through the work of such legendary figures as Konstantin Stanislavskii. For much of its relatively short history, however, periods of artistic creativity and experimentation have been shadowed by suspicion, persecution and control – factors that have given events on the Russian stage a broader significance as a barometer of social and political life.

The origins of the Russian theatrical tradition lay in the work of the *skomorokhi*, or jesters of the Middle Ages, who toured the country with acts that included trained bears and puppet shows; and in mystery plays on religious themes. At the level of the court, the first performance did not occur until 1672, when the Tsar Alexis was won over by the theatrical art. The birth of the Russian national theatre subsequently took place in the middle of the 18th century: the first professional theatre in Russia was established in the city of Yaroslavl' in 1750 by **Fyodor Volkov**. After this, a growing number of aristocrats took to setting up their own private theatres, which made use of serfs as actors, in plays that imitated French and Italian styles.

Elite and popular theatre in the 19th century

Despite the appearance of some notable plays by writers such as Griboyedov, Gogol' and Ostrovskii (see p. 49), government control and censorship stifled the development of the theatre for much of the 19th century, with a state monopoly over theatres in Moscow and Petersburg in place until 1883. Meanwhile, popular entertainment in the country as a whole developed from the *narodnye gulyaniya*, or fairs, that were seasonal celebrations with roots stretching back to pagan rituals and which included lively performances of folk tales and other dramatized stories. From the 1860s on, a growing number of popular theatres appeared, as part of the intelligentsia's efforts to bring culture to the common people. This extended into the concept of the *narodnyi dom*, or people's house, a building that housed a stage for productions, reading facilities and other amenities for the enlightenment of the population. By 1917 there were many examples of these people's houses.

Stanislavskii and Meierkhol'd

The lifting of the state monopoly opened the way to a new era for Russian theatre, with new companies opening across the country. The most significant of these was the *Moskovskii Khudozhestvennyi Teatr* (Moscow Art Theatre), set up in 1898 by **Konstantin Stanislavskii** (1863–1938) and **Vladimir Nemirovich-Danchenko** (1858–1943). Stanislavskii was to gain an international reputation as a director for his development of the 'method' approach to acting, in which actors develop a close psychological insight into the characters they are playing, assuming the identity of the character on the stage. The Moscow Art Theatre joined up with **Anton Chekhov** (see Unit 3) and it was here that his plays were first performed.

After playing various roles in performances at the Moscow Art Theatre, **Vsevolod Meierkhol'd** (1874–1940) took Russian theatre in new directions as the head of a studio that Stanislavskii put him in charge of, to investigate alternatives to the realistic style. Meierkhol'd began to develop the notion of **biomechanics**, which moved away from the psychological approach and placed emphasis on visual performance, with the actors (who were trained like gymnasts) moving in a puppet-like, mechanistic fashion around a bare stage. Meierkhol'd's productions removed the sense of illusion in theatre, doing away with the curtain, for example, and engaging the audience in the spectacle of performance in various ways.

The spirit of experimentation in the pre-revolutionary years gave rise to a host of avant-garde works, including the 'Suprematist' performance *Victory over the Sun* (1913), by **Aleksei Kruchonykh,** in which the painter Kazimir Malevich collaborated. After this period of liberation, though, since the lifting of tsarist restrictions, the Bolshevik Revolution would dramatically change the way in which theatre would be seen in Russia.

Mass spectacles and *agitprop*

Following the Revolution there was a trend for holding mass spectacles, in which key events in the revolution and the civil war were re-enacted on the streets, with the aim of freeing drama from the supposedly bourgeois theatres and taking it to the people. The most memorable spectacle of this kind was the *Storming of the Winter Palace,* staged in 1920 by **Nikolai Evreinov** in the spot in St Petersburg (at this time named Petrograd) where the revolution had begun. There were some 8,000 members of the cast and an estimated 100,000 people in the audience!

Theatre was also used for *agitprop,* from the desire of those who supported the revolution to take its message to the country through 'agitation' (touching on the grievances of the population) and propaganda. The *Sinie bluzy* (*Blue Blouses*), named for the workers' shirts they appeared in, was a famous *agitprop* group, whose performances included the presentation of symbolic shapes (such as factories) formed by the actors linking together in acrobatic fashion. The prototype for similar groups that sprang up later in other countries, the Blue Blouses came to an end after their satirical work incurred the wrath of the Stalinist regime in the late 1920s.

The fate of the avant-garde

Meierkhol'd and others were able to continue to enjoy considerable artistic freedom in the early 1920s and Meierkhol'd himself held an influential position within the official cultural establishment. He took advantage of this further to pursue his ideas on biomechanics, combining them with the

'Constructivist' notions seen in art and architecture at the time, with stage sets becoming machines, as the industrial age was glorified. **Yevgenii Vakhtangov** (1883–1922) also presented innovative productions, drawing both on Stanislavskii and Meierkhol'd's work, while at the Moscow Art Theatre, Stanislavskii put on **Mikhail Bulgakov**'s powerful play *Dni Turbinykh* (*Days of the Turbines*), dealing with the effect of the revolution and civil war on a middle-class 'White' family.

TSIRK! THE CIRCUS!

The circus is revered as a form of entertainment in Russia and there are circus troupes based in many towns. Although they were under the control of the state during the Communist era, the tradition of family dynasties was, perhaps surprisingly, still common.

There are special schools around the country for training in the various circus acts, with this system providing the foundation for the breathtaking agility of the high-wire artists, among others. Over the years Russian circus acts – such as the legendary clown, **Popov** – have won many friends among old and young alike on their foreign tours.

By the late 1920s, however, the same darkness that had descended on the other arts was seen in the world of theatre: attempts to stage Bulgakov's subsequent plays were hampered or foiled, while **Vladimir Mayakovskii** (1891–1937) – the energetic purveyor to the masses of poetry and dramatic productions (such as his *Mystery Bouffe* of 1918), found his latest offerings for the stage came under strong attack in the officially controlled press, a factor that must have contributed to his suicide. Meierkhol'd continued to hold to his right to engage in experimentation, a course that led him inevitably to conflict with the authorities – with terrible consequences. He was arrested in 1939 and executed in 1940 (his wife, an actress, was murdered shortly after his arrest).

The later years of Soviet drama

The long night of Stalin's terror prevented any meaningful progress in the theatre, which did not begin to recover until the late 1950s. In the early 1960s, the Vakhtangov Theatre in Moscow was able to stage the plays *The Shadow* and *The Dragon*, written in the early 1940s by **Yevgenii Shvarts**

(1896–1958), and **Yurii Lyubimov** began his long spell as head of the **Taganka Theatre** in Moscow, with Vladimir Vysotskii (see Unit 5) as one of his stars. Theatrical freedom was still far from guaranteed, however, and producers, actors and audiences learned to communicate meanings (including veiled criticism of the Soviet system) in a subtle, between-the-lines manner. This was a skill that also needed to be mastered by variety performers, comedians and satirists, such as the people's favourite comedian, **Arkadii Raikin** (1911–1987).

The glasnost' revolution reduced this need significantly and playwrights, producers and actors found that they were able to deal boldly with themes that had long been taboo. Previously banned plays were resurrected, while new drama grew ever more adventurous and a large number of small studio theatres appeared, serving as a venue for a fresh wave of experimentation. Comedians such as **Mikhail Zhvanetskii** (b. 1934) and **Mikhail Zadornov** (b. 1948) brazenly and brilliantly shot stinging satirical commentary towards the regime in front of packed houses.

The ending of handsome state subsidies and a fall-off in theatregoing in the early 1990s, led to the same talk of crisis that was seen in the film industry. There were strong signs by the start of the new millennium, however, that the Russian theatre was surely getting its act together, with the long and proud traditions of acting excellence still gaining plaudits from critics and audiences alike. Meanwhile, a sense of returning to pre-revolutionary times came with the reappearance of cabaret as a form of entertainment.

Media

The Russian media have come a long, long way since the Bolsheviks and other revolutionary groups churned out their underground newspapers to stir the masses. The tsarist censorship and sanctions imposed on the media before 1917 evolved in the Soviet Union to become the embodiment of the Orwellian nightmare of 1984, seen at its worst in the publication of admissions of crimes against the Soviet state by the victims of Stalin's purges.

Newspeak – Soviet control of the media

For seven decades the media were the principal weapons of the Communist party in its ongoing – and, as it turned out –

unwinnable battle to convince the world, and its own people, of its infallibility and righteousness. At the height of the system, with people denied for the most part any access to alternative sources of information, there is no doubt that the propaganda did go a considerable way to achieving its desired effect, as Soviet citizens came to believe, for example, what they were told about the inequalities of life in the West. There was even a practice of reporting disasters such as a train crash that had actually taken place in the USSR by stating that an accident had occurred in some foreign country instead, such was the desire of the authorities to avoid negative news relating to the Soviet Union.

The almost farcical, yet also deeply tragic disregard of the truth (and the readership) in the Soviet media is summed up in the Russian anecdote about the two principal daily newspapers, the party's paper *Pravda*, (which means truth) and the government's paper *Izvestiya* (*The News*): '*V "Pravde" net izvestii i v "Izvestiyakh" net pravdy*' ('There's no news in the *Truth*, and no truth in *The News*').

SMEKH SKVOZ' SLYOZY – LAUGHTER THROUGH TEARS

Russians have a great sense of humour – and it's worth learning the language just to find out what everyone else is laughing about! It's often a stoical, ironic type of humour, with lots of self-parody thrown in (we think it's pretty similar to British humour – but maybe you'd disagree...).

The most well-known Russian jokes to outsiders are those of the political variety, from the Soviet era – when the bumbling antics of the puppet-like Brezhnev and other ageing leaders provided plenty of material for **anekdoty**. ('What was the main difference between Brezhnev and Chernenko?' 'Brezhnev ran off the mains supply, but Chernenko worked on batteries.')

Jokes about the system and its 'successes' were also popular, e.g. Q: 'What are the four main problems of Soviet agriculture?' A: 'Spring, Summer, Autumn, Winter.'

Other jokes are more difficult for the foreigner to get. There are loads of jokes about real and fictitious characters: for instance, the Soviet agent **Shtirlits**, from the TV serial *Seventeen Moments of Spring*, has provided the inspiration for literally thousands of puns (most of them unprintable here!). Other 'targets' include the civil war hero Chapaev and Rzhevskii, a young officer from the time of the Napoleonic wars.

Many Soviet citizens became astute at reading between the lines, at coming to their own conclusions as much on the basis of what was not reported, as on what was. (The case of the war in Afghanistan, 1979–1989, is a stark example of this – for the first few years of the campaign no mention of a war was made in the media, despite the mounting number of casualties.) In contrast to the surprisingly low level of knowledge sometimes found among the populations of long-standing democracies, where information of all kinds is freely available, many Russians are incredibly knowledgeable about a whole range of subjects – despite the limitations on access to information and on travel seen during the Soviet period. Some people also gleaned news and ideas from beyond the officially controlled realm – Western radio stations such as Radio Liberty and the BBC's Russian service beamed their programmes in Russian and English towards the Soviet Union, offering an alternative view of world events to that presented by the Communist party.

Finding a voice

In the late 1980s, Gorbachov's policy of glasnost' announced that the paranoia that the Soviet regime had felt for all those years with regard to the opinion of the people would no longer be used as a pretext for denying media freedom. Journalists quickly took advantage of these new-found freedoms. The TV news/talk show *Vzglyad* (Glance), with **Vladislav Listyev** and **Aleksandr Lyubimov**, attracted an audience of many millions, appealing especially to younger people with its blend of witty yet penetrating social commentary, lively discussions and music features. In St Petersburg, the programme 600 Seconds gave a rapid-fire review of the news in ten minutes, highlighting cases that revealed the extent of social problems in Russia, gaining fame for its controversial presenter, **Aleksandr Nevzorov**. The thirst among the population for information that became more and more abundant and open allowed popular newspapers such as *Argumenty i fakty* and *Komsomol'skaya pravda* to enjoy enormous circulation figures – both papers are listed in the *Guinness Book of Records* for their peak circulations, reached in 1990, of 33.5 million for the weekly *AiF* and almost 22 million for the daily *Komsomolka*.

The entertainment side of television and radio also improved dramatically from the glasnost' years on. Up to then, the variety of programmes available on the Soviet network had been pretty limited. Some shows did stand out for their popular appeal, including the student skit programme *KVN – Klub Vesyolykh i Nakhodchivykh* (The Club of the Happy and Resourceful, which in 2001 celebrated its 40th anniversary); certain dramatized TV serials, such as the eternally popular *Semnadtsat' mgnovenii vesny* (Seventeen Moments of Spring) from the early 1970s, about a Soviet agent's undercover work inside Hitler's Germany; and the *Vokrug smekha* comedy review.

Sport was covered extensively and there were many well-produced children's programmes. There were strict limits, however, with regard to the nature of material that could be shown – the puritanical side of the Soviet regime prevented portrayal of sex and violence from becoming too graphic or explicit. Images of the West were limited and, for the most part, shown in a negative light; in order to get a glimpse of Western pop groups, young people would stay up to record the short montage of videos that were shown in the early hours of New Year's Day. Apart from such treats, a good deal of air time was given over to programmes that depicted the achievements of the USSR in a positive light, praised its institutions (as in the programme 'I serve the Soviet Union', devoted to the armed forces), or singled out a slack factory, office or farm for criticism for failing to reach the highest standards of socialist work. The focus was on the system – not on the individual and her or his needs.

Variety – and freedom?

The increased variety and improving quality of television programmes from the late 1980s transformed the viewing habits of the population. Most people across Russia now had access to at least most of the major channels – the state-owned ORT, the independent NTV, RTR, as well as Moscow's TV6 and the Petersburg channel, and there are many regional and local stations. The tastes of the population are now catered for much more fully than before, with programmes dealing with issues of everyday life (relationships, health, education), providing light entertainment (music of all kinds, comedy shows), and increasingly daring and thought-provoking documentary programmes. Game shows are a big hit, with *Pole Chudes* (Field of Wonders, based on 'Wheel of Fortune') and the Russian version of 'Who Wants to Be a Millionaire' attracting large viewing figures, as do soap-operas, including the seemingly endless Brazilian shows that have hooked many old and young Russian fans. Advertising – almost unknown in the USSR before perestroika – is now a big business.

The transition to a situation where the state has no monopoly over the media has not always proved smooth and serious disputes have flared up at times, as the interests of media tycoons such as **Boris Berezovskii** and **Vladimir Gusinskii** have clashed with those of the government (partly explained by NTV's critical coverage of the first war in Chechnya). Concerns over media freedom are expressed and need to be taken seriously, but should also be set against the context of the enormous changes that have taken place in Russia in recent years – the country has undergone an incredible transformation and it is inevitable that this will lead to certain problems. But there is now a plurality of opinion and analysis available, from the more liberal papers such as *Nezavisimaya gazeta* and *Kommersant*, through Communist and opposition publications such as *Pravda*, to the tabloid *Moskovskii komsomolets*.

Role of the internet

The fact that Russia has a strong tradition in the field of information technology (see following section, 'Science and technology') has helped with the rapid growth of internet access and use in the country. Many newspapers and other publications are now available online, while increasing numbers of people, especially urban youth, are taking advantage of the much improved telecommunications network to surf the net and chat. This is a major factor in offsetting the problems people have traditionally had in keeping in touch with friends, family and colleagues across the huge expanse of Russia and the other successor countries of the USSR, and the internet is also an important source of information about the wider world. The skill of Russian web designers can be seen in the wide and expanding range of attractive sites springing up around the country.

Science and technology

Russian science and technology have produced some of the most stunning and important achievements in the world, leading the way in space exploration, pushing back the frontiers of our understanding of psychology, mathematics and physics. Yet there is also a legacy of the Soviet era that is all too clearly seen today, of what can happen when scientific advance is pursued at any cost. Here we look at both the highs and the lows of Russian science and assess the position that science and technology hold in Russian society.

Early achievements: science and technology before 1917

Although Russia's education system was slow to develop in comparison with those of other major European countries, it nevertheless produced a number of scientists of international renown. Here is a roll call of the most prominent of them:

A GREAT RUSSIAN SCIENTIST – IVAN PAVLOV
(1849–1936)

Pavlov's work in the field of physiology – and especially his experiments with the 'Pavlov dogs' – brought him international fame, not just among the scientific community but among the public alike. His groundbreaking research on the human brain led him to develop his 'doctrine of superior nervous activity', but it is his work on conditional reflex, in which he trained dogs to salivate in response to varied prompts, that most captured the imagination. He was the first Russian to be awarded the Nobel Prize (1904) and he was an active campaigner for peace and justice.

- **Mikhail Lomonosov** (1711–1765), the writer, and founder of Moscow University (which bears his name), was also an accomplished chemist, astronomer and geologist.
- **Nikolai Lobachevskii** (1792–1856). His work on geometry made a major contribution to mathematics and theoretical physics.
- **Dmitrii Mendeleyev** (1834–1907) established the periodic table of chemical elements in 1869.
- **Aleksandr Popov** (1859–1906) was a pioneer of the radio, which he first demonstrated in 1895.
- **Ilya Mechnikov** (1845–1916), a biologist, was an early Russian recipient of the Nobel Prize. He received the coveted award in 1908 for his work on immunity.
- **Konstantin Tsyolkovskii** (1857–1935) was a leading figure in the development of astronautics, producing theoretical work on human space travel and rocket propulsion long before others worked on these issues.

Progress in the name of Socialism

Russian ingenuity continued to make its mark after 1917. Ivan Pavlov's work in physiology (see box) is the most famous example, but other names of note are:

- **Nikolai Vavilov** (1887–1943) made a major input into our understanding of genetics and biology.
- **Aleksandr Friedman** (1888–1925) was a mathematician and cosmologist who conducted groundbreaking work on theories concerning the expansion of the universe.
- **Pyotr Kapitsa** (1894–1984) discovered superfluid helium in 1941, and received the Nobel Prize for physics in 1978.

But these achievements also need to be set in the political context of the day. After the October Revolution, achievements in science and technology had become intertwined with the image of the state and Socialism's march forward towards a 'bright future'. The scene at the end of the film version of Pasternak's *Doctor Zhivago*, where the young couple embrace against a backdrop of a mighty hydroelectric dam, sums up the image of relentless and successful progress that the Soviet government wanted to present to the outside world and its own population.

At its worst, the supremacy of ideology and the demands of the party over scientific ethics and common sense led to the abuse of science and considerable human suffering. The construction of the Belomor Canal, another of Stalin's pet projects, led to the deaths of thousands of forced labourers. The Russian countryside is strewn with the legacy of environmental abuse, most ominously that of radioactive waste from tests of weapons that went on for years with little control over the effect on the surroundings, as well as discharges from power stations and arbitrary dumping of waste. And so the list goes on. But surely the affair that symbolizes most strikingly the arrogant cynicism of the depths of Soviet science is shown by Lysenkoism.

Trofim Lysenko (1898–1976), an agronomist, won the backing of the party leadership for his claims about increasing crop production and became a dictator in the field of biology, ruining the careers of those with whom he disagreed (some of whom were to die in camps). In another field, the brilliant aircraft designer **Andrei Tupolev** (1888–1972) was arrested (on trumped-up charges) and spent six years in a special GULAG camp along with other aviation specialists – his reward for making a major contribution to his country's need to arm itself before World War II.

These events cast a shadow on the pages of Russian scientific history, but the achievements of other Russian scientists still shine out for their contribution not just to their specialist field, but also to humanity. Indeed, for many in the USSR, the world of the hard sciences and mathematics was a haven that was, on the whole, much less contaminated with ideological control than other academic areas, especially the social sciences. This is why so many dissidents, human rights activists and for that matter rock music stars have come from a background of science or mathematics.

The most famous scientist-dissident was **Andrei Sakharov** (1921–1989), a leading member of the team of Soviet scientists that discovered the theory of nuclear fusion, which opened the way to the development of the hydrogen bomb. Sakharov's conscience led him to leave the privileged, cocooned life of the scientific elite and begin a campaign to warn the world of the awesome threat of nuclear war and also to fight against the suppression of human rights. This path led to persecution and internal exile, but Sakharov lived long enough to play a high-profile role as democracy began to take root under Gorbachov's reforms.

The importance placed on science – at least for the purposes of serving the state – was reflected in the setting up of a town dedicated to science – **Akademgorodok** near Novosibirsk in Siberia. From the 1950s on this served as the home for a community of scientists, far away from Moscow. Apart from the high-profile Akademgorodok, there was also a network of 'secret' towns, known by a number attached to the name of the nearest town or city (e.g. Arzamas-16), where the most sensitive scientific work (such as that on the nuclear arms programme) was carried out. Needless to say, these towns were off limits to ordinary Russians, let alone foreigners (they did not even appear on maps).

Science in Russia today

The (non-secret) products of Soviet science and technology were proudly displayed at the famous exhibition centre in Mosow, known as *VDNKh* (*Vystavka Dostizhenii Narodnogo Khozyaistva* – Exhibition of the Achievements of the National Economy). By the end of the Soviet Union, however, the world of science, like VDNKh itself, was more than a little jaded – the sustained effort to match the USA in the arms race had proved too great a burden to bear, draining the civilian economy of resources. Russia had fallen behind as the computer age had sped technological advance on faster than ever.

In the post-Soviet era, Russian science is trying to adjust to life without the state subsidies it used to enjoy and to reorientate its resources to the civilian sector. The high quality of education in science, maths and computing is still something to be proud of, but the 1990s saw a significant brain drain, as more and more Russian specialists found that their skills were in demand abroad – and with a much more lucrative lifestyle attached (in contrast, many colleagues in Russia were finding themselves having to moonlight by taking extra jobs, such as taxi driving, as they were unable to live on their increasingly meagre salary). If concerns over the continuation of Russia's proud and long tradition of scientific excellence are to be answered, a great deal of investment will be needed to shore up the infrastructure of the system and make sure that young Russian talent is encouraged to stay in Russia to work.

Space

When **Yurii Gagarin** (1934–1968) called out *'poekhali!'* ('let's go!') and blasted off on ***Vostok-1*** ('East-1') to become the first person in space, on 12 April 1961, he flew into history and worldwide stardom. A Hero of the Soviet Union, he was feted by politicians and public alike, with streets named after him across the USSR, which was also awash with photographs and

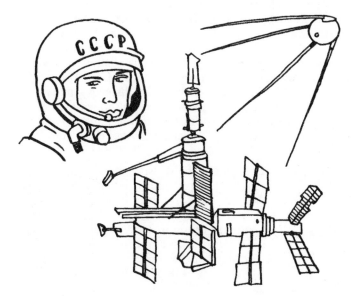

Soviet space exploration: Yurii Gagarin, Sputnik, *Mir* space station

portraits of Gagarin, as well as other souvenirs marking the event. Gagarin, who had joined the air force after spending his early years on a collective farm, was the symbol of scientific advance, of Soviet achievement – and of triumph in the race with the USA. He and the cosmonauts who followed, such as **Valentina Tereshkova** (b. 1937), the first woman in space, became household names not just in the Soviet Union but abroad as well, while such monuments as the towering Cosmos statue in Moscow served to reinforce the feeling that the USSR – and, by extension, Communism – was reaching for the stars.

Gagarin's flight had followed the launch of *Sputnik*, the first unmanned satellite in 1957 and *Sputnik 2* in 1958, carrying the dog **Laika**, events that stunned the American establishment, causing a flurry of nervous overreaction in that country to the perceived gap that had grown between the USSR and USA in the field of science. The space race continued apace during the 1960s, with more Soviet 'firsts' taking place (such as the first space walk, by cosmonaut **Aleksei Leonov** in 1965). US pride would not be restored until the Apollo mission landed on the moon in 1969.

The Soviet Union, meanwhile, continued to pump enormous material and human resources into its space programme – which continued relentlessly, despite several fatal accidents. Notwithstanding the spin-offs of the space programmes for civilian science and the high public profile of these missions, space exploration was seen by both sides first and foremost as an issue for national security, with defence requirements taking priority. This was the new front line of the Cold War, with the USSR and USA playing out their rivalry through scientific duels set in the futuristic landscape of space – although the period of détente in the early 1970s did lead to the famous rendezvous between the Soviet *Soyuz 19* and US Apollo 18 craft, which docked in July 1975.

The greatest achievement of the Russian space programme was the *Mir* space station, launched into orbit in 1986. Over the years the station was the site for a great deal of scientific work and hosted British and US astronauts at various times. (**Helen Sharman** became the first Briton in space, spending a week on *Mir* in May 1991.) Among the list of records associated with the station is that set in March 1995 by **Valerii Polyakov**, when he returned to Earth after a 438-day mission, a new space endurance record.

After the fall of the Soviet Union the financing of the space programme, which had for so long been the status symbol par excellence of the USSR, was cut dramatically, as the new Russian government diverted funds into more earthly demands. This, and the condition of the ageing station, were factors in a number of incidents seen on *Mir* in the 1990s and it was eventually decided to decommission the station. It came back to earth in February 2001 in a blaze of publicity, its final descent caught on live television. *Buran*, the Soviet equivalent of the US Space Shuttle, had managed only one unmanned test flight in space before it and its sister ships were left to become monuments to the high-flying ambitions of the Communist regime – *Buran* itself is now an attraction in Gorkii Park in Moscow.

The vast amount of expertise amassed by Soviet and Russian scientists and cosmonauts means that they will continue to play a key role in the future of space exploration (Russia is participating in the International Space Station initiative, for instance). Meanwhile, new commercial opportunities are opening up, bringing much needed funds into the Russian programmes: in April 2001 American businessman Dennis Tito became the first space tourist, aboard the Russian *TM-32 Soyuz* craft, paying $20 million for the privilege!

GLOSSARY

КИНО (n.)	*cinema*
агитпроп (m.)	*pro-Bolshevik propaganda through film, theatre or other art forms*
актёр/актриса (m./f.)	*actor/actress*
киностудия (f.)	*film studio*
мультфильм (m.)	*cartoon, animated film*
немое кино (n.)	*silent movie*
режиссёр (m.)	*director*
снимать фильм (vb.)	*to shoot a film*
сценарий (m.)	*screenplay*
ТЕАТР (m.)	*theatre*
авангард (m.)	*avant-garde*
декорации (pl.)	*scenery*
зрители (pl.)	*spectators*
постановка (f.)	*production*
сцена (f.)	*stage*

СРЕДСТВА МАССОВОЙ ИНФОРМАЦИИ (СМИ)

(pl.)	*mass media*
газета (f.)	*newspaper*
журнал (m.)	*magazine, journal*
журналист/журналистка (m./f.)	*journalist* (male/female)
заголовок (m.)	*headline*
пресса (f.)	*press*
реклама (f.)	*advertisement*
свобода слова (f.)	*freedom of speech*
телевидение (n.)	*television*

НАУКА (f.)	*science*
достижение (n.)	*achievement*
нобелевская премия (f.)	*Nobel Prize*
открытие (n.)	*discovery*
Российская Академия Наук (f.)	*Russian Academy of Sciences*
учёный (m.)	*scientist*

КОСМОС (m.)	*space*
космонавт/космонавтка (m./f.)	*cosmonaut* (male/female)
космический корабль (m.)	*space ship*

Taking it further

Books

Beumers, B. (ed.) *Russia on Reels: The Russian Idea in Post-Soviet Cinema* (London: I B Tauris & Co. Ltd, 1999).

Borovsky, Victor and Leach, Robert (eds) *A History of Russian Theatre* (Cambridge: CUP, 2000).

Hall, R. and Shayler, D., *The Rocket Men: Vostok and Voskhod, the First Soviet Manned Spaceflights* (New York: Springer Verlag, 2001).

Harvey, B., *Russia in Space: The Failed Frontier?* (New York: Springer Verlag, 2001).

Johnson, V. and Petrie, G., *The Films of Andrei Tarkovsky : A Visual Fugue* (Bloomington, IN: Indiana University Press, 1994).

Kenez, P., *Cinema and Soviet Society from the Revolution to the Death of Stalin* (London: I B Tauris & Co, 2001).

Mickiewicz, E., *Changing Channels: Television and the Struggle for Power in Russia* (Durham, NC: Duke University Press, 1999).

Rudnitskii, K. and Milne, L. (eds) *Russian and Soviet Theatre: Tradition and the Avant-Garde* (London: Thames & Hudson, 2000).

Taylor, R., Graffy, J. and Iordanova, D. (eds) *Bfi Companion to Eastern European and Russian Cinema* (London: British Film Institute, 2001).

Video

If you are very lucky – and stay up late at night – you might just see a Russian film screened on television in your own country. Otherwise, try looking for recordings of Russian films on video cassettes (many are available with subtitles).

Websites

News about the Russian film industry is given on the 'Nika' site, home of the Russian film awards:

www.kinonika.ru/

Many Russian newspapers and periodicals now have online versions and there are some internet-only publications (such as **www.gazeta.ru**). Some of these – such as Moscow News – have English editions or are part-translated into English.

The main TV channels (such as NTV) are also moving into internet broadcasting, offering both live and archive material.

For information on Russian science, see the 'Virtual Guide to the History of Russian and Soviet Science and Technology' at

http://web.mit.edu/slava/guide/

To check out the latest on the Russian space programme or to find out more about the history of Soviet space exploration, go to Space Russia:

http://users.ev1.net/~larin/space_russia/

08

politics and institutions

In this unit you will learn
- about Russia's fledgling democracy
- about Russia's political parties
- about elections and state institutions
- about the symbols of Russia

Russian political life is anything but boring – an attempted coup in 1991, tanks on the streets of Moscow again in 1993 to bombard the parliament building, corruption scandals leading up to the very highest level, fist fights in parliament, intrigues and conspiracy theories galore, a president who was famous for getting drunk… It all makes the kind of goings on in UK or US politics seem quite tame and mundane!

After the 'stagnation' of the Brezhnev era, when one-party rule seemed immovable and political opposition was suppressed, the country has come a long way – but just how secure is democracy in the New Russia? The new political system is still just that – a very recent innovation – and the process of building traditions is still in its early stages. After all, no matter how long ago the Cold War era may seem to us now, it really isn't so many years since the Hammer and Sickle were flying over the Kremlin. The following survey therefore looks back at the events of the past 20 years or so, to see just how Russia has progressed from one-party state to democracy. We also take a look at the state of the armed forces, the security services (the successors to the dreaded KGB), and policing and crime in Russia today – just how strong is the so-called *Mafiya*?

The transition: from one-party rule to fledgling democracy

The phrase *v printsipe* (in principle) is used a lot in Russia. In principle, the Soviet Union's political system ran according to democratic procedures – for example, Stalin's 1936 constitution can, if taken at face value, be considered to provide a model of democratic values and the promotion of human and civic rights. Yet…

Mikhail Gorbachov, Boris Yel'tsin, Vladimir Putin

While elections were held in the USSR, therefore, and turnout at voting tended to be an impressive 98 per cent or so of the electorate, in fact the procedure was pretty much a sham. The elections were for the soviets (councils) that existed at all levels from municipal through regional, and republican, to the Supreme Soviet of the USSR. But there was only one candidate on the ballot paper – the party's candidate, of course. And while the soviets were supposed to act as the seat of power, in fact it was the parallel set of institutions of the **Communist Party of the Soviet Union** (CPSU) that really called the shots (and who was there to argue with this, at least out in the open?) As far as turnout was concerned, it was seen as a civic duty that Soviet citizens really had to perform. Even so, by the early 1980s, disillusionment and apathy had set in so much that voters in some areas were enticed to the polling booths by having *defitsit* goods on sale (in other words, products that normally were hard to find in the shops).

And then a relatively young reformer from the southern city of Stavropol' came to break the stranglehold of the old guard and set in motion changes that would cause a revolution in political life. **Mikhail Gorbachov,** who became General Secretary of the CPSU and leader of the USSR in April 1985, saw change in the country's political structures and culture as essential if the revival in the economy that his *perestroika* programme had been introduced for was to be achieved. Alongside the slogan of *glasnost'*, or openness, *demokratizatsiya* (democratization) was also stressed as a key aim for the government and for society – although it soon became clear that what Gorbachov had in mind, at least in the beginning, was not the interpretation that others in the population had with regard to introducing change in the political sphere. Gorbachov's statements in the early perestroika period called for a return to Leninist principles, to rejuvenating the Communist party and its programme for the country. Events in the USSR, however, soon began to take a more radical course, as the momentum for independence in the 15 republics of the USSR (and in a number of smaller autonomous republics within them) grew and as various 'informal' movements in society, such as the popular fronts that sprang up in several republics, pressed for wholesale change and the introduction of pluralism and democratic elections.

Gorbachov did indeed react to the mood in the country and in 1989 the first more or less free elections since the 1920s took place in the USSR, as the Congress of People's Deputies was set up. Although new political parties had not been set up by this

RUSSIA'S LEADERS: MIKHAIL SERGEYEVICH GORBACHOV (b. 1931)

Much criticized at home towards the end of his tenure in office, abroad Gorbachov enjoyed greater popularity, with 'Gorbymania' seen in the West as a result of his radical change of direction in foreign policy. Famously described by Margaret Thatcher as a man 'we can do business with', Gorbachov and his high-profile, glamorous wife Raisa seemed to break the mould of the aloof, out-of-touch and aged Soviet leadership when he became General Secretary in 1985. But the changes that his glasnost' and perestroika policies set loose went further than he appeared to have intended and he struggled to keep abreast of the growing demands for more radical reform in the country, and in the end he was upstaged by his rival Boris Yel'tsin.

His attempts to re-enter political life in the post-Soviet era have met little success, although he has retained a prominent public role, with his Gorbachov Foundation acting as a forum for discussion of the political, economic and social changes taking place in Russia and abroad.

stage, the deputies represented a wide range of political stances, from those who wanted to push forward with perestroika, to those who wanted a return to the pre-Gorbachov situation, others who called for wide-scale democratic change and others who adopted a nationalist agenda. The congress was more than ready to direct criticism at Gorbachov and it provided a platform for Boris Yel'tsin, a former member of the Politburo, to emerge as the leading advocate of democratic reform in Russia. Yel'tsin was duly elected President of the Russian Republic in the summer of 1991 and, as we saw in Unit 1, his authority was increased by his energetic and bullish resistance to the coup attempt in August of that year. This gave Yel'tsin the momentum he needed to undermine his rival Gorbachov and bring an end to the USSR through the Belavezh agreement with the heads of Ukraine and Belarus.

Political flux – towards the White House show down

Yel'tsin was so determined to make sure that the course of change could not be reversed and to ensure that his own position was secure, that constitutional reform and fresh elections did not follow the achievement of independence.

Instead, both the parliament and the president relied on the mandate they had been given in elections held in 1991, from the population of what was then the Russian Republic of the USSR. Perhaps Yel'tsin's reluctance to introduce change in the political system at a time of such general uncertainty and flux was understandable, but difficulties began to mount, especially in the relationship between the president and the parliament. The latter came increasingly to criticize the government for the problems encountered in the shock therapy economic policies it had introduced and tried to block Yel'tsin's reform agenda. The matter was not resolved by a referendum held in April 1993, in which Yel'tsin asked for and received public endorsement of his presidency (although the support for his government's policies was less enthusiastic) and by the autumn of that year a crisis situation had been reached as executive and legislature came to loggerheads. As we saw in Unit 1, the crisis reached its peak when members of the parliament, led by the Speaker **Ruslan Khasbulatov** and Yel'tsin's former Vice-President, **Aleksandr Rutskoi,** blockaded themselves in the White House – only to be arrested and imprisoned after Yel'tsin and his Minister of Defence, **Pavel Grachov,** used tanks to bombard the building, in what was not the most convincing demonstration of the spread of democratic values.

Russian politics since 1993

With the old parliament out of the way, Yel'tsin was able to oversee the introduction of a new constitution, which the electorate was asked to approve in a referendum held on the same day as elections to the new Russian parliament, the *Gosudarstvennaya Duma* (State Duma, thus adopting the name of the pre-revolutionary parliament) were held in December 1993. How has the new Russian political system worked in practice?

The constitution

The *Konstitutsiya Rossiiskoi Federatsii* (constitution of the Russian Federation) adopted at the end of 1993 replaced the Soviet constitution that had been introduced under Brezhnev in 1977 and which had been much amended in 1990. The considerable powers it invests in the president reflects Yel'tsin's desire to have the upper hand in relations with the parliament (which the president has the right to dismiss in certain circumstances). The haste with which the constitution was drawn up inevitably meant that it contains certain loopholes and ambiguities, which the constitutional court exists to consider and pass judgement on, with relations between the federal government and the regions keeping it particularly busy.

THE RUSSIAN POLITICAL SYSTEM

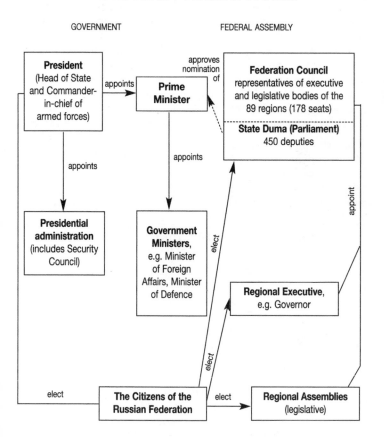

The executive branch

The president of the Russian Federation, who is also the head of state and commander-in-chief of the armed forces, is chosen through direct elections for a four-year term of office. If one of the candidates receives an absolute majority in the first round, s/he is duly elected; if not, then the two leading candidates from the first round fight it out in a second, deciding round.

According to the constitution, an incumbent president can put her/himself forward for re-election once (as in the US system), although there were rumours that Boris Yel'tsin at least toyed with the idea of breaking this rule and trying for a third term. There is no vice-president – if the president is incapacitated for some reason, the prime minister takes over as acting president until new elections are held. The president nominates a candidate to be *premyer ministr* (prime minister or head of the government), who is presented to parliament for approval. This can give parliament an opportunity to try to put a stick in the spokes of the executive's wheel, as was seen in the case of the Duma's attempts to reject Yel'tsin's proposal of the young and inexperienced **Sergei Kiriyenko** as prime minister in 1998 – only after some aggressive and stubborn manoeuvring by Yel'tsin did the Duma pass the president's choice of PM.

While there is no strict division of responsibilities, on the whole the president looks after foreign and security policy and relations with the regions, while the PM takes care of the day-to-day management of the government, and economic policy in particular. Under Yel'tsin the post of prime minister was

RUSSIA'S LEADERS: BORIS NIKOLAYEVICH YEL'TSIN
(b. 1931)

After an early career as an engineer (and as a top-class volleyball player), Yel'tsin's political career took him to the top of the party apparatus in the Sverdlovsk region, before moving to Moscow in 1985, where Gorbachov soon gave him the key post of Moscow party boss. He became a thorn in Gorbachov's side though, eventually becoming president of an independent Russia when the Soviet Union collapsed.

As leader of Russia from 1991–1999, he oversaw a troubled period of transition to democracy and market economy. He profited from the fact that he was seen by many in Russia and abroad as the only realistic candidate for the democratic cause and was prone to slip into autocratic actions at times. His health deteriorated during the latter half of the 1990s as he suffered various heart and other problems, exacerbated by his infamous drinkings bouts (on one occasion he was too 'ill' to get off his aircraft on an official visit to Ireland). Feted by many as a champion of democracy, especially during the August 1991 coup, yet also heavily criticized for his role in the Chechen crises, corruption scandals and political intrigues, Yel'tsin left a mixed legacy on quitting the Kremlin.

especially important, as a safe pair of hands was needed to compensate for the President's frequent lapses into ill-health and his tendency to rely on populist bluster rather than skilful politicking and careful management of the country. **Vladimir Putin,** who was himself Yel'tsin's last prime minister before using this as a launch pad into the Kremlin, is a more energetic figure who is more directly involved in the day-to-day affairs of the government.

Other key figures in the government are the *ministr inostrannykh del* (minister of foreign affairs), *ministr oborony* (minister of defence), *ministr vnutrennykh del* (minister of internal affairs) and the *ministr finansov* (minister of finances). The *Sovet bezopasnosti* (security council) includes the heads of the 'power ministries' (defence, foreign affairs), as well as other key players in the administration (such as the head of the FSB). The Security Council reports directly to the president and at times its influence has been substantial, acting as a decision-making body for issues beyond the already broad realm of security.

FREEDOM OF SPEECH?

There is no doubt at all that there is far greater freedom of speech in Russia now than ever existed in the USSR, although the country is still getting used to the new state of affairs. Political satire – as in the popular TV show *Kukly* (puppets), similar to the UK's *Spitting Image*, is presented openly, while campaign groups are able to put their views across in the media, in public meetings and on the internet. Meanwhile, Russia's press and TV have seen a new generation of investigative journalists, whose search for hot stories has unearthed much sensational material – and sometimes put the journalists' life in danger, as in the high-profile murder of **Dmitrii Kholodov**.

Some might say there is even too much freedom in the media, with extremist groups able to put their views forward with few restrictions imposed and pornography widely available with few safeguards about who can get access to it. These and other factors (such as political rivalry or criticism of the government) can cause the old reflexes of the state and its security apparatus to intervene in a heavy-handed fashion at times, as in the controversial law on religious faiths and the Putin government's open conflict with the media mogul **Vladimir Gusinskii**, owner of the independent NTV channel, which raised concerns about the extent of media freedom in the New Russia.

The presidential administration is another important body, that reports directly to the president and which under Yel'tsin became the centre of considerable political clout. At times Yel'tsin relied on, and gave a good deal of power to, close advisers, including his bodyguard, General **Aleksandr Korzhakov** (who later revealed his version of the goings on inside Yel'tsin's Kremlin in his memoirs).

Parliament

The bicameral *Federal'noe sobranie* (Federal assembly) comprises the *Sovet Federatsii* (Federation Council), an upper chamber whose 178 seats are made up of representatives of the executive and legislative bodies of the country's 89 regions, who meet in Moscow once a month; and the *Gosudarstvennaya Duma* (State Duma), whose 450 full-time *deputaty* (deputies) are elected by popular vote for four-year terms. Half of the seats in the Duma are elected from single-member constituencies and half by proportional representation from party lists. For its members to gain seats through the proportional representation route, a party has to pass a threshold of 5 per cent of the total vote (the experience of elections since 1993 has shown that, as a rule, only four to six parties manage to do so).

The first Duma to be elected, in December 1993, was an interim one that would serve just two years, before elections were held in 1995 for a full four-year term. Yel'tsin was no doubt pleased that this was the case, for the results of the 1993 elections shocked his government, as well as the liberal reform camp in Russia and the international community, particularly the US Clinton administration and others who had continued to back Yel'tsin as their choice for Russian leader ever since he had jumped onto that tank during the August 1991 coup. For in 1993, the ultra-nationalist (and completely misleadingly named) Liberal Democratic Party of Russia, under the flamboyant and outrageous **Vladimir Zhirinovskii**, scored a stunning success, picking up almost a quarter of the vote, with the Communist party coming second and liberal reform parties faring less well. The relative power of the president, though, meant that while he did remove some of the more reform-minded members of the government, the overall policy course was not that greatly affected by the election results. In the second Duma, elected in December 1995, the Communists came out on top, a reflection, it seemed, of the population's weariness of struggling with the economic and social problems the country was enduring. Again,

CORRUPTION

In the Soviet system officials, particularly at the higher echelons, grew accustomed to enjoying perks, such as access to better housing, special shops that stocked goods just not available outside and a range of other comforts that were kept out of the public eye as far as possible.

When he became Moscow party boss, Boris Yel'tsin made a big point of doing without such privileges, travelling by public transport and criticizing Gorbachov for the luxuries that he enjoyed. However, as the USSR broke up and control over state assets was relaxed, some made the most of this opportunity to acquire ownership of these assets for themselves, with literally billions of dollars finding their way into the pockets of officials, entrepreneurs and criminal gangs (certain members of the KGB were particularly well placed to conduct such 'operations').

Yel'tsin, for all his populist show of disgust at Gorbachov's lifestyle, succumbed as well. He and his family (in particular his daughter and image adviser Tatyana Dyachenko) were widely reported to have made huge amounts of money during his time in office, with their activities the subject of investigations by Swiss as well as Russian prosecutors. Other leading figures to have fallen foul of corruption scams include **Anatolii Chubais**, former head of the privatization policy. Of course, the taint of corruption goes hand in hand with politicians of all countries, it seems – witness recent scandals in the UK, Germany and France, for example. However, the scale of the problem in the Russian case does give cause for concern and raises questions about the consolidation of democracy in the country. It also explains the appeal to the general public of someone like Vladimir Putin, who came to office vowing to take tough and uncompromising measures to fight crime and corruption.

the parliament's ability to exert a major influence on government policy was limited, as Yel'tsin selected his ministers from the political centre ground, but a working relationship was established between president and parliament, with the latter beginning to perform its role as a debating forum for new legislation more effectively. On several occasions, however, the Duma did attempt to flex its muscles, with no-confidence votes brought against the government over its monetary policy and its handling of the first Chechen war – but the votes cast fell short of the majority needed to inflict a defeat on the government.

In the 1999 Duma elections, the Communist party again gained most votes, although it was closely followed by the *Edinstvo* (Unity) party that had been set up immediately prior to the elections, and which was linked with the then Prime Minister Vladimir Putin. This has helped Putin to enjoy a more stable relationship with the Duma than had been the case under Yel'tsin.

And who are the *deputaty*? As you might expect, the Duma is a male-dominated arena: only some 7.7 per cent of deputies in the Duma elected in 1999 were women (34 compared with 407 men), while in the Federation Council there were no women at all, and in 2001 there was just one female minister occupying a prominent post. (By contrast, the supreme soviet of the USSR had between 25–30 per cent female members – although this was a somewhat symbolic gesture to equality, as the real power then, as now, lay firmly in male hands.) The average age of the deputies of the 1999 Duma was almost 49 years old. As far as their backgrounds go, 51 came from engineering, while the second most numerous group was made up of former officers of the armed forces and security service (39). Strangely enough, the law-making chamber of the Duma only contained two lawyers... As far as the benefits of holding a seat in parliament go, the *deputaty* receive certain perks with regard to housing in Moscow and other material rewards, but they also have immunity from prosecution. This has been used by a number of politicians to steer clear of the attention of prosecutors and has also acted as a disincentive when parliament is considering options of impeaching the president or passing a vote of no-confidence in the government, as the president's response might include the dismissal of the Duma and the lifting of immunity on its deputies.

Political parties

The situation with political parties in Russia has been fluid, with large numbers of parties created (189 parties registered for the 1999 elections!), but few at all able to garner support in the country, with the result that many have disappeared, or merged with others. According to many political commentators, this situation gives cause for concern over the consolidation of democracy in Russia, for which a stable and well-functioning party system is seen as a prerequisite.

One reason for the slow development of a party system stems from the fact that both Yel'tsin (in particular) and Putin, as President, have maintained a position of independence from party politics, as have, on the whole, government ministers. Prime ministers, for example, have tended to start off without a clear party affiliation and then move towards forming a party, or bloc, only when they have been in office for some time (or already left the post). Often personalities rather than policies and principles have been the key elements in elections.

The major parties to have played a role in Russian politics to date include:

Agrarnaya Partiya Rossii Agrarian party of Russia
Represents the agricultural community.

Kommunisticheskaya Partiya Rossiiskoi Federatsii (KPRF) Communist Party of the Russian Federation
The successor party to the old CPSU, the Communists are the most well-organized party across the country and they still enjoy considerable support at the polls, especially among the older generation, who are attracted by their message of protecting social welfare, restoring Russia's status in the world, renationalization of industry. Their leader, **Gennadii Zyuganov** was runner-up in the 1996 and 2000 presidential elections.

Otechestvo–Vsya Rossiya Fatherland–All Russia
This bloc was formed by Moscow mayor **Yurii Luzhkov** and the veteran politician **Yevgenii Primakov** (the former foreign and prime minister), with the support of several major regional leaders. It occupies a position in the centre of the political landscape.

Liberal'no–Demokraticheskaya Partiya Rossii Liberal Democratic Party of Russia (Zhirinovskii Bloc)
Is Vladimir Zhirinovskii, the leader of this ultra-nationalist party that stands for anything but liberal or democratic ideas, a clown, a dangerous neofascist or a clever manipulator of public opinion? The colourful and forever controversial Zhirinovskii has provided headline writers and cartoonists with a steady supply of material since he emerged on the scene. The clip of the TV interview in which he threw the contents of his glass at liberal politician Boris Nemtsov is well known abroad, while he has also been known to engage in brawls in the Duma (again, caught on camera). He espouses a mix of populist promises (such as plentiful vodka – he has his own brand – and a husband for every woman), xenophobia and racism, and a tough anti-West, pro-Russia-as-great-power stance. His party, however, has seen its appeal wane since the early 1990s.

Nash Dom – Rossiya Our Home is Russia

Viktor Chernomyrdin, Prime Minister between 1992–1998 formed this party before the 1995 elections and it was thus seen as the party of government, but it failed to achieve great success then or subsequently.

Soyuz Pravykh Sil Union of Right Forces

A coalition of the centrist parties of the reform-minded **Sergei Kiriyenko**, **Boris Nemtsov** and **Anatolii Chubais**, and including the influential female deputy **Irina Khakamada**, this group supports the interests of business and free market reforms.

Edinstvo Unity (also known as *Medved'* – Bear)

Established on the very eve of the 1999 elections, as a Kremlin-backed attempt to draw votes away from Fatherland-All Russia and the Union of Right Forces, this 'virtual' party achieved a stunning result at the polls, coming a close second to the Communists in terms of votes cast. Linked with President Putin, its only senior politician was its leader, the popular **Sergei Shoigu** (the high-profile Minister for Emergency Situations), with the Olympic gold-medallist wrestler **Aleksandr Karelin** its number two candidate.

Dvizhenie Zhenshchin Rossii Women of Russia Movement

Under its leader **Yekaterina Lakhova** this party hit the headlines in the early to mid 1990s, with policies designed to promote not just the interests of women but also those of the family, improved social welfare and an end to the conflict in Chechnya.

Yabloko (Apple)

The title of this bloc was formed from the names of its founders – *Ya*vlinskii, *Bo*ldyrev and *Lu*kin. **Grigorii Yavlinskii** is an economist who rose to prominence in the perestroika period, devising a 500-day economic reform programme that was eventually rejected by Gorbachov. Yavlinskii and Yabloko occupy a central position in Russian politics, promoting liberal reform that incorporates adequate welfare policies.

Centre and regions

The regions

The Russian Federation contains 89 political units, which include:

Units defined by ethnicity
respublika – Republic (21)
avtonomnyi okrug – Autonomous district (10)
avtonomnaya oblast' – Autonomous oblast or region (1)

Units defined by territory
krai – (6)
oblast' – region (49)
2 federal cities (Moscow and St Petersburg), which enjoy the status of *oblast'*

The sprawling mass of the USSR, with all its linguistic, cultural and ethnic diversity, provided a huge administrative challenge for the Soviet government. Its answer was to attempt a highly centralized approach to running the country, with Moscow dictating much of the pattern of political life, from major decisions down to minute details of organization. Moscow also used its power to demand that other regions sent it the best produce of their region – hence the joke that many Russian cities have, asking 'what is long, green and smells of sausage? The train from Moscow to our city!', reflecting the regular trips that locals had to make to Moscow in order to buy the best products, including those that had been 'exported' from their own region.

RUSSIA'S LEADERS: VLADIMIR VLADIMIROVICH PUTIN (b. 1952)

Putin served as a KGB officer in East Germany, rising to the rank of colonel, before joining the staff of St Petersburg mayor Sobchak during the later stage of perestroika. He was brought to Moscow and became head of the FSB, and later Prime Minister, before being chosen as the Kremlin's preferred candidate to replace Yel'tsin as president and he duly scored a resounding victory in the 2000 elections.

His meteoric climb to the top, his past in the secret police, his youthful and athletic appearance and his tough-talking image attracted much comment at home and abroad, although in office his approach has been more cautious and conciliatory than rhetoric and reputation suggested.

The Gorbachov reforms released this grip somewhat, and by the end of his time in office there was already a momentum towards fragmentation, not just among the 15 republics that were soon to become independent states, but also within the Russian

Federation itself. This trend continued in the 1990s and the desire shown by some regions for more and more freedom from Moscow's control seemed at times to threaten the integrity of the Federation as a whole, with the conflicts in Chechnya the most striking example.

The top political position in the regions is usually the *gubernator* (governor), who is chosen by direct elections (at the start of the post-Soviet era Yel'tsin tended to appoint them himself). In Tatarstan and certain other places the top person is a *prezident*, reflecting the status of that region. In many cases during the 1990s the name on the door of the governor's office was the same as during the late Soviet period, as many former Communist party bosses managed to retain their position. Like in the old Soviet days, some governors still use their popular mandate to act as if they were in charge of their own fiefdom, wielding considerable power often in an autocratic fashion. **Yevgenii Nazdratenko**, the *gubernator* of the Primorskii Krai, the Pacific coast region in Russia's Far East, gained a notorious reputation during his time in office, before being squeezed out by Putin in 2001 after one scandal too many.

As part of its strategy of maintaining control over the regions, the Yel'tsin administration oversaw the signing of a federal treaty in 1992, which tried to establish the parameters of relations between the centre and the regions, and the 1993 constitution sought to clarify these further. In practice, though, many regions saw fit either to take advantage of loopholes in these arrangements or ignore them altogether. This was especially true of some of the richer regions, such as the huge republic of Sakha (which covers some 3 million square kilometres), which owns diamond reserves and the oil-rich republic of Tatarstan, which even produced its own constitution which its president claimed was higher in authority than the federal one! The presidential representatives that were sent to monitor events in the regions also proved less effective than Yel'tsin wished. A more useful tool for the centre was the use of economic carrots and sticks – the poorer regions depended on Moscow to bail them out with subsidies, while even the richer republics proved willing to negotiate on items such as the payment of taxes to the centre, in return for certain political concessions.

The biggest challenge to Moscow's authority, however, came from **Chechnya**. This republic has long had a troubled relationship with the centre, since it was conquered by tsarist troops in the 19th century. Many still alive today remember the deportation of the Chechen people conducted by Stalin in 1944 and there was considerable support for the declaration of independence of Chechnya made in 1990 by its leader, the former Soviet air force General **Dzhokar Dudaev**. By 1994, Chechnya's defiance of Moscow, the amount of criminal activity in the republic and Yel'tsin's personal enmity with Dudaev proved too much for the Russian leadership and a bloody war was launched, which had cost tens of thousands of lives (mostly innocent civilians) by the time a ceasefire was achieved in mid-1996. In the ensuing troubled peace of the next three years, lawlessness grew out of control in Chechnya, with kidnappings, torture and executions of Russian and Western citizens hitting the headlines, while the Russian authorities did little to try to rebuild the shattered country. Then, in the autumn of 1999, another conflict was launched by the Russian federal forces, again with much bloodshed and considerable amounts of human rights abuses seen on both sides. Although the war ended in 2003, with elections held soon after, the troubles remain unresolved. The motivation for the conflict? The Russian government points to the need to establish order on its territory and the fear that allowing one republic to secede from the Federation could lead to further attempts at secession elsewhere, with potentially violent and highly unstable consequences. Other factors that lie beneath the surface of the conflicts include claims that this is a response to a perceived (but often exaggerated) 'threat' of Islamic-based extremism, and economic imperatives – Chechnya is not too far away from the site of substantial oil fields, from which Russia, along with other countries, is vying to control the rights to transportation via pipelines to gain lucrative export income.

Fortunately, the level of conflict and tension between Moscow and other parts of the Federation has been a long, long way from the bloodbath of the situation in Chechnya. After he became President, Putin sought to rein back the regions and impose a more effective and stronger level of control from the centre, with the introduction of seven so-called federal districts, led by presidential representatives. Although some saw this as an anti-democratic move, reviving the governor-generals of the tsarist times, the early results showed that the federal districts' initiative was having a more or less positive impact.

Local politics

At the municipal level, elections are held to district and town or city councils, which have also taken to using the title *Duma* (formerly they were known as **gorodskoi sovet** – town soviet or council). The name of the head councillor has changed too, with the Western term of **mer** (mayor, pronounced 'mehr') used. The top dogs in the larger cities can be influential figures not just on a local but also national level – **Gavriil Popov** and **Anatolii Sobchak** of Moscow and Petersburg played prominent roles in the democratic movement at the very start of the post-Soviet period, while Moscow's mayor since 1992, **Yurii Luzhkov,** has proved a tenacious and outspoken character on Russia's political scene, single-mindedly overseeing Moscow's transformation as it has benefited from receiving the vast majority of foreign investment in Russia.

Elections and voters

Making an effort to win over the public has been a part of Russian politics since Gorbachov's staged walkabouts at the start of the perestroika period. In the 1990s, Russia's political parties and presidential candidates quickly acquired the art of electioneering, with sophisticated media campaigns employed (Prime Minister Chernomyrdin's team even brought the German supermodel Claudia Schiffer to Moscow in support of their cause in 1995!). Although President Yel'tsin never attempted the morning jog of US presidents, he did get up on stage at a pop concert during his presidential campaign of 1996 and stomped around – unwisely as it turned out, as the strain it put on his heart almost finished him off.

There has been a lot of analysis and speculation about just how far Russian elections can be seen to be free and fair, with many pointing to dirty tricks campaigns in which presidential candidates have been discredited, overt bias in the coverage of pro-Kremlin TV stations and a certain amount of evidence of result rigging on election day (although there were smiles on many faces in Russia after the debacle at the US presidential elections in 2000 and the revelations of shortcomings there, as the US administration and organizations had spent a lot of time teaching lessons to Russia on how to build democracy).

All of this has not done much to enthuse Russian voters. After the upsurge in political activism seen in the late 1980s and the high level of interest shown in the events in the Congress of People's Deputies, there has been a steady decline in interest in politics among the population at large, with this apathy seen most acutely among the young people, who often feel alienated from the political process. The antics of deputies in the *Duma*, the scandals, the corruption and the cynical disdain for the voters that many perceive to see among a good number of the political elite just serves to reinforce the gap that exists between the person on the street and those who are supposed to be the representatives of the people. The low regard with which politicians are held can be seen in the results of opinion polls, in which they consistently achieve only miserably low confidence ratings (although President Putin's consistent popularity proves an exception to this rule).

A MODERN MARTYR: GALINA STAROVOITOVA
(1946–1998)

Starovoitova was a tireless fighter for the democratic cause, linked with the dissident movement during the Soviet era (she even had the audacity to sue the newspaper *Pravda* for libel in 1990), she served as adviser on ethnic affairs under Yel'tsin for a time. Her outspoken manner and willingness to take on any opponent won her admirers but enemies as well. Her murder in St Petersburg in 1998 shocked the nation (the killer was never found and the motive remains unclear).

State institutions

Security organs

The question of security has always been a priority for the Russian state over the centuries, both with regard to defence against external attack (the experience of invasion and occupation has left what seems to be an indelible scar on the political mindset in Russia) and inside the country as well, where the FSB, successor to the KGB, still has a powerful presence.

The armed forces

The Soviet armed forces formed a central pillar of the USSR's claim to superpower status and both the Soviet government and the CIA (for different motives) presented them as a highly efficient and potent machine that was at least a match for the militaries of the NATO countries. It is true that the huge nuclear arsenal of the USSR in particular posed an awesome threat, but the true strength of the Soviet Red Army was by no means as great as the propaganda of both sides would have it.

In the post-Soviet era, the improvement in international relations that Gorbachov's policies kicked off in the late 1980s and which has continued (despite some notable disputes) ever since, has meant that the Russian government can afford to pay more attention to pressing economic and social issues and spend less money on the armed forces. The Russian military has duly undergone a painful and sobering process of downsizing, with numbers falling from almost 3 million personnel in 1992 to some 1.2 million by 2001, with further reductions inevitable. The lack of funds has led among other things to restrictions on training and problems in maintaining equipment (including, ominously, nuclear missiles). The prestigious and privileged position that the military once occupied has been eroded and officers and enlisted personnel have seen a dramatic drop in living conditions. These have been accompanied by a rise in crime and corruption within the organization (up to and including the sale of weapons to the highest bidder) and a breakdown in discipline, with the problem of brutality and abuse frequently found in the ranks of conscripts, as highlighted by press reports and campaign groups, notably the 'soldiers' mothers' organizations that campaign for improvements in conscript service (or its abolition). Because of exemptions granted by parliament, only some 18 per cent of young men between 18 and 27 years old now find themselves eligible for military service, which has become ever more unpopular, especially during the two conflicts that have taken place in Chechnya.

The Chechnya wars (or counter-terrorist operation as the Russian authorities like to name the second conflict) have embroiled Russian forces in the most serious conflict since the Afghanistan war (1979–1989), but Russian troops have also been involved in combat and peacekeeping missions in various countries of the Commonwealth of Independent States. The excessive use of force that has been seen at times has drawn criticism from within Russia and from the international community, although the latter has played a less than energetic role in trying to resolve the many conflicts that have flared in the region since the late 1980s.

Although some in Russia, including President Putin, have continued to talk about the need to re-establish Russia's great power status and rejuvenate its armed forces, the reality is that this would prove enormously expensive and is thus probably beyond the country's means – especially if it is to deal with the more pressing and important questions of economic recovery and the provision of reasonable living conditions for the population. For many, the tragic sinking of the nuclear-powered submarine *Kursk* in the Barents Sea in August 2000, as the result of an explosion, symbolized the state of the Russian military, although the extensive nature of the media coverage, which reflected the level of public concern for the fate of the sailors and which influenced the government's handling of the affair, also showed just how much Russia had changed.

There has been much speculation about the potential for a military coup in Russia, fuelled by the events of 1991 and 1993. However, research among military officers shows that while many might not be happy with the political situation in the country, they are opposed to military intervening in politics (and, indeed, accuse the politicians of abusing their position to use the military for political goals). Apart from anything else, there is a fear that any attempt on the military's part to play a more active political role might split the organization, which already suffers from fragmentation of identity in its dispirited officers corps. There have, though, been a number of high-profile 'military' politicians, notably the Afghanistan war hero Aleksandr Lebed', who brokered a ceasefire in Chechnya in 1996. President Putin has also tended to appoint former members of the armed forces and the security services to key political posts.

The security forces

Unfortunately, no book on Russia would be complete without mention of the work of the secret police. The atmosphere of suspicion both of outsiders and of internal dissent that has pervaded much of Russian history and which provided a platform for the activities of security forces from Ivan the Terrible's *Oprichnina* to the KGB of the Soviet era, has definitely receded greatly since the fall of the USSR, but old habits die hard. The KGB's successor in the New Russia, the *FSB* (*Federal'naya Sluzhba Bezopasnosti* – federal security service) is still a huge organization that enjoys considerable powers and which has one of its own people in the Kremlin, in the form of President Putin (a former KGB colonel). The FSB is a sprawling body whose functions mirror those of both the CIA and FBI in the USA, and its key role in combating organized crime and terrorism gives it a high public profile, but concerns are raised over the degree of its involvement in politics and business, the methods it employs and the difficulties of ensuring its accountability before the law.

The militia

The Russian police force has faced the most severe of challenges in the post-Soviet period, in trying to cope with the upsurge in criminal activities of all kinds. Police personnel are relatively poorly paid and often have to struggle with outdated and limited equipment that is no match for the more sophisticated technology and weapons used by criminal gangs. The black-uniformed OMON special police units, however, that were introduced in the late 1980s, have a tougher reputation and are better equipped.

The lack of adequate material rewards on offer for what has become an increasingly dangerous job has compounded what is an ongoing and serious problem of corruption within the police force itself (something that existed in the Soviet system). This has undermined the public's confidence in the police and must be dealt with as a matter of priority if Russia is to be able to break the grip of the criminal elements at all levels in society.

Crime and punishment

Crime wave

Whereas during the Cold War the grey suits and granite faces of ruthless KGB agents made frequent appearances on Western cinema screens, the favoured villains of Hollywood action movies nowadays include the so-called Russian *Mafiya*. The image presented in such movies and reinforced by many Western media reports on Russia, makes it sound as though it is impossible to walk along a street in Russia without being caught up by the crime epidemic. The reality is somewhat different, although there is no escaping the fact that there is a huge crime problem and the authorities are struggling to cope with it. The upsurge in crime of all kinds that accompanied the start of the post-Soviet era had stabilized by the mid-1990s and crime rates fell during the second half of the decade. However, there are still numerous contract killings that are reported in lurid detail by the media and the pressures of social problems and economic instability contribute to ongoing problems of violent crime, prostitution and theft in society at large, with young children particularly vulnerable to the lure of criminal activity, especially if there seems no other way out of a poverty trap. To reiterate, however, the situation is not as bleak as our Western media would have us believe.

The justice system and prisons

This is an area that needs radical reform in Russia, as the fundamental approaches to the application of the law of the land have undergone little change since the Soviet times, with the result that the prosecution still enjoys a great advantage in the courts, witnessed by the high level of convictions of those who undergo trial. The prison system, too, desperately needs an overhaul – there are more than one million persons in various kinds of detention centres and the justice machine simply cannot cope with the huge number of cases. Often an accused person can be held in a pre-trial unit for many months (sometimes over a year), as bail is still almost unheard of in Russia. The conditions here, and in the prisons themselves, are often terrible – there is extreme overcrowding, disease (such as tuberculosis) is rife, brutality among inmates is common. No wonder that even a short term in prison is often regarded as akin to a life sentence. Perhaps the most striking example of the problems the country faces in dealing with crime and its consequences lies in the juvenile correction centres, which have been filled to bursting in recent years by young offenders, who often drift into criminal activity out of desperation with the lack of hope provided by the conditions they and their family live in.

In light of these problems, it is no surprise that President Putin's promise to establish the 'dictatorship of law' after his election was a factor in his attraction to the Russian voters. To some Western observers this sounded like a return to the police state, but we need to put ourselves in the position of Russian citizens. It is doubtful that people living in stable democracies such as the UK or USA, where, despite obvious problems, the justice system is seen to operate fairly well and the police enjoy a good degree of respect and support from the population, would be prepared to tolerate the level of breakdown of law and order that has been seen in Russia without wanting to see order re-established.

Symbols of Russia

National anthem

At the end of 2000 the *gimn* (national anthem) of Russia changed back to the rousing melody that had been used for the USSR since 1944 and which had rung out at major sporting events around the world as Soviet athletes racked up gold medal after gold medal. This was the fourth time the anthem had been changed since 1917. The pre-revolutionary 'God Save the Tsar' had given way to the 'International' after 1917, before the 1944 theme took over (with a line dedicated to Stalin removed later), before Yel'tsin's government rejected this along with other symbols of the Soviet era, choosing instead the 'Patriotic Song' of 19th-century composer Mikhail Glinka. The trouble was that there were no words to go with the new anthem, no one could ever remember the tune and many people still preferred the sound of the old Soviet anthem. The final straw came when Russian gold medallists at the Sydney Olympics in September 2000 had to stand silently by while their anthem was played. The reintroduction of the old tune was not without controversy, despite the fact that new words were used to replace the original lines about the USSR, Communism and Lenin.

National Anthem of Russian Federation (from 2001)
Words – S. Mikhalkov

Rossiya – svyashchennaya nasha derzhava,	Russia – our sacred power,
Rossiya – lyubimaya nasha strana.	Russia – our beloved land.
Moguchaya volya, velikaya slava –	Your mighty resolve, your great glory –
Tvoyo dostoyanie na vse vremena!	Are yours for ever!
Slav'sya, Otechestvo nashe svobodnoe,	Glory to our free Fatherland,
Bratskikh narodov soyuz vekovoi,	Ancient fraternal union of our peoples,
Predkami dannaya mudrost' narodnaya!	Our national wisdom passed down by our ancestors!
Slav'sya strana, my gordimsya toboi!	Our glorious country, we take such pride in thee!

The bear, the eagle and the hammer and sickle

At home and abroad, the symbol of the bear has traditionally been used to refer to Russia – powerful, sometimes slumbering, sometimes acting quickly and aggressively, wise and a fearless defender of its territory and its offspring.

In the Soviet times the hammer and sickle were among the many symbols used to represent the Soviet state and the march towards Communism, adorning the red flag of the USSR, showing the unity of the workers and the peasants.

In the post-Soviet era the pre-revolutionary symbol of the two-headed eagle of the tsars is now used on Russian coins and various emblems of the state.

GLOSSARY

адвокат (m.)	*barrister, attorney*
вооружённые силы (ВС) (pl.)	*armed forces*
выборы (pl.)	*elections*
гласность (f.)	*glasnost – openness*
демократия (f.)	*democracy*
демократизация (f.)	*democratization*
депутат (m.)	*deputy*
избиратели (pl.)	*voters*
заключённый (m.)	*prisoner*
Коммунистическая Партия Советского Союза (КПСС) (f.)	*Communist Party of the Soviet Union*
голосовать (vb.)	*to vote*
Государственная Дума (Госдума) (f.)	*State Duma*
губернатор (m.)	*governor*
конституция Российской Федерации (f.)	*constitution of the Russian Federation*
коррупция (f.)	*corruption*
лидер (m.)	*leader*
милиция (f.)	*militia (police)*
милиционер (m.)	*police officer*
многопартийная система (f.)	*multi-party system*
партия (f.)	*party*
перестройка (f.)	*perestroika – change, restructuring*
политбюро (n.)	*Politburo*
президент (m.)	*president*
преступник (m.)	*criminal*
призыв (m.)	*draft, conscription*
призывник (m.)	*conscript*
прокурор (m.)	*counsel for prosecution*
служить в армии (vb.)	*serve in the armed forces* (lit. in the army)
Совет безопасности (m.)	*security council*
суд (m.)	*court*
судья (f.)	*judge*
тюрьма (f.)	*prison*

Taking it further

Mass media

Although the intensity of coverage of Soviet politics in the Western media seen during the perestroika period has gone, events in Russian politics still capture the headlines from time to time and stories relating to Russian current affairs appear in the Western press on a regular basis. Check out the hard copies and internet sites of the major Western newspapers and TV networks, as well as the English and Russian-language versions of their Russian counterparts, including **www.smi.ru**, **www.polit.ru** and the government backed site **www.strana.ru** (see Unit 7 for further suggestions).

Books

There are thousands of books available on Soviet and Russian politics, ranging from academic studies through political memoirs to accounts by Western and Russian journalists.

For a comprehensive selection of essays on the current state of Russian politics, see White, Stephen, Pravda, Alex and Gitelman, Zvi (eds) *Developments in Russian Politics 5* (Basingstoke: Palgrave, 2001).

Among the books on Gorbachov is *Gorbachev*, written by the man himself (New York: Columbia University Press, 2000). Boris Yel'tsin gives his account of events during his presidency in his *Midnight Diaries* (London: Weidenfeld, 2000).

Liliya Shevtsova, a leading Russian political analyst, gives a brilliant insight into the workings of the new Russian political system in *Yel'tsin's Russia* (Washington, DC: The Brookings Institution, 1998).

If you want to take a peek into the dark underworld of Russian organised crime, then try Varese, Frederico, *The Russian Mafia* (Oxford: OUP, 2001).

If you're in Russia...

You can sample the political atmosphere of the new Russia and the Soviet Union at the Museum of Russian Political History, St Petersburg: Ulitsa Kuibysheva 2/4. Metro: Gor'kovskaya. Tel. 812 233 7189.

You might also like to visit one of the many other museums dedicated to the lives of prominent Russian and Soviet politicians – a good travel guidebook will give you the details you need to find them.

09

the basics for living

In this unit you will learn
- about education in Russia
- about health and housing
- about social welfare
- about transport

Soviet era jokes

What is the definition of Socialist amnesia? It's when you're standing outside a shop with an empty bag and you can't remember whether you're just about to go into the shop or have just come out of it.

A woman is checking the delivery date for the new car she has ordered. 'On September 5th in five years' time,' replies the salesman. 'Morning or afternoon?' she enquires. 'What difference does it make?' 'Because I've got a plumber coming in the morning!'

The image of everyday life in the USSR as often presented in the West was of a bleak struggle against both an oppressive regime and economic hardship, the latter highlighted by the ever present queues found outside shops. The reality, of course, was somewhat more complex than this. Yes, political freedoms were restricted and those who stepped out of line could find themselves in considerable trouble with the authorities (although the instruments of terror seen under Stalin were largely replaced after his death by more subtle forms of control and sanction). But most people were careful not to stray outside the corridor of 'acceptable' behaviour and their daily concerns were pretty much the same as those of people anywhere – finding somewhere to live, doing well at school, choosing a career, bringing up children.

And yes, the relative shortage of consumer goods and, at times, of more basic commodities, did mean that Soviet citizens would have to spend a good deal of time standing in queues – often joining the end of one as soon as they saw it, even before they found out what was on offer. People learned to be patient, but also skilful at finding ways to bypass obstacles and take a shortcut to obtaining the things they needed and they also (as the two earlier jokes demonstrate) often had to just put on a brave face and laugh off their frustration at the problems of *defitsit* (shortage) goods – sometimes there weren't even enough telephone numbers to go around!

At the same time, the system of social welfare, education and health provision was comprehensive and ensured that people could get access to the services they needed for free, as the Soviet state attempted to put into action the Communist adage: 'From each according to his means, to each according to his needs.' This lofty goal would never be achieved in the Soviet times – but in the turmoil of the transition from USSR to democratic Russia, the social welfare safety net has proved extremely fragile, as the authorities have been unable or at times unwilling to maintain provision of sometimes even basic services for its citizens. A stark example was given in the winter of 2000–2001, when people in the Russian Far East endured incredible hardships as heating and water supplies were severely disrupted for months, while the region suffered an extremely severe winter with temperatures of –40° Celsius or worse on occasion. Having been used to relying on the state for so long, Russians are having to get used to utilizing their own resources more and more – although for some, this is proving more than an uphill struggle. Despite signs of adjustment to the new realities and some evidence of recovery in certain aspects of social welfare, this remains an area that the Russian federal and regional authorities will need to give considerable attention in the years to come, in order to restore confidence in the system among the population at large.

In this unit we trace these developments by looking at the nature of education, health, social welfare and housing in Russia, highlighting not just the evident problems, but also the considerable achievements seen in these sectors. We also take a tour of the different forms of transport used in Russia – including a trip on the fabled Trans-Siberian railway!

Education

The Soviet system

'*Uchit'sya, uchit'sya i uchit'sya!*' ('Study, study and study!') – yet another phrase uttered by the Soviet *vozhd'* (leader), Lenin, and this time one which the population responded to with vigour. In the years following the October Revolution huge efforts were made to eradicate illiteracy and produce an educated and skilled workforce that would be equipped to drag the USSR from the backward conditions found under the tsarist regime and make it a real competitor for the more advanced capitalist nations.

The Bolshevik government attempted to introduce radical change in the school system after 1917, moving away from the traditional didactic and authoritarian basis of the tsarist school, adopting instead a child-centred approach, using project work to emphasize the merging of academic and vocational work and introducing an element of democracy into the system. But these developments never caught on in the country as a whole and were turned around in the 1930s, as Stalin's drive for industrialization and bringing the population to heel was accompanied by a return to the pattern of schooling seen before 1917. This resembled the French and German models it had been based on, with an emphasis on rigorous academic training, rote learning and strict discipline, a pattern that would remain at the basis of the Soviet school until the 1980s.

One notable feature of the Soviet system was its uniformity, with a common syllabus being followed (without any deviation allowed, officially) across the country. As designed, the system was quite inflexible with regard to catering for the needs of individual pupils, with everyone expected to work at the same pace and cover the same material. Those who did not conform to the 'norm' – such as children who tried to write with their left hand – were brought either gently or firmly back into the fold (although it should be remembered that similar things happened in Britain and elsewhere in the past). While the education system may have suited the more academically inclined, therefore, it catered less well for students with particular learning difficulties. However, beneath the rigid sameness seen on the surface, many teachers did manage to adopt an approach that differentiated between the needs of their pupils – although they had to take care not to step too far beyond the bounds allowed by the education authorities.

Another aspect of the Soviet system that struck the foreign visitor was the apparent saturation of all aspects of education with the Communist ideology. From the *detskii sad* (kindergarten) to university level, young citizens were left in no doubt as to the approach to life that the Communist party deemed appropriate for them to adopt, with the message put across both subtly and explicitly. The subject of history was one of the most 'ideological,' with pupils (and teachers) expected to go along unquestioningly with the official line. But was the indoctrination effective? Perhaps during the Stalinist years there was a greater amount of acceptance and compliancy among students (at least on the surface), but by the 1980s the Communist message had lost its significance among the young, who would repeat its slogans in school, but then happily tell jokes about the party leaders in the schoolyard. The pioneers (*pionery*), a scout-like organization for young children, was ostensibly there to promote Communist values, but many children saw it just as a group where they could get together, go on camps and have fun.

EDUCATIONAL ESTABLISHMENTS IN THE RUSSIAN FEDERATION

Postgraduate education – *Aspirantura*

Studying for...

Doctorate *doktorskaya stepen'*
Candidate's degree *kandidatskaya stepen'* equivalent to PhD

Higher education *vysshee obrazovanie* Degree courses between 4–6 years, leading to the *diplom* (degree)	*universitet institut*
Secondary specialized education *srednee spetsializirovannoe obrazovanie* 15–19 years	*kolledzh tekhnikum uchilishche*
Secondary education *srednee obrazovanie* 6–17 years*	*shkola* (school) *gimnaziya* (gymnasium) *litsei* (lycée) *spetsializirovannaya shkola* (specialized school for in-depth study of languages, or maths, or sport, etc.) *vechernyaya srednyaya shkola* (evening school, 15–17 years)
Pre-school education *Doshkol'noe obrazovanie*	*yasli* (crèche) *detskii sad* (kindergarten)

*A reform is currently being introduced to move the school system from an 11-year to a 12-year model, in which students would graduate from secondary school at the age of 18.

If we leave the ideology to one side, we can perhaps also see that the Soviet system did actually provide a high level of education, particularly in the sciences and mathematics. Pre-school provision was widespread in the USSR, with the majority of children attending *yasli* (crèches) and *detskie sady* (kindergartens) between the ages of about one and six or seven. Apart from general secondary schools, there was also a network of *spetsializirovannye shkoly* (specialized schools), which gave intensive instruction in subjects such as foreign languages, maths or sport. There was a large number of vocational establishments (*uchilishcha* and *tekhnikumy*) that provided secondary specialized education in various trades, while at higher education level a range of *instituty* and *universitety* provided intensive five-year programmes leading to the *diplom o vysshem obrazovanii* (higher education degree), after which selected students could enter *aspirantura* or post-graduate study.

All change? Education in Russia today

Education was the subject of intense public debate in the late 1980s, as it became a focal point for discussion about the need for change in Soviet society. A wave of grassroots innovation that emphasized the need for students to develop as individuals capable of critical thought, rather than concentrating on memorizing large quantities of information, was taken up by reformers within the establishment. Soon after Russia became an independent state, the reformers' agenda was adopted in the 1992 Law on Education. The new policies were designed to counteract what was seen as the negative legacy of the Soviet period and aimed at the diversification of educational provision, the decentralization of the system, as well as the so-called 'humanization' of the school, to render it more democratic and child centred. The Communist ideology was also removed from the classroom – subjects such as history could now be taught and studied using a plurality of viewpoints, with students encouraged to engage with the material.

The reforms opened the way for the introduction of 'new' types of establishment, including private schools and universities and a wave of lycées (*litsei*) and gymnasia (*gimnazii*) emerged. Sometimes the change involved was merely down to a school changing the name plaque outside its front gate, but in other cases the new or renamed institution did indeed adopt an innovative approach to education – sometimes catering for elite students with a rigorous academic programme, in other cases following Montessori or Waldorf-type pedagogy and in others (such as the 'Dialogue of Cultures School', where students learn through cross-subject projects that are based on historical and contemporary cultures). Where such experiments have worked well, they have resulted in a fresh and exciting way of teaching and learning.

For the most part, however, the education received by Russian pupils continued pretty much in the same vein as it had in the Soviet system, albeit with the bust of Lenin removed. The system faced an increasingly severe funding crisis and found it ever more difficult to persuade young teachers to join the profession and experienced ones to stay, a scenario that was also experienced in the higher education sector. For a time in the 1990s, it seemed that young people in Russia had lost faith in education – or at least that which was offered at university – as enrolments dropped, with opportunities in the commercial world proving more attractive. By the late 1990s, however, numbers of students entering university were returning to previous levels, a reflection both of the changes taking place in the system to make degree programmes more suited to new demands and the realization among young people of the long-term value of education.

Health

If you happen to show any signs of being ill when among Russian friends, you are likely to meet a barrage of concerned questions and practical advice on how to get better – and perhaps even be offered a traditional herbal cure for your ailment. Russians tend to take health issues very seriously and still make good use of old-fashioned remedies.

In the USSR, healthcare was provided free of charge and most of the population had quite easy access to a good range of medical services. The first port of call would usually be the local *poliklinika*, which was often attached to (and given material support by) a factory, farm or other institution. Here you would see your general doctor (*terapevt*), who could refer you, if necessary, to a small range of specialists who were also located in the same clinic or, for more specialized care, to a larger regional clinic. Longer term care, major operations, accident and emergency treatment and maternity care were catered for in a variety of hospitals (*bol'nitsy*). There was also a network of *sanatorii*, which were often supported by trades unions, factories or other bodies. They were located in spa resorts, in the clean air of forests, or perhaps the pleasant climate of the Black Sea coast and provided treatment for various conditions.

At its best, the level of care could be excellent, although provision could vary across the country, with more remote regions less well covered. The health system did suffer from funding shortages, exacerbated in later years by the growing expense of equipment and medicine. While the medical profession was respected within society, an ordinary doctor (*vrach*) was paid only a modest salary, reflecting the fact that, as was the case with the teaching profession, the vast majority of general doctors were women.

The healthcare system in post-Soviet Russia still looks pretty much like the old system, although the difficulties associated with the transition to the market economy have added to the funding problems that already existed within the system. Hospitals and clinics have found it increasingly difficult to maintain the standards of care they would like and have taken to charging patients for aspects of service and for medicines and treatment – a fact that has hit hard those who can ill afford to pay. This comes at a time when the nation's health is deteriorating – the combined effect of worsening environmental problems, the stress endured by people as they live through Russia's economic crisis and the decline of healthcare and preventive medical provision have led to disturbing upward trends in rates of illness, with tuberculosis becoming prevalent again and experts warning of an AIDS epidemic.

Drug taking has become as prevalent among young Russians as it is in the West, with all the attendant consequences, while alcohol consumption remains at an incredibly high level.

SVYATOSLAV FYODOROV (1927–2000)

A prominent eye surgeon and, in later life, politician, Fyodorov turned to medicine after his plans to become an aviator ended when he lost a leg in a crash.

He developed the process of radial keratotomy, an innovative and extremely effective means of correcting eyesight problems. He gained international recognition and fame for his achievement, and Western patients benefited too from operations that he and his team carried out at his high-tech centre in Moscow and on a converted cruise liner. In an ironically tragic twist, he died in a helicopter accident in 2000.

Gorbachov's anti-alcohol campaign of the late 1980s, which sought to deal with Russia's age-old drink problem through the rather ill-advised approach of reducing the amount of alcohol available in the shops, led to more *samogon* (moonshine) alcohol being made, but now with its quality uncontrolled by any authorities, leaving the problem unresolved. Now a much greater variety of alcoholic drinks is available in Russia, but there is still little sign that the old habits of excessive drinking of vodka are changing.

Housing

The traditional charm of the *izba*, or village house described in Unit 6, is still present in Russia's rural areas and on the outskirts of the towns, but most people nowadays live in apartment blocks in housing complexes. Many families do own a *dacha* in the countryside, however. These are far removed from the exclusive dachas that the nomenklatura enjoyed out of sight of the general population during the Soviet times – instead, they are often little more than a wooden hut, although some are more substantial brick buildings. They are usually located within a reasonable distance of home (close enough for you to spend the weekend there before returning on Sunday evening ready for work on Monday). Many people spend much of the summer in the dacha, taking in the fresh air, and looking after their plot of land (most town-dwellers have no garden).

PROPISKA

The **propiska** is a stamp in the internal passport that all Russian adults have to carry (as a form of identity card). Without it the person cannot officially hold down a job or enjoy other benefits of being a citizen.

It has its origins in tsarist times, and was in place throughout most of the Soviet period as an effective means of controlling the movement of the population. Despite calls for it to be abolished completely, it remains part of Russian life even today.

The housing situation in the towns and cities has undergone a certain amount of change since the end of the USSR. In the Soviet period, the authorities had to engage in a massive housing programme in order to deal with the problems caused by the devastation of the civil war and, later, the Great Patriotic War, combined with the exodus of village folk to the towns. The earliest measure taken to deal with the need for housing after 1917 was the creation of 'communal' flats (the *kommunalka*), which were often made by placing several families in a house or apartment that the Soviet authorities had appropriated from its previous owners. Later, ambitious building programmes led to the appearance of the housing developments mentioned in Unit 4. While they didn't add much to the country in aesthetic terms, they did provide a cheap and effective means of getting roofs over the people's heads. Those with a job (which was everyone, in principle) could claim some kind of access to accommodation through their workplace – in this way, for instance, someone who worked in a factory would receive (after a period of waiting) an apartment for free, after which they would have to pay an extremely low level of rent and payment for gas, electricity and water. The new housing developments were designed to act as self-standing communities, with kindergartens, schools, medical centres, shops, sporting and other facilities all close at hand. One interesting feature of Soviet housing was the social mixture that could be found in most apartment blocks, with educated professionals living next door to unskilled workers, for example, a situation that is quite different from that often found in the West. Another characteristic of life in the USSR was the practice of having three generations of one family living in the same flat, with young people usually continuing to live with their parents while still in education and beyond.

BLAT – USING CONNECTIONS

As in every society, getting things done in Russia sometimes depends on whom you know. Particularly during the Soviet period, when many goods were in short supply, the use of *blat* to *dostat'* (obtain) some hard-to-get consumer goods or services was quite common (although, contrary to the image sometimes presented by certain Western observers, it is not the case that everyone in Russia was or is engaged in doing things *po blatu* (through connections)).

If a family wanted to move to a larger flat, or to a different district of the city, perhaps, they would try to arrange an exchange (*obmen kvartir*), with another family (there were often adverts to be found on bus shelters and other suitable spots on the street, giving details of the flat being offered). While most housing in the Soviet period was state owned, there was a certain amount of private house ownership (mainly in the rural areas), as well as so-called cooperative housing projects, in which a group of citizens would pool their own money to purchase an apartment block (through a loan scheme). In the post-Soviet period, the former restrictions on private ownership of property have been lifted and there has been a trend towards the privatization of formerly state-owned flats. Initially, residents were able to purchase their flat for next to no cost, although there has been talk of charging people the market price – which will be beyond the means of many ordinary citizens, as housing prices have increased dramatically. There is a considerable property market now, with a range of new housing springing up, including more exclusive apartments and individual houses for those who can afford it. There has also been a trend of 'New Russians' (*novye russkie*), the nouveaux riches, buying up communal apartments and returning them to their original status as a single house or apartment.

At the same time, there has been a disturbing rise in the number of homeless people in Russia, with the plight of children particularly emphasized (albeit sometimes exaggerated) in the media. There are an estimated 4 million homeless people (*bezdomnye*) in Russia, who have ended up in this position through a variety of causes, including migration from former Soviet republics and moving to larger cities in search of work.

Social welfare

The homelessness problem highlights the extent of the social problems facing Russia today and the degree of strain that its welfare safety nets are under. At the turn of the 21st century the estimate of the number of Russians living below the officially set poverty line stood at the ominously high level of 40 per cent (in the USA it was 12.7 per cent, in the UK 17 per cent). As we have seen, the question of guaranteeing education, healthcare and housing is proving far from an easy task. While efforts are being made to respond to this situation, for example by reforming the nature of the welfare system (*sotsial'noe obespechenie*), with the introduction of social workers (*sotsial'nye rabotniki*), for instance, many people have to rely on their own resources, developing survival strategies that they hope will see them through to more stable times.

Transport

The size and the climate of Russia can make getting around a real logistical nightmare – in the time of the autumn rains and spring thaw, the country roads can turn into an impassable quagmire, with villages located in the middle of nowhere accessible only by helicopter! The inhabitants of these areas, like those in the Australian Outback, have to rely on flying doctors in the case of a medical emergency.

Rivers

Many of Russia's larger rivers are used extensively for commercial purposes, with barges plying them during the summer months, although many rivers are frozen over during the winter. River cruises are extremely popular, with passenger ships travelling the length of the mighty Volga, for instance, while hydrofoils and other smaller craft cater for local traffic, both for pleasure purposes and as river buses.

Trains

Russia has an extensive rail network, which uses a larger gauge than that found in the rest of Europe. The huge distances between major cities means that many trains can take several days to reach their destination, so the carriages are all used for sleeping in – with a choice of either *platskartnyi vagon* (an open-plan carriage with bench seats) or a place in a *kupe* (coupé), with four or two people in an enclosed compartment. Each carriage has a *provodnik* (male) or *provodnitsa* (female) attendant, who brings round glasses of tea, while more substantial refreshments can be found in the restaurant car (although many people take their own food and drink aboard). Russian trains tend to travel quite slowly, although they do usually arrive pretty much on time, despite the lengths of the journeys. In general, getting around the USSR by train was a cheap and usually comfortable experience.

Prices have risen substantially since 1991, however, and some people find it hard to afford to buy tickets for longer journeys and thus have to curtail trips to see relatives, for example. At the same time, there have been improvements in the service provided, with an increase in the number of so-called *firmennye poezda*, which are trains that carry a name. They are used for journeys between certain cities and offer a better standard of

Along the shore of Lake Baikal on the Trans-Siberian railway

TRANS-SIBERIAN RAILWAY

The mention of this route conjures up images of a romantic and mysterious journey across the steppes of Russia. The longest train journey in the world takes seven days to cross Russia, from Moscow to Vladivostok, although you can also travel to Beijing or Ulan Bator. Highlights of the trip include the sight of Lake Baikal in Siberia.

BAM – the Baikalo-Amurskaya Magistral' – is a lesser known route that was a huge construction project in the 1970s, with thousands of volunteers joining the teams of workers to lay the line through the inhospitable terrain of Siberia, 'spurred on' by many *agitprop-*style uplifting songs!

---

accommodation (for a more expensive price). There is also good provision of local trains (***elektrichki***), which serve the suburban and semi-rural areas.

Urban public transport

Russian towns enjoy a good level of provision of public transport on the whole, which is still very cheap to use by Western standards, despite ticket prices having risen considerably since the Soviet times, when they were ridiculously cheap (a bus or metro ride then would cost just 5 kopeks – just a few pennies – no matter the distance).

Planes

Aeroflot, the Soviet airline, was the largest in the world, although most of its flights took place entirely within the Soviet Union and the Communist bloc, of course. The organization was split into many smaller companies after the collapse of the USSR and alongside the new Russian Aeroflot there are several other Russian and foreign-owned airlines operating in the country now. In the Soviet days, internal flights were very cheap, but prices have crept towards world market levels since 1991. Whereas in the old days many of the destinations on the departure board in Moscow's *Sheremetyevo-2* international airport were capitals of 'Socialist' countries, now aircraft are more likely to be heading for Turkey, Cyprus or other favourite holiday venues. Flying to Russia from abroad has become easier, with prices dropping over recent years, and routes to Russian regional airports increasingly available.

Cars

It's fair to say that Russian cars have not got the best reputation abroad – the cars of the mark known as Lada in the West were seen as outdated and slow in comparison with their foreign rivals and their exhaust emission levels led to a ban on their import by the European Union in the late 1990s. (At least Russian cars tended to be spared as a target for the worst jokes about cars from the Communist bloc, with the Czechoslovakian 'Škoda' holding this honour!) Some 20 million Lada cars have been made since 1971 at the huge factory in the town of Tolyatti, near Samara in central Russia, whose Italian sounding name comes from that of an Italian Communist party leader, testimony to the fact that the original Lada design was copied from an old Fiat, the rights of which were sold by the Italian concern to the USSR. While they may seem ungainly, they have – despite their southern European heritage – proved a match for the severe Russian winter! Other Russian makes include the ubiquitous *Volga*, used as taxis and for transporting state officials, the *GAZ* jeep, and the *Chaika* and *ZIL* limousines, used for senior politicians. In recent years, thousands of imported cars have also appeared on Russia's streets, which are now struggling to cope with an amount of traffic for which they were just not intended. There is a huge problem with pollution and traffic jams in Russia's cities, with Moscow suffocating at times from the fumes of the 2.7 million cars that sit bumper to bumper during the *chas pik* (rush hour) and beyond.

The harshness of the climate, and the sheer difficulty of maintaining roads across such a huge country, has meant that Russian roads tend to provide something of a challenge for drivers, especially in the more rural areas, with freezing winter conditions adding further problems. This calls for a certain degree of skill, which most Russian drivers indeed possess – although it may seem that they are ignoring all the rules of the road when wildly switching lanes in the towns! In the past, especially, drivers also had to be adept at looking after their car themselves, as spare parts were in short supply, although nowadays there is a good choice of commercial garages.

GLOSSARY

ОБРАЗОВАНИЕ (n.) *education*	
аспирантура (f.)	*post-graduate study*
воспитание (n.)	*upbringing*
детский сад (m.)	*kindergarten*
коммунистическая идеология (f.)	*Communist ideology*
Комсомол (m.)	*Komsomol* (Communist youth organization)
пионеры (pl.)	*Pioneers* (children's organization)
поступить в университет (vb.)	*to enter university*
сдавать/сдать экзамен (vb.)	*to take/pass an examination*
школа (f.)	*school*
университет (m.)	*university*
ученик (m.)	*pupil*
учитель (m.)	*teacher*
учиться (vb.)	*to study*
ясли (pl.)	*crèche*
ЗДОРОВЬЕ (n.) *health*	
аптека (f.)	*chemist, pharmacy*
больница (f.)	*hospital*
врач (m.)	*doctor*
заболеть (vb.)	*to fall ill*
здравоохранение (n.)	*healthcare*
лечение (n.)	*treatment*
медсестра (f.)	*nurse*
поликлиника (f.)	*polyclinic* (healthcare centre)
санаторий (m.)	*sanatorium*
специалист (m.)	*specialist (consultant) physician*
терапевт (m.)	*family doctor* (UK – general practitioner)

ЖИЛЬЁ (n.) *housing*

бездомный (m.)	*homeless person*
бомж (без определённого места жительства) (m.)	*person 'without fixed place of abode'* (colloquial expression derived from official police definition)
город (m.)	*town, city*
дача (f.)	*dacha (country cottage)*
деревня (f.)	*village*
коммунальная квартира (f.)	*communal flat*
обмен квартир (m.)	*exchange of flats/apartments*
общежитие (n.)	*hostel*
посёлок (m.)	*village*
прописка (f.)	*stamp in internal passport showing permanent address*
снимать квартиру (vb.)	*to rent a flat*
частный дом (m.)	*private house*

СОЦИАЛЬНОЕ ОБЕСПЕЧЕНИЕ (n.) *social welfare*

бюджетник (работник бюджетной сферы) (m.)	*state sector employee*
выйти на пенсию (vb.)	*to retire*
льготы (pl.)	*benefits*
малоимущие семьи (pl.)	*low-income families*
пенсионер (m.)	*pensioner*
пособие по инвалидности (n.)	*disability allowance*
прожиточный минимум (m.)	*poverty line*
социальная защита (f.)	*social welfare* (lit. protection)
социальный работник (m.)	*social worker*

ТРАНСПОРТ (m.) *transport*

автобус (m.)	*bus*
железная дорога (f.)	*railway*
движение (n.)	*traffic*
загрязнение воздуха (n.)	*air pollution*
машина (f.)	*car*
общественный транспорт (m.)	*public transport*
поезд (m.)	*train*
пробки (pl.)	*traffic jams* (lit. corks)
троллейбус (m.)	*trolleybus*
час пик (m.)	*rush hour*

Taking it further

If you really want to take things a lot further, why not go for a journey on the Trans-Siberian railway? There are many package deals available, so check the internet for the best offers. Or why not go for a relaxing cruise on the mighty Volga or another of Russia's rivers?

Books

Field, M. and Twigg, J. (eds) *Russia's Torn Safety Nets* (Basingstoke: Palgrave, 2000).

Hesli, V. and Mills, M. (eds) *Medical Issues and Health Care Reform in Russia* (New York: Edwin Mellen Press, 1999).

Ledeneva, A., *Russia's Economy of Favours* (Cambridge: Cambridge University Press, 1998).

Manning, N., Shkaratan, O. and Tikhonova, N. (eds) *Work and Welfare in the New Russia* (Aldershot: Ashgate, 2000).

Thomas, B., *Trans-Siberian Handbook* (5th ed) (London: Trailblazer Publications, 2000).

Webber, S., *School, Reform and Society in the New Russia* (Basingstoke: Palgrave, 1999).

White, Stephen, *Russia Goes Dry* (Cambridge: Cambridge University Press, 1995).

10 Russians at work and play

In this unit you will learn
- about the Russian economy
- about work and unemployment
- about sport and leisure

The economy

Russia has huge natural and human resources at its disposal – vast deposits of gas and oil, diamonds and other precious stones, timber, large expanses of arable land, as well as an educated and skilled workforce. Yet Russia has always been an underachiever in economic terms, eternally struggling to catch up with the more developed West, but finding at each step that the West was moving ahead more rapidly. If we think about Russian products that Russia is famous for outside the former Socialist bloc, the list is rather modest – apart from its raw materials, its exports include caviar, vodka, cars and other vehicles (and even they had limited appeal). And the militarized Soviet economy also managed to develop and sell a range of advanced military hardware (including the favourite weapon of freedom fighters, the Kalashnikov automatic rifle). But that's about all – not a great record for a country with such potential. Can it now, having rid itself of centralized planning and taken the leap towards the free market, turn round the legacy of the Soviet period and become the strong player it has always had the promise to be on the globalized economic stage?

The Soviet legacy

When Boris Yel'tsin's team of reformers, led by the Prime Minister and economist **Yegor Gaidar** (b. 1956), took over the Russian economy after the Soviet Union had quietly disappeared at the end of 1991, they might have been forgiven for thinking that they were about to commence an impossible task. The scale of the problems left by the Soviet legacy was almost too much to contemplate:

- The centralized economic planning system overseen by *Gosplan* (state planning committee), with its five-year plans, was too rigid and inflexible, incapable of responding to changing consumer and industrial demands.
- Too many resources were pumped into the *voenno-promyshlennyi kompleks* (*VPK*) (military–industrial complex), at the expense of the civilian sector.
- The huge factories that had been the pride of Stalin's industrialization drive had become increasingly inefficient and despite Soviet achievements in the field of science, the USSR's economy was too slow moving to keep pace with the technological advances seen in the West, especially in the application of computers in production techniques.

- Despite the enormous natural resources that the country had at its disposal, it never managed to make full use of them. In agriculture, for instance, although the USSR had the potential to supply itself with plentiful food supplies, a combination of ineffective methods of farming and poor transport and storage facilities led at times to food shortages – and on occasion the Soviet Union even had to import grain from the USA and Canada.

- The inadequacies of the official economy led to the growth of the *tenevaya ekonomika* (shadow economy), which fed off the state-run sector – but also, ironically, helped to prop it up, helping goods to change hands more quickly and effectively, albeit illegally. But this meant that the tradition of running business concerns outside of the official rules of the game were well entrenched by the time New Russia began the climb towards the free market – a situation that would hold implications for the establishment of open, fair and law-abiding business practices in the 1990s.

Shock therapy

Gorbachov's perestroika programme had attempted to save the Soviet economic system by introducing a limited amount of competition and by loosening, but not removing altogether, the state's control over the economy. The attempt had failed – too little, too late to deal with the *zastoi* (stagnation) of economic life seen in the late Soviet period, not bold enough to acknowledge and deal with the fundamental flaws inherent in the command economy. Instead, by 1991 Soviet industry and agriculture were in crisis, shortages even of basic goods were becoming chronic and there was talk of hunger in Moscow, while the USSR ran up debts as foreign credits arrived to shore up the Soviet coffers.

When it took over the reins of power in Russia, the new government under Yel'tsin and Gaidar was determined to avoid the mistakes it felt Gorbachov had made. They were committed to sweeping the decaying structures of the Soviet command economy aside and making a headlong rush towards the free market – notwithstanding the social cost that might result. One of Gaidar's first moves was to liberalize prices on 2 January 1992. Although there had been a mounting inflation problem in the last year or so of the USSR, for most of the Soviet era prices had been suppressed at an almost absurdly low level, particularly for food (consumer goods such as electrical items, cars and good-quality clothing, meanwhile, had often been very expensive when compared with the average salary). Now, all of a sudden, Russians were facing *shokovaya terapiya* (shock therapy) and hyperinflation and many found their life savings wiped out overnight. Subsequent measures included a programme of mass privatization, as the government sought to break up the unwieldy state monopoly of ownership of industry and foster competition and economic growth. Every adult received a set of vouchers that they could use to invest, but not everyone knew how to put them to good use, while the process of privatization as a whole ran into various setbacks. Some entrepreneurs were finding it easy to make a profit in the rapidly changing and confusing conditions of capitalism, while others fell by the wayside, unable to adapt to the very new demands of the nascent market economy.

1992	1993	1994	1995	1996	1997	1998	1999	2000
–14.5	–8.7	–12.5	–4.1	–3.4	0.9	–4.9	3.5	7.7

Growth rate of the Gross Domestic Product (GDP) in Russia

These radical and, for many, painful economic reforms allowed Russia to secure financial backing from the International Monetary Fund, which continued to plough billions of dollars into the Russian economy throughout the 1990s. But while there were some success stories of factories that managed to convert their production to in-demand consumer goods, in many other cases enterprises continued to struggle on much as before, often keeping afloat by not paying their workers for months on end. Although there has been a considerable amount of foreign investment in recent years, particularly in the gas and oil sectors, Russian industry continues to suffer from a shortage of funds essential for overhauling obsolescent machinery – and as every year passes Russia's companies fall more and more behind their international competitors. The country has, up to now, lacked a stable, well-established middle class that could provide the financial backing industry needs to get itself back on its feet. The banking system, too, needs to develop into a more solid foundation of economic security, although it has already made rapid progress having begun almost from scratch in 1992.

In the agricultural sector, as with industry, there has been a good deal of resistance to change – stemming from a mixture of uncertainty about what change might bring, as well as the reluctance of the bosses of the old *kolkhozy* (collective farms) to give up their positions, and the drawn-out process of resolving the complex issue of land reform. In the Soviet period, while most of the land (after the *kulak* peasants had been eliminated – see Unit 1) had belonged to the state, there was a tiny proportion of land reserved for private use – but this had been exploited so effectively that it yielded a disproportionately high amount of the foodstuffs sold at markets across the country. There was hope in the early 1990s that this could serve as a basis for the emergence of private farmers (*fermery*), free from the mass farming approach of the *kolkhoz* – but so far these hopes have not been realized to a great extent.

From the '98 crash – to recovery?

The fragility of Russia's economic position was brought home graphically in August 1998, when the economy suffered a serious crash and the rouble was devalued. This came after a period of apparent stabilization in the mid-1990s, but now the achievements of those companies that had begun to show real signs of success in the market were under threat and many businesses suffered substantial losses. The underlying causes of the crash were complex, but it reflected among other things the dilemma faced by Russia during the transition – the government was finding it more and more difficult to afford to pay for commitments such as the welfare system and was under pressure from some quarters to keep the purse strings tight, but it could not ignore completely the social consequences that pulling back further from those commitments would bring. While the economy was able to drag itself up after the '98 crash and begin to show more stable patterns of growth, this dilemma is ever present in Russia.

What of the prospects for the future? There has been much foreign investment in Russia since 1991 (although the vast majority is concentrated in the capital, Moscow), while some of Russia's domestic companies (such as the giant gas producer *Gazprom*) have also developed their financial muscle. But Russia still has to rely too heavily on its natural resources, while industry and agriculture continue to suffer from a lack of modernization. As time passes, so it will become ever more difficult to revitalize Russia's industries and make them internationally competitive.

Percentage of GDP by sector

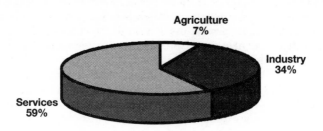

Agriculture
7%

Industry
34%

Services
59%

(Source: CIA World Factbook 2001)

Work and unemployment

In the Socialist state of the USSR it was actually illegal to be unemployed – all adults of working age who could work had to. Or at least they had to have an official place of work. What they did there, however, could vary from having to work extremely hard, perhaps even in tough conditions (as in the case of miners), to situations where a much more relaxed attitude to work could be found, with some employees able to go shopping, chat for hours or even earn money through a job on the side, all during the working day. This was the result of various factors, including the size of the bloated bureaucracy, in which a proportion of *chinovniki* (officials) found themselves twiddling their thumbs, while in the industrial and retail sectors, there was much less of a need to be truly competitive or to respond to consumer demands, than found in market economies. There were incentives of a kind – the authorities encouraged so-called *sotsialisticheskoe sorevnovanie* (Socialist competition), to see which team could harvest most wheat, for example, or assemble most engines in a given time. Usually at the end of the month, there would be a mad rush to fulfil (or over-fulfil) the quota of work – but often this would be jeopardized by supply and other problems, so the figures had to be massaged. The vast majority of people did work scrupulously and honestly, but the faults of the system were stacked against them. And symbolic rewards for the success of a *brigada* (team of workers) in a particular month did not make up for the overall lack of financial incentives, as salaries remained at low levels.

At the same time, there was not the awful threat of unemployment hanging over the head of the workforce. Instead, they could take advantage of the often extensive range of benefits that their employers offered as part of their employment 'package' – in the case of factories, this could include sport complexes, *bazy otdykha* (rest camps, often in the forest for cross-country skiing, and other pursuits) and *sanatorii*, a kindergarten equipped by the factory and a range of cultural and sporting clubs, as well as the apartments that the employer provided for its workforce. Given the value of these benefits, it is not surprising that Russians have been reluctant to give them up as the country has moved towards the free market and employers have sometimes cut back on expenditure on such matters.

Changing the work culture?

What is the difference between capitalism and communism? The former is the exploitation of man by man – the latter is just the opposite!

Although the transformation of the Russian economy is proving to be a long process, with old practices still very much in evidence in most sectors, there are growing numbers of examples of companies (some Russian owned, others with foreign management) where new approaches to doing business are found that are more akin to those found in the long-established market economies of the West. Is a change in work culture taking place, therefore? To some extent yes, it is, as employees find that they are expected to put in long hours as they work towards ensuring profitability for their company (although Russia has, fortunately, yet to fall victim to the kind of exploitation of its professionals through encouraging the kind of workaholism seen in the UK and USA). The rise of small business helps in this, as employees can engage more closely with an organization, something that was much harder to do with the faceless monolith of Soviet state enterprises. In the service sector and in shops, a new, customer-is-always-right approach is beginning to emerge with a smile, in stark contrast to the dismissive and often downright offensive attitudes shown by staff towards customers during the Soviet era.

The age-old habits of the bureaucrats, however, are taking longer to change. Meanwhile, the number of people who do second or even third jobs to supplement their inadequate official salary has risen. State employees such as doctors and teachers can often be found working overtime, then going off to do another part-time job, perhaps completely unrelated to their professional skills. Meanwhile, there is a considerable amount of underemployment with, for instance, workers still officially employed in factories, but receiving little or no salary as the company is bankrupt.

Unemployment – a new disease

The problems of Russian industry in the 1990s, with the dramatic slump in GDP, the layoffs of workers resulting from privatization and the overwhelming difficulties involved in trying to rescue factories from inactivity, made it seem for a time that Russia was bound to suffer unprecedented levels of unemployment, with predictions that this would lead to mass poverty and a social explosion. Yet the official unemployment level peaked at around 12.5 per cent in 1999, and since then has declined to as little as 1.4 per cent by 2001– although this can be explained as much by the effects of Russia's worsening demographic situation as by any upturn in economic fortunes. Government ministers now state that Russia won't have any unemployment to mention very soon – and there might not be enough people even to fill vacancies.

Those who are unemployed are supposed to register with the authorities at the *birzha truda* (employment exchange). Here they will receive a certain level of financial and other benefits (*posobie po bezrabotitse*), and will be offered a selection of jobs that, in principle, match their qualifications. If the person declines too many of these offers, they will lose a proportion of their benefit entitlement.

Sport and leisure

Competitive sport

Today's Russian sportspeople can proudly look back on the long and distinguished heritage of success and achievement of their predecessors. World records galore, Olympic and world championship gold medals by the ton, the list of legendary sporting names goes on and on. Of course, sport was another arena for both sides in the Cold War to flex their muscles and aim for domination, and the Soviet state pumped considerable resources into its sporting infrastructure to ensure that its sportsmen and women had the best possible chance of winning.

The use of sport for political purposes reached its height during the boycott of the 1980 Moscow Olympics by the USA and some other countries, as a protest over the invasion of Afghanistan by Soviet forces. Revenge was taken by the USSR and the Eastern bloc (apart from Romania) when they did not turn up to compete at the 1984 games in Los Angeles.

But this should not detract from the incredible exploits of the individuals and the teams, who over the years helped to show the world a human face from beyond the Iron Curtain. Russian gymnasts such as **Lyudmila Turishcheva**, **Yelena Mukhina**, **Natalya Shaposhnikova**, as well as the brilliant Belarussian **Ol'ga Korbut**, charmed audiences with their breathtaking and graceful skills, as they gained success after success on the international stage. In the ice-skating arenas, the names of **Irina Rodnina**, **Yekaterina Gordeyeva**, **Sergei Grin'kov**, **Oksana Grishuk** and **Yevgenii Platov** are among the many legendary figure skaters to have come from the Russian school to conquer the world over the years. The ice was also the battlefield for memorable East–West clashes between the Red Machine, the Soviet Union's formidable ice hockey team, and its rivals from the USA.

Tennis superstar Anna Kurnikova

The extensive training facilities and programmes that the Soviet Union provided for its top athletes (including a network of sports secondary schools attended by gifted children) have continued to bear fruit in the post-Soviet era, as Russian sportspeople are still very much present on the top step of winners' rostra. Among them are the incredible **Aleksandr ('Alex') Popov,** who successfully defended his 50m and 100m freestyle titles at the 1996 Olympic Games, and the charismatic gymnast **Aleksei Nemov**.

And nowadays Russian sports stars are able to enjoy the lucrative benefits their talents attract, unlike the situation in the old days. Then, although top sportspeople did have certain substantial benefits – not least the opportunity to travel to international destinations in order to compete – opportunities to profit from their sport in financial terms were limited by the Soviet state. Even those who did earn prize money in international competitions (such as tennis players) had to hand their winnings to the Soviet authorities. Now they are free to keep their prize money, sign contracts as highly paid players and enjoy lucrative sponsorship deals. In 2001, the ice hockey star **Sergei Fyodorov** of the Detroit Red Wings NHL team was said to be the third highest paid sportsperson in the world, while the 20-year-old pin-up idol and tennis player **Anna Kurnikova** was raking in millions of dollars for advertising a range of products.

Recreational sport

SHAKHMATY – CHESS

Stroll through a Russian park, even in the middle of winter and you'll probably come across a game of chess going on – a sign of the popularity of this sport in Russia. Chess came to Russia in 820 AD, before it caught on in Western Europe and the intellectual fascination of the game has remained ever since, with Russia producing many of the world's greatest chess champions, including **Viktor Korchnoi**, **Anatolii Karpov** and **Gari Kasparov**. During the Cold War, the game even got mixed up in the East–West rivalry, as seen in the controversial matches between American Bobby Fischer and the Soviet champion Boris Spasskii.

Many Russians are avid sports fanatics, both as spectators and as participants. The major football and ice hockey teams (such as Moscow Spartak) enjoy solid support from their *bolel'shchiki* (fans), for example, while many thousands of Russians take advantage of the country's sports facilities and its natural assets to engage in a range of pursuits, from cross-country and downhill skiing, to handball, ice speedway on motorbikes, gymnastics, climbing, parachuting and so on. The harsh climate can produce hardy souls – there are those who will go out jogging in shorts and T-shirt at –20° Celsius and then there are the famous **morzhi** (walruses), people who like to go swimming in the middle of winter by cutting a hole in the ice on a river – and plunging in! There is often a **klub morzhei** (walrus club) in a town and those who take part maintain that the chilly shock of their winter dips is good for their health... Rather them than us!

Physical education is also an important aspect of the school and, until recently, higher education curricula, with students required to get through sporting tests (such as a 20 kilometre cross-country skiing course) within a certain norm in order to gain a suitable pass grade. This was all right for those who were fit, but for students who for one reason or another struggled to meet the norm, **fizkul'tura** could prove an uncomfortable experience.

Dosug – day-to-day leisure

Like people everywhere, Russians pursue a whole range of hobbies – taking dance or music classes, restoring old cars, amateur archaeology, taking part in clubs and societies. In the Soviet period, these would be located in buildings lent by the local factory or town authorities. For children, a lot of activities were organized in the **Dvortsy pionerov** (pioneer palaces) or **Dvortsy kul'tury** (palaces of culture), which also catered for adults and which were found in most towns. As we saw in Unit 9, in the summer many children would head off to summer camp. State subsidies of leisure facilities have diminished in the free market conditions of post-Soviet Russia and factories often struggle to maintain sports halls and other venues to the same standard as was previously the case. The token fees that used to be charged in the past have increased substantially – but many people still continue to make good use of the facilities on offer.

Russians love to use any excuse to get out into the countryside (**poekhat' na zelyonuyu**) for a **piknik** or **shashlyki** (kebabs), or to gather mushrooms (**sobirat' griby**) – a hobby that for some people is something of an obsession, with the real connoisseurs taking pride in their intimate knowledge of the many delicious varieties of mushroom to be found in the forests.

As for night life, this has changed a lot in recent years, at least in the larger cities. There were numerous bars and discos to be found in the Soviet times, but they could be quite basic, even unappealing, while the sound and light equipment available to DJs was often not of great quality. Now, more and more nightclubs are springing up, with all the trappings of the scene found in Western cities, while new bars have also appeared (the memory of the anti-alcohol campaign that Gorbachov's administration attempted, when formerly pleasant bars were suddenly able only to sell ice cream 'cocktails' and soft drinks, has long disappeared). The cinema, too, remains popular, although inexpensive video hire has lured some away from the *kinoteatry*.

Eating out is also now a very different proposition from what it used to be. In the old days, if someone told you that your home-cooked food tasted like restaurant food, this could be a great insult! Some of the restaurants that were open to the general public (as opposed to those where the *nomenklatura* dined) could be dismal places – menus that listed meals you couldn't order, poorly prepared food, little ambience to speak of. And that was if you got in the place – sometimes hungry Russians could tear their hair out arguing with a doorman who was telling them that the restaurant was full, when there were plenty of places (or there might even be a sign on the front door saying 'closed for lunch'!!). Things have definitely changed and taken a turn for the better in this respect, as larger cities especially now have a wide spectrum of restaurants, cafes, diners, take-away and delivery restaurants, covering everything from traditional Russian, through Georgian, Chinese and Indian food to fast-food joints. (McDonald's now has dozens of restaurants across Russia, while the home-grown *Russkoe bistro* chain serves up *kvas*, *pirozhki* and other Russian favourites in a fast-food format.) Going out to eat can prove pricey, however, and regular trips to restaurants are still something that is beyond the means of many Russians.

Entertaining at home is still preferred by a lot of people, therefore – and if you are lucky enough to be invited to someone's flat, you'll be sure to taste the warm hospitality that Russians are renowned for. Friends will call in to see one another frequently, often unexpected, and will be given endless cups of tea, perhaps with cakes, or beer or vodka, with some bread, perhaps some fish or sausage.

Vacations

The traditional holiday destinations (*kurorty*) for Russians during the Soviet period were, of course, mostly found in the USSR, although some were able to travel further afield to other countries in the Socialist bloc (such as Bulgaria). The top spots for getting away from it all within Russia were found in **Sochi** and the surrounding Black Sea coastline, a beautiful area that is blessed with a Mediterranean-type climate; the mountain air of such places as the town of **Mineral'nye Vody;** or somewhere in the mountains or forest areas of the country. Other destinations in the USSR as a whole included the Crimea, the coastline of the Baltic States, or perhaps the exotic cities of the Central Asian republics.

Many people would try to book a stay in a *sanatorii* or a *Dom otdykha* (resort hotel), most of which belonged to *profsoyuzy* (trade unions). The union would distribute *putyovki* (a 'route' ticket, the equivalent of a package deal), which was set at an affordable price, or sometimes even for free, and for which you applied in January each year at your workplace, with those with medical conditions given priority. Otherwise, rail and air travel was inexpensive and families were able to visit relatives no matter how far away they lived.

In the free market conditions of the New Russia, vacation habits have changed somewhat. Internal travel is more expensive now and quite a number of people find it difficult to afford to travel as often as they used to. The cost of taking a vacation on Russia's Black Sea coast has also risen quite sharply, although it is always possible to find a room to rent from a family, rather than stay at a hotel or *sanatorii*. Surprisingly, it is often cheaper nowadays for Russians to go abroad on vacation – for example to Turkey or the Greek islands. And even holidays in destinations further afield are becoming more affordable.

Meanwhile, the tourist industry within Russia has seen an upsurge in foreign visitors, but it remains an underdeveloped sector. In the future Russia could well begin to make use of the fabulous cultural heritage found in its cities and its beautiful and varied countryside, to attract greater numbers of tourists from around the world.

GLOSSARY

ЭКОНОМИКА (f.)	*economy*
военно-промышленный комплекс (m.)	*military-industrial complex*
командная экономика (f.)	*command economy*
предприниматель (m.)	*entrepreneur*
приватизация (f.)	*privatization*
пятилетка (f.)	*five-year plan*

рыночная экономика (f.)	*market economy*
фондовая биржа (f.)	*stock exchange*
РАБОТА И БЕЗРАБОТИЦА (f.)	*work and unemployment*
биржа труда (f.)	*employment exchange office*
зарплата (заработная плата) (f.)	*salary*
подать заявление на должность (vb.)	*to apply for a job*
пособие по безработице (n.)	*unemployment benefits*
профессия (f.)	*profession*
профсоюз (m.)	*trade union*
специальность (f.)	*specialization* (e.g. enginer, accountant)
устроиться на работу (vb.)	*to get a job*
СПОРТ (m.)	*sport*
болельщики (pl.)	*fans, supporters*
команда (f.)	*team*
лыжный спорт (m.)	*skiing*
тренер (m.)	*coach (trainer)*
фигурное катание (n.)	*figure skating*
шахматы (pl.)	*chess*
ДОСУГ И ТУРИЗМ (m.)	*leisure and tourism*
Дворец культуры (m.)	*palace of culture*
каникулы (pl.)	*vacation* (for students)
курорт (m.)	*resort*
отпуск (m.)	*vacation/leave* (for those in employment)
путёвка (f.)	*holiday package*
турагентство (n.)	*travel agency*

Taking it further

Books

There are numerous books out there on Russia's economic transformation. Try the following selection:

Clarke, S., *New Forms of Employment and Household Survival Strategies in Russia* (Coventry: Centre for Comparative Labour Studies, 1999).

Granville, B. and Oppenheimer, P. (eds) *Russia's Post-Communist Economy* (Oxford: Oxford University Press, 2001).

Gustafson, T., *Capitalism Russian-style* (Cambridge: Cambridge University Press, 1999).

Silverman, B. and Yanowitch, M., *New Rich, New Poor, New Russia* (Armonk, NY: M.E. Sharpe, 1997).

Websites

For information on the achievements of Russia's sports stars (as well as facts and gossip on their personal lives!), the internet is the best place to look. Try out the following sites – but there are many, many more…

For a tribute to the Red Machine, the USSR's ice hockey team,

http://soviet.virtualave.net/

is worth a visit. The official site of hockey star Sergei Fyodorov is found at

www.sergeifedorov.com/

and if it's Anna Kurnikova you're after

www.kournikova.com/

is the official site – though there are hundreds of other sites dedicated to her, by fans attracted by her tennis playing skills or for other reasons.

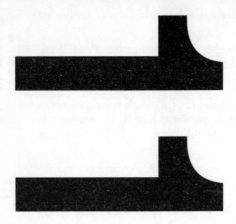

the people

In this unit you will learn
- about Russians and their stereotypes
- about family, gender and sexuality
- about religion in Russia
- how Russians are faring in the new era

Who are the Russians?

The Russian character

Who are the 'Russians'? What are they like? The sad fact is that during Russia's long isolation from the outside world it was extremely difficult for outsiders to get to know either the culture of the country or its people. Even for those Westerners who spent prolonged periods of time working and living in Russia, establishing friendships with Russians could be a tricky affair, given the suspicion that this aroused among the authorities and the risk that this entailed for the Russian person concerned. Fortunately, the pointless paranoia and mistrust of foreigners has, if not completely disappeared, then reduced to an unprecedented low level and its legacy of ignorance and misunderstanding gradually swept away as more and more Russians have come into contact with people from outside. This has definitely helped to debunk some of the myths and extreme stereotypes – contrary to the image presented in Cold War spy movies, they are not cold, steely-eyed, ruthless, unsmiling automata. But there are certain traits that we can say are typically Russian.

For one thing, it is not inaccurate to say that Russians do not seem to smile that much – at least in public. This comes at least in part from the peculiar pressures of life in the USSR. People everywhere tend to have a public and a private persona, but this divide was perhaps especially marked in Russia where, as we have seen, you had to be cautious with regard to what you said or did in public during the Soviet times. Russians tended to be more than a little wary of revealing too much to new acquaintances, until they got to know them better, a characteristic that is still present today. But then, once a friendship is forged, it tends to be a strong one: *Druzya poznayutsya v bede* (a friend in need...). Russians can rely on their friends to help them out in all matters and no one turns friends away, no matter what time of day or night they turn up or what state they're in!

What else can we say about Russians? They like to be sincere and are often forthcoming both in their helpfulness and their criticism – Russians won't take offence at what might seem to a foreigner to be a pretty blunt statement or rebuke. They are also quick to intervene in the affairs of others when they think it is necessary – again, something that the more reserved British, for instance, might find intrusive. But it often comes from the heart, a spontaneous gesture of proffering help or advice. Steve (co-author of this book) recalls his first trip to Russia, to the then Leningrad, in an extremely cold winter. He was wandering aimlessly around, no doubt inadequately dressed – when two young students came up to him and started rubbing his nose with their gloves. Not, as it turned out, some sort of greeting ritual, but a concerned attempt to prevent the hapless foreigner from getting a frost-bitten *nos*!

Russians tend to be generous to the point of carefree abandon – *poslednyuyu rubashku otdast* (they will give up their last shirt). They will not hesitate to provide their guests with a seemingly endless flow of food and drink – using any excuse to start a celebration.

As anyone who has arranged meetings with Russians will have found out, they don't take punctuality as seriously as people from Anglo-Saxon countries – *tochnost'-vezhlivost' korolei* (punctuality is the virtue of royalty – i.e. ordinary folk can take it easy!). They can also, as Bismarck once noted, take some time to be roused – but then spring into action with a vengeance: *Russkie dolgo zapryagayut, da bystro pogonyayut* (Russians take a long time to saddle up, but ride quickly).

Not surprisingly, given the trials that Russia's tortured history has made its peoples undergo, they also have a reputation for extreme resilience, combined with a readiness to adapt stoically to new challenges and display enormous resourcefulness. This is also reflected in the fatalistic attitude that Russians often hold, referring frequently to *sud'ba* (fate) and patiently shrugging their shoulders as they endure yet another setback or delay.

Yet despite all the things that fate has thrown at them, Russians have never lost their sense of fun and humour, their ability to forget it all and enjoy life. Underneath the apparent pessimism and resignation in the face of everyday problems, there is an eternal optimism that has carried Russians across the centuries.

Russkaya dusha – the Russian soul

The characteristics just listed are all said to form part of the mysterious Russian soul, that has proved such an enduring source of fascination for foreigners and which many Russians themselves like to think of as a unique trait that marks Russia out as a special culture. Of the many Russian writers who have tried to capture the essence of the Russian soul, none comes closer than Fyodor Dostoyevskii, particularly in his novels

Crime and Punishment (*Prestuplenie i nakazanie*) and *Brothers Karamazov* (*Bratya Karamazovy*). But a Russian will often tell a foreigner that it's impossible for an outsider truly to understand the depths of the Russian soul. It is indeed a complex and logic-defying spiritual world, in which suffering and retribution intermingle with a yearning for an unattainable idyll. There can also be an expression of belief in Russia's special place in the world, her messianic destiny to provide a moral lead to others. As Russian society has been turned upside down by the changes of recent years, so many people have clung to the notion of the special nature of the Russian soul to provide a means of maintaining their spiritual integrity and their sense of identity.

Collectivism and individualism

As we saw in Unit 9, one of the fundamental precepts of Soviet Communism was the promotion of a collectivist spirit, in which members of a community were expected to pool their resources for the benefit of all. But this drew on deep-rooted Russian peasant traditions, in which the *mir* (a multi-faceted word that here refers to community, but which also means 'world' and 'peace') played a key part in the lives of Russians up to and for some time after the October Revolution. As the saying went, impoverished Russians would *po miru poidyot* (go around the *mir*), as they would be sure that *dobrye lyudi pomogut* (good people would help) in their time of need.

This traditional collectivist attitude continued well into the Soviet period and can still be seen today, although its influence has gradually diminished, as a result of the harsh realities of Soviet life and now the rampant free-for-all of the post-Soviet free market. Beneath a veneer of residual collectivism (which can still be quite powerful on occasion), Russian society has seen an increasing amount of 'atomization', in which the people see to their own individual needs first and foremost: *sam o sebe ne pozabotishsya, nikto o tebe ne pozabotitsya* (if you don't look after yourself, no one will look after you).

A multiethnic society

At this point we'd better clarify just who the 'Russians' are. The Russian Federation is actually made up of an amazingly rich and diverse tapestry of cultures and peoples. While Russians make up the majority of the population of the Federation (81.5 per cent), there are in fact more than 60 different ethnic groups in the country, including Slavic nationalities (Ukrainians 3 per cent and Belarussians 0.8 per cent, as well as many non-Slavic groups, such as Tatars (3.8 per cent), the Chuvash (1.2 per cent), Moldovans, Bashkirs, Komi, Germans, Chechens, Karelians, Jews, Udmurty and so on. And you can add to this list the nationalities and ethnic groups found in the former Soviet republics, which for so long were part of the same country and whose populations intermingled, gave and borrowed from one another. The extent of these influences on Russian culture is clearly visible in its food, drink, literature and culture and the attitudes to life itself among Russian people. The position of Russia, straggling as it does both Europe and Asia, has had enormous significance on the makeup of its population.

The result of the contact between the majority Russian group and the many other groups found in Russia means that it's actually quite difficult, if not impossible, to say that anyone is really an 'ethnic' Russian. If we take the case of Tatyana (co-author of this book), she has Belarussian, Polish, Bashkir and Greek ancestors – quite a mix, but one that is not at all uncommon for 'Russians', many of whom can point to an even more elaborate and exotic heritage. In the case of the smaller ethnic groups, there has been a general tendency over the decades and centuries for assimilation into the dominant Russian culture, both willingly and through a policy of enforced Russianization that reached its peak with the drastic measures of Stalin, with ethnic cultures and languages suffering repression for periods under Soviet rule. In recent years there has been something of a revival of cultural traditions, with the federal government itself supporting the teaching of ethnic languages (there are over 100 languages spoken in Russia, with the number of speakers of some measured only in the hundreds). The results of these attempts at cultural restoration have been mixed, due to lack of resources in some cases, perhaps a lack of interest among the young for whom Russian (or even Western) culture is more attractive and a problem of forgotten skills, lost during the years of neglect. But despite such problems, if you travel the length and breadth of Russia today you will still see plenty of evidence of the fascinating heritage of the many peoples of this huge country.

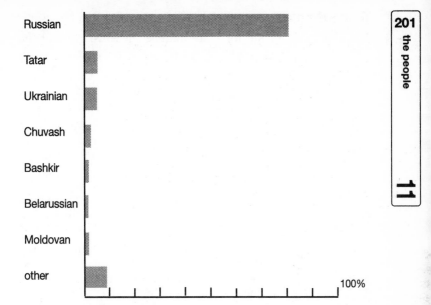

Ethnic composition of the Russian population

Racism

One of the slogans of the Soviet Union was that of *druzhba narodov*, the friendship of nations, exemplified in the USSR's ethnic composition. But slogans were never strong enough to affect attitudes across the board and there is, as is the case just about everywhere in the world, a certain amount of racism, chauvinism and xenophobia present in Russia. In recent years, the troubles in the northern Caucasus region have led to a backlash among the general Russian population, with *litsa kavkazskoi natsional'nosti* (people of Caucasian origin) often targeted as scapegoats, blamed for organized crime and the problems in Chechnya and beyond. Western visitors are also often shocked by the readiness of even liberal, educated friends in Russia to make crude racist comments about blacks, Jews and other minorities – a sign indeed of a degree of intolerance towards others, that is seen at its ugliest in the presence of ultra-nationalist sentiment and neofascist groups. But it is not possible to say that such problems are more widespread or such attitudes more ingrained than in Western Europe or North America, where overt racism is much less common now, but implicit discrimination still very much in evidence.

Towards a demographic catastrophe?

The conditions of life for many families in Russia during the Soviet period – living in what was often cramped housing, with limited financial and material resources and with increasing cases of divorce and single-parent homes – led to a shift away from the larger families with several children that had been the norm in the countryside towards a situation where it was more and more common just to have one child. There were attempts by the authorities to encourage parents to have more children, with the title of *mat' geroinya* (mother hero) and a range of benefits. If a family had three children, they might be able to bypass certain queues for goods, while a *mnogodetnaya semya* (family with many children), with five or more offspring, would qualify for more substantial 'rewards', including a medal and perhaps even a small minibus!

But while it was still common for families in the Central Asian republics to have four or five children or more, it proved impossible to persuade urban dwelling couples in Russia to have more children – having just one was simply easier to manage.

In the uncertainty and instability of the post-Soviet period, however, even the rate of one child per couple has dropped, as people have put off the idea of having children out of anxiety about the future in general and worries in particular about not being able to provide for a child. Those expectant mums who do turn up in once busy maternity wards find themselves surrounded by eager staff, pleased to have someone to look after for once!

This drop in the number of births has come at the same time as the death rate has gone up – in almost one-third of Russia's regions some two to three times more deaths are recorded than births. Life expectancy has fallen sharply for men in particular, now standing at the frighteningly low figure of 58 years, the result of an increase in heart and lung disease, alcohol abuse, traffic accidents, murders and suicide. (The figure for women is a more reasonable 72 years.) Ominously, there are noticeable upward trends in the number of chronic illnesses suffered even by the youngest babies.

All of this means that a real demographic catastrophe seems to be looming for Russia. Already the Russian population is shrinking at an alarming rate – forecasts predict that by 2016 the number of people in the country will have dropped by more than 10 million from the total of 146 million in 2001. To reverse this slide will take an enormous effort from the Russian government, in order to improve the health conditions of the nation and reinstall the confidence in the future that people need to have in order to want to raise a family. This makes gloomy reading, of course, and for many in Russia this human cost of the years of transition is something that it is difficult even to bear thinking about. We can only hope that things improve in the years ahead.

Family, gender and sexuality

Semeinaya zhizn' – family life

The traditionally close-knit extended family structure that existed in rural Russia before the October Revolution was gradually, and at times violently, broken up by the various upheavals that took place in Soviet society. From the ravages of the civil war (where brothers could end up fighting on opposing, Red and White, sides), to the exile endured by many during Stalin's terror, the devastation of the Great Patriotic War, and the practice (continued right to the end of Soviet times) of *raspredelenie*, or 'distributing' newly qualified specialists to far-flung corners of the USSR, many people found that they were separated from their relations. In addition, there was the exodus from the rural to urban areas, which also saw the younger members of a family in particular heading off to the towns, leaving their roots and their parents behind. The end result was that many families found that their relatives were scattered across the huge expanse of the Soviet Union, thus limiting both the amount of contact between family members and the support that they could offer each other.

The onus, then, was on the nuclear family – although it remains common that grandparents will continue to play a major part in the lives of their children way beyond marriage, often living in the same apartment with them and their grandchildren. It is taken for granted in such cases that the *babushka* (grandmother) will 'sit' with the children while they are young, releasing the mother to hold down a full-time job. But the presence of three, or sometimes even four generations in one small apartment can have its strains of course. On the humorous side, this is noted by the plethora of mother-in-law jokes that Russians can roll off:

A mother arrives at her daughter's apartment having made a long and arduous journey from the other side of the country. She rings the doorbell, the son-in-law opens the door, and his jaw drops. The mother-in-law sees that he is not too happy to see her, and reassures him: 'Don't worry, I won't stay long.' 'But won't you even have a cup of tea before you leave?', he asks slyly!

On the more poignant side, though, it is reflected in the level of domestic conflict seen in Russian families, a factor in the high divorce rate. The lack of private space for the individual also causes problems as children grow into young adults and start to date – finding time to be alone can prove difficult. Traditionally Russian parents have tended to be quite protective of their offspring and the fact that young people tend, out of necessity, to have to continue to live at home often until well into their twenties, can add to the frustration of the young at their apparent lack of independence. This is undergoing some change nowadays, as growing numbers of young people are taking advantage of opportunities to leave home earlier and as cohabitation becomes more common (although many parents, even those who are themselves still relatively young, find this notion hard to accept).

Gender balance?

The position of women in Russian society has always been ambivalent, as the following lines written by the 19th-century poet **Nikolai Nekrasov** show. On the one hand, a Russian woman's natural spirit means that she will *Konya na skaku ostanovit, v goryashchuyu izbu voidyot...* (Stop a horse in full flight, or enter a burning house). And on the other, Nekrasov lamented that *Dolyushka russkaya, dolyushka zhenskaya, vryad li trudnee syskat'* (You could not find anything harder than the lot of a Russian woman). In other words, no matter how strong, brave, kind or wise a woman might be, her life would inevitably be more difficult than that of a man.

In symbolic terms, the figure of the mother (*mat'*), and women in general, has served as a central, defining element in Russian culture, with the country itself frequently referred to as *Mat' Rossiya* (Mother Russia), or as *rodina*, or motherland (from the verb *rodit'*, to give birth). The country is also known, though, as *otechestvo*, fatherland, as well as a range of other male symbols (such as the tsarist two-headed eagle, now readopted in post-Soviet Russia). Tsarist Russia was, like many societies, one

Portrait of a 'New Soviet Woman' from a 1920s poster

in which the males held the dominant position in most areas of life – would this change after the October Revolution?

That was indeed the intention of such leading female revolutionaries as **Aleksandra Kollontai** (1872–1952). Freely available abortion and much more liberal attitudes towards marriage and divorce were intended to prise women away from the shackles that had bound them to husband and home for so long. Yet while some of the principles established in those early years were to survive throughout the Soviet period (such as the provision of a very cheap and comprehensive network of childcare), the policies of the Stalinist regime once more placed restrictions on the freedom of women. They were expected to play a full part in the industrialization of the USSR, at the same time as fulfilling their social duty as mothers, providing young citizens to meet the needs of the state. Abortion was made illegal in 1936 and divorce laws were tightened once more.

This double burden continued throughout the rest of the Soviet period, with the weight on women's shoulders intensified by the effect of the losses suffered in the Great Patriotic War. While many women had themselves fought and died in the front line, the male population was the worse hit, resulting in a sizeable imbalance in the proportion of women and men in the country for decades afterwards. (In fact, this imbalance still exists, now affected by the 14-year difference in life expectancy between men and women highlighted on page 202 – according to experts, the Russian population is 6 million men 'short' of where it would have been, if normal death rates had occurred).

Other factors contributed as well to the strain on women. While it is a problem that some women suffer from as well, the prevalence of alcoholism among men and associated problems (marital conflict, sometimes involving domestic violence) have long been a curse on Russian family life. Further, the need to hold down a full-time, often demanding job at the same time as bringing up children, perhaps single-handedly, brought additional tensions. Despite the fact that these various challenges meant that Russian women had to be resourceful, resilient and quite tough, this was still not enough to overcome the barriers to equality found at the workplace, with very few women managing to climb up the career ladder to senior positions. As a small consolation, the retirement age for women was 55, while men had to work for a further five years to reach their retirement.

What effect has the transition to post-Communism had? There have been signs of the emergence of a greater degree of equality between the sexes, with young men seeming to be more prepared nowadays to share the domestic responsibilities (reflected as well by the appearance of TV shows in which traditional gender roles are challenged, as in the cookery programme of rock star **Andrei Makarevich**). At the same time, there has been a certain amount of pressure from some quarters for women to return to their roles of mothers and housewives again, with the Orthodox church as well as some conservative voices in the media stating that *zhenshchina prezhde vsego dolzhna byt' mater'yu i zhenoi* (A woman should first and foremost be a mother and wife). Some women have indeed been content to do just that, taking advantage of the greater financial security received from their high-earning husbands. Other women, however, have been able to make good use of the opportunities that now exist to engage in business activity, perhaps even owning their own company, with the result that women are finally starting to have more of a direct say in the development of the economy. Others, meanwhile, continue to try to juggle responsibilities at work and at home, on a salary that is just inadequate even to provide some of the basics that their family needs.

While women have always been seen as *khranitel'nitsy semeinogo ochaga* (keepers of the family fire), Russian men have been expected to be *zashchitniki* (protectors, defenders) of people close to them and of their motherland. As we mentioned in Unit 8, in the USSR most young males had to perform two, sometimes three years of military service after the age of 18. For various reasons the conditions of service deteriorated during the 1970s, with abuse and violence among conscripts in the barracks becoming widespread. The risks were compounded from 1979 by the chance of being sent to fight in Afghanistan. Conscription is still in place in Russia today and the problems of abuse have worsened; furthermore, the conflicts in Chechnya and elsewhere have taken a large toll in deaths and injuries among young soldiers. Despite the official urgings that young boys needed military service to become 'real men' (a view that was echoed by some in society as well), increasing numbers have looked for any means they could find to evade service – and their mothers, in particular, have often played a large part in helping them to do so (some even starting to gather medical certificates to prove their sons' unsuitability for military service before they are even ten years old).

'U nas net seksa!' ('We don't have sex!')

This unfortunate (and clearly inaccurate!) remark, made by a matronly Russian woman during a *telemost* (TV bridge) between the USSR and USA that took place at the start of perestroika, is both amusing yet also sadly revealing of the prevailing public discussion (or lack of one) on this topic. Sexuality was repressed, treated as a taboo subject. There was very little information available on any issues relating to sex, while contraception was scarce. For many women abortion was the main form of birth control, with some undergoing as many as ten operations by their early thirties, despite the humiliating treatment they often found awaiting them in the clinic.

The collapse of the Soviet Union has also seen something of a rejection, by some in society at least, of the puritanical mores promoted by the Communists. To some extent the pendulum has swung too far, with pornography freely available with few restrictions placed on access and blatant exploitation seen in the media, and at times in the workplace, of women as sexual objects. This has in turn been met by a conservative reaction from the Russian Orthodox Church. But what is needed now is the emergence of a balanced approach to sexuality in Russian society, in which the subject can be treated frankly and the needs of the population (such as effective sex education for the young) given due attention.

In fact, the chance to display their femininity more openly (through wearing more adventurous clothes and makeup, even taking part in beauty contests) has been seen by some women as a means of liberation, of expressing their identity as women and protesting against the material and moral constraints of the past. While the pattern of feminist protest seen in such countries as the UK, USA and elsewhere has not been seen on anything like the same scale in Russia, therefore, it can be said that Russian women have managed to make their point to society to a degree – although there is clearly a fine line between freedom and exploitation at times.

The relative freedom of post-Soviet Russia has allowed gay culture to emerge from hiding, however. During the Soviet times there was almost zero tolerance of gay relationships, with homosexuality seen as a criminal offence that earned a prison sentence. While there is still a good deal of prejudice against gay relationships in society at large, the previous level of official persecution has gone and gay communities are starting to flourish in larger urban centres.

Religion

Russia's cultural diversity is reflected in the broad range of religious faiths found in the country, with Orthodoxy, Islam, Judaism and Buddhism the most established and widely followed: Muslims number some 10 per cent of the population of the Federation, while there are still some 700,000 Jews in Russia, despite the various waves of emigration that took place in the late Soviet period and which continue to a lesser degree today. There are also communities of *starovery* (Old Believers), a group that broke away from the Orthodox Church in the 17th century. Catholicism has maintained a following in parts of Russia, as have many Protestant-based churches, including Lutherans, Baptists, Mormons and Jehovah's Witnesses, while in some areas shamanism is still practised.

While it was initially thought that the collapse of the atheist Communist state in 1991 would lead to a new dawn of religious plurality in Russia, subsequent events have cast doubts on this, as echoes of the persecution and intolerance of earlier years have been heard.

Extinguishing belief?

We have seen in earlier units that the Russian Orthodox Church was by far the most powerful in the country, tied closely to the state until the time of Peter the Great, but continuing to exert a considerable influence on the political and social life of Russia until the events of 1917. The *svyashchennik* or *pop* (priest) was a key figure in the local community, a figure of great authority, which he could often wield in a strict manner: *Na tsarya, da na popa suda net* (No one can judge the tsar or the priest).

During the years of Soviet rule, atheism was actively promoted, while the state tried to persuade the population, at times through violent repression, to give up any attachment they might have to religious faith – the 'opium of the masses', as Marx had called it. It is indeed ironic that the ways in which Communism was presented to the people bore all the hallmarks of the kind of religious worship that the authorities declared they were seeking to eradicate. Just look at the way Lenin became a god-like figure, his embalmed body visited by millions of 'worshippers' in the mausoleum on Red Square in the decades since his death. Look at the *Kodeks stroitelya kommunizma* (*Code of the Builder of Communism*), whose instructions on how a good Communist citizen should behave in many ways resemble the ten commandments. And look at the way the population was supposed to accept unquestioningly the dogma presented to them by the Communist party.

It proved to be impossible to suppress, let alone eradicate religion – and during the Great Patriotic War (World War II), Stalin even had to turn to the church for support in an effort to rally the population in the struggle for victory. Further evidence of the ambivalent and hypocritical attitude of the party towards religion is provided by the trend in later years of the Soviet period for members of the *nomenklatura* to have their own children baptized.

A post-Soviet spiritual revival

As the hollow message of the Communist faith was increasingly ignored, then abandoned dramatically by the political centre in the events leading up to the dissolution of the USSR, so a moral vacuum emerged, accompanying the uncertainties and the dangers of the transition to democracy and the free market. For many people, especially those who found themselves in the most vulnerable situations, there was a need to find a haven away from the trials of everyday life – a need that led increasing numbers to turn to religion of one form or another. For many this meant the Orthodox Church – some 40 per cent of Russians state that they associate themselves with this church, although only some 7 per cent go to church every month, while Islam has also experienced a revival. There has also been a wave of 'new' religious movements, often involving visiting activists from abroad, with many US citizens spending extended periods in Russia, for example, promoting the work of their church and attempting to recruit new members. While there have been examples of more extreme 'cults' operating in Russia, for the most part these new religious organizations have come from well-established, respected and benign churches – some of which have actually had a presence in Russia for many decades, if not centuries. However, the sight of these groups – especially those which stood out as being strikingly different, such as the Hare Krishna movement – attracted a great deal of comment in the Russian media and from the Orthodox Church, which began to warn of the corruption of Russian spirituality through imported, alien beliefs.

Clamping down on religious freedoms

Religious intolerance has a long history in Russia. The word *pogrom* comes from Russia, a reflection of the ongoing vein of anti-Semitism that has lain near the surface of Russian society for centuries. As social discontent mounted during the 1990s, feeding into growing nationalist sentiment, some of it extreme in nature, so prejudice has at times spilled over into active persecution, with Jews, Muslims and Christians targeted.

The placing of restrictions on religious freedom has also been conducted at the level of the state, through the 1997 law on religion, which established a strict set of guidelines regarding the ability of religious organizations to operate in Russia. The Orthodox Church – which helped to draft the law – is privileged as the dominant faith in Russia, while Judaism, Buddhism and Islam also receive more or less adequate protection. But many faiths that were seen as foreign 'imports' and thus potentially threatening to the religious and moral fabric of the country, found themselves having to try to pass through an array of bewildering bureaucratic obstacles in order to preserve the right to remain in Russia – with a number of legal cases subsequently brought against some of them by federal and regional authorities.

Church, state and society in the 21st century

It is now a common sight to find the Patriarkh of Moscow and All Russia, Aleksii II, present alongside the Russian president and other key figures during important state occasions. However, while the church's profile has been restored to a high position, as yet its actual influence remains somewhat limited, both at the level of the state and in the community, where, for example, schools are still secular in character (although religious studies do form part of the curriculum). Whether or not this influence will increase in the years to come is not clear.

Russians in the newly independent states

One of the features of the establishment and maintenance of the Russian and then Soviet empires was the settlement, either long term or temporary, in the various republics of the USSR of large numbers of Russians. Until 1991, of course, this fact mattered relatively little, as the Soviet Union was just one big country. But the dissolution of the USSR changed all that, and 25 million Russians – a huge figure – suddenly found that they were now citizens of a newly independent state. This was seen by some as potentially a significant issue, as in certain states the Russian population was sizeable – in Kazakhstan some 38 per cent of people were Russian, while in the Baltic states of Estonia and Latvia the figure was around 30 per cent.

There was, accordingly, a lot of speculation at the start of the 1990s about the problems that might develop with regard to these Russian populations. Would they, as some predicted, create obstacles to the consolidation of independence of these countries? Would Russia itself see fit to intervene, perhaps even using military force, to protect the interests of its 'own' people (possibly with the ulterior motive of regaining control over these countries)?

It is true that the Russian government has made angry noises at times in response to the denial of certain key citizenship rights for Russian speakers by the governments of these states, although such criticism has been echoed, to some extent, by the European Union, which is using the fact that these states are applying for EU membership to try to exert an influence on the establishment of equal citizenship rights for all inhabitants. The warnings made by some in the early 1990s, however, that Russia would use the problems encountered by the Russian-speaking populations here to intervene more forcefully (or that these populations would themselves display open unrest) have failed to materialize (fortunately, people on the ground tend to be more sensible than some rather sensationalist analysts give them credit for...).

For the most part, a similar pattern has been seen in the other countries where significant numbers of Russians live, with the overwhelming majority of Russians living in these states more than content to consider themselves citizens of that country – and contribute to and benefit from its economic development. However, in those places where the situation has been more volatile (as in the case of Tajikistan, with its brutal civil war in the early 1990s), Russians have left in large numbers, usually looking to 'return' to Russia, either to family members or as refugees with no obvious place to head for. The problem is that many such people have relatively few direct links with Russia, as many were born and raised in another part of the USSR (and perhaps are members of a family that had been there for several generations). While some Russians have been able to make a comparatively smooth transition to living in Russia, therefore, others have found the process much more difficult.

GLOSSARY

РУССКИЕ – КТО ОНИ? *Who are the Russians?*

добродушные (adj. pl.)	*kind hearted*
коллективизм (m.)	*collectivism*
национальное меньшинство (n.)	*ethnic minority*
национальность (f.)	*nationality*
рождаемость (f.)	*birth rate*
русская душа (f.)	*Russian soul*
судьба (f.)	*fate*
щедрые (adj. pl.)	*generous*

СЕМЬЯ, ОТНОШЕНИЯ МЕЖДУ ПОЛАМИ, СЕКС
Family, gender, sexuality

брак (m.)	*marriage*
гражданский брак (m.)	*cohabitation*
дискриминация (f.)	*discrimination*
поколение (n.)	*generation*
равенство (n.)	*equality*
развод (m.)	*divorce*

РЕЛИГИЯ *religion*	
атеизм (m.)	*atheism*
вера (f.)	*faith*
верующий (m.)	*believer*
Ислам (m.)	*Islam*
священник (m.)	*priest*
Христианство (n.)	*Christianity*
церковь (f.)	*church*

РУССКИЕ В НОВЫХ НЕЗАВИСИМЫХ ГОСУДАРСТВАХ
Russians in the newly independent states

беженцы из бывших советских республик (pl.)	*refugees from former Soviet republics*
миграция (f.)	*migration*

Taking it further

Of course, the best way to get to know what Russians are like is to make some friends! The fact that there are many more Russians living outside of Russia nowadays means that this is not the difficult task it used to be.

Books

Ashwin, S. (ed.) *Gender, State and Society in Soviet and Post-Soviet Russia* (London: Routledge, 2000).

Barta, P. (ed.) *Gender and Sexuality in Russian Civilization* (London: Routledge, 2001).

Costlow, J., Sandler, S. and Vowles, J. (eds) *Sexuality and the Body in Russian Culture* (Stanford: Stanford University Press, 1998).

Gerhart, G., *The Russian's World: Life and Language* (Orlando, FL: Harcourt Brace, 1994).

Markowitz, F., *Coming of Age in Post-Soviet Russia* (Urbana, IL: University of Illinois Press, 2000) (looks at the lives of young people in the 1990s).

Melvin, N., *Russians Beyond Russia: The Politics of National Identity* (London: Royal Institute of International Affairs, 1995) (on the issue of Russians living in former Soviet republics).

Milner-Gulland, R., *The Russians* (Oxford: Blackwell, 1999).

Pilkington, H., *Migration, Displacement and Identity in Post-Soviet Russia* (London: Routledge, 1998).

Smith, H., *New Russians* (New York: Random House, 1990). Smith had previously written a book titled *The Russians*, published in 1973, based on his experience as a newspaper correspondent in Moscow. This later book takes a look at how much Russia had changed in the intervening period.

Sutton, J., *Traditions in New Freedom* (Nottingham: Bramcote Press, 1996) (a survey of religious education in Russia and Ukraine).

Thubron, C., *Among the Russians* (Harmondsworth: Penguin, 1985) (based on the author's experience of driving across Russia).

Zhel'vis, V., *A Xenophobe's Guide to the Russians* (London: Oval Books, 2001) (written by one of (co-author) Tatyana's former lecturers).

12 Russia in the wider world

In this unit you will learn
- about Russia's relations with the West
- about Russia's relations with her neighbours
- about Russia's image in the world
- about the future for Russia

Relations with the West

Is Russia still a 'great power,' with influence that extends way beyond its borders? Is it a spent superpower, now impoverished and considered irrelevant on the world scene? Or has it become just another country, ready to contribute to and benefit from strong and open economic and cultural links with the outside world and ready to play a full part in the increasingly globalized environment of the post-Cold War era?

These questions have been at the core of debates both inside Russia and further afield since the end of the 1980s, with Russia's foreign policy swinging between eager cooperation with the West and a more cautious, inward-looking stance and even at times a cool hostility that conjures up echoes of the past. At the start of the 1990s there was a kind of honeymoon period with the West, as the momentum of goodwill and expectations fostered by Gorbachov's policies carried on under the New Russian regime of Boris Yel'tsin. There was confident anticipation among Russia's reformers that the West, and the USA in particular, would now step forward to help Russia through the transformation, as a reward for having brought down the USSR and embraced the notions of democracy and the market. The almost naive idealism of Gorbachov's hopes for a new world (he had spoken of a 'Common European Home' and a nuclear-free planet) could be detected in Russia's initial policy directions, with foreign minister **Andrei Kozyrev** (b. 1951) earning the nickname 'Mr Yes', for his apparent willingness to go along with the suggestions of his Western counterparts (in contrast to the stony-faced Soviet foreign minister **Andrei Gromyko** (1909–1989), who had gained a reputation as Mr *Net* ('Mr No') during his marathon tenure in this post (1957–1985), for his stubbornness in dealings with the West).

But the honeymoon didn't last for long. As the scale of the economic and political investment needed to support the transition started to become clearer, Western governments grew more cautious about the amount of material assistance, as opposed to moral support, that they were prepared to offer. In Russia, meanwhile, the success of the nationalist and Communist opposition parties in elections in 1993 and 1995 helped to push Yel'tsin into adopting a more assertive stance in Russia's foreign policy.

Since then, Russia's relations with the West have hit a number of lows. The conduct of the wars in Chechnya, for instance (1994–1996 and from 1999) has provoked considerable criticism in Western Europe in particular, with Russia's membership of the Council of Europe suspended for some time. The Russian elites have, for their part, mostly stood opposed to the policy of the enlargement of the North Atlantic Treaty Organization (NATO), of which the countries of East–Central Europe, including the former Soviet republics of Estonia, Latvia and Lithuania have applied to become members. This is presented by many in Russian policy circles as a threat to Russia's security, although its symbolic impact is more telling, with the former Cold War adversary now approaching Russia's borders. While NATO tried to patch up the rift by signing (in 1997) a founding act of cooperation with Russia and setting up a Permanent Joint Council to provide a forum in which Russia can air its views with alliance members, the extent of the differences of opinion between the two sides on European security was highlighted during and immediately after the Kosovo conflict, with relations taking a turn for the worse for some time.

Although the Russian–NATO dispute serves as a reminder of the difficulty of shaking off the suspicions of the Cold War, in many other ways the years since 1991 have seen much more positive and constructive interaction between Russia and the West. The European Union, for instance, has funded a range of assistance and exchange programmes designed to help Russia in the process of transition, with similar schemes supported by the US government, as well as various charities, funds and other organizations. The **Soros Foundation**, set up by the Hungarian–American business tycoon George Soros, has ploughed millions of dollars into Russia and other former Communist countries, notably in the field of education. Meanwhile, the ex-president of the USSR, Mikhail Gorbachov is the figurehead of the **Gorbachov Foundation**, which promotes a range of activities aimed at fostering civic culture, glasnost' and democracy in Russia and elsewhere.

At an institutional level, Russia has continued to receive loans from the International Monetary Fund (IMF) and advice and assistance from the London-based European Bank for Reconstruction and Development (EBRD). As a gesture to ease the process of its integration into the world community, Russia has also been given a place in the informal G-8 (G-7 before Russia joined) group of the world's leading economies.

Russia's status has been maintained as well through its inheritance of the USSR's seat on the Security Council of the

United Nations and it has played a significant role in a number of international crises and diplomatic disputes, notably during and after the Kosovo crisis, when former Prime Minister Viktor Chernomyrdin was sent to negotiate with Yugoslav leader Slobodan Milosevic. While tension mounted when Russian airborne troops drove into Prishtina airport in Kosovo ahead of NATO forces, subsequently Russian units cooperated effectively with those of NATO as part of the K-FOR peace restoration force in Kosovo.

Cooperation also occurred, despite an amount of suspicion and the uttering of wild accusations on the part of the Russian navy, in the aftermath of the tragic sinking of the *Kursk* nuclear powered attack submarine in August 2000, with the loss of all 118 hands. Apart from the involvement of Western navies and companies in the initial rescue attempt and then the salvage efforts, the incident also seemed to spur all sides to pay more attention to the question of nuclear safety in Russia, with several countries promising multi-million dollar assistance packages to help with clean-up operations.

At the presidential level, Boris Yel'tsin enjoyed a good relationship on the whole with his Western counterparts, who often seemed willing to ignore his outspoken remarks (such as promising to retarget nuclear weapons against the West), his tendency to take authoritarian measures at home and his worsening health problems that left him incapacitated at times. Vladimir Putin's arrival on the scene as acting, then actual president, was met with considerable caution in the West, with the media in particular making much of his past as a KGB officer and the part that the second war in Chechnya played in his rise to power. Despite some tough talk about Russia's great power status, however, Putin has also sought to develop relations with the West, studying English in order to be able to converse directly with Western leaders (he already had a fluent command of German), something no doubt appreciated by Britain's Prime Minister Tony Blair, with whom Putin seems to have struck up a good relationship.

Relations with neighbours

After centuries of being the centre of the Russian empire and decades as the leading power in the Warsaw Pact of Communist states in Eastern Europe, Russia found itself in January 1992 as just one of 15 Soviet successor states and with its former satellite countries in the Communist bloc already heading for what many termed a 'return to Europe' (along with applications for membership of NATO and the EU). While it is undeniably the most powerful state among the former Soviet republics, Russia's leadership and its population have had to come to terms with the fact that their erstwhile compatriots now elect their own presidents of their own sovereign states. The learning curve for Russia and its neighbours has been steep and not without significant difficulties.

Having urged the dissolution of the USSR, Yel'tsin and his government quickly realized that it would nevertheless be in Russia's interests to retain some kind of institutional framework to bind together the successor states. The result was the emergence of the Commonwealth of Independent States (CIS) in 1992, a body that was intended to act as a forum for discussing political, economic and other forms of cooperation in the region. The Baltic states of Estonia, Latvia and Lithuania, however, refused point blank to join, while Ukraine, notably, was cautious, unwilling to submit to what it saw as an attempt to assure Russian domination once more. This inauspicious start to the CIS has been reflected in its subsequent development, for while it has served as a vehicle for a certain degree of interaction and decision making, it has never become an effective mechanism for widespread cooperation. Instead, states have tended to form a range of ad hoc groupings with other countries, both former Soviet republics and countries from outside the region (such as Turkey and Iran in the case of the Central Asian states and Azerbaijan, and Poland and the Baltic states in the case of Ukraine).

Russia's relations with Ukraine have been thorny at times, particularly in the early 1990s, as some in the Russian elite (and population at large) apparently found it hard to come to terms with the fact that Ukraine was now an independent state, that was eager to demonstrate this fact to Russia and the rest of the world. There was a particularly acrimonious dispute regarding the fate of the Black Sea fleet, which both sides laid claim to as their rightful inheritance from the Soviet military. This was eventually resolved later in the 1990s, although disagreements rumbled on over the status of the Crimea, a territory in Ukraine that had been part of the Russian Federation until Khrushchov made a present of it to the Ukrainian republic in 1954. Other disagreements have centred on economic relations, including the question of Russia's gas exports to Ukraine.

With Belarus, a very different story has been seen, at least with regard to state-to-state relations. Various agreements have been signed between Russia and Belarus since 1996, with the declared aim of moving towards a form of union of the two countries, for instance through establishing joint armed forces and a common currency. The Russian side has been more reluctant to press ahead with this process than the authoritarian leader of Belarus, **Alyaksandr Lukashenka**, however.

The three Baltic states have been embroiled in a range of disputes with Russia since 1991 – over the withdrawal of Russian troops left there after the collapse of the USSR, over borders, and, as we saw in Unit 11, over the status of the Russian-speaking population in these countries. The nationalist rhetoric of certain elements in Russia notwithstanding, for the most part Russia has made little attempt to intervene in the affairs of the Baltic States (although if these countries are offered NATO membership the Russian reaction is likely to be more forthright). In other parts of the former Soviet Union, Russia has adopted a far more active line, openly interfering at times in the domestic affairs of such countries as Georgia, in order to gain more influence on the political and security situation in the region (the issue of access to oil and gas fields and the routing of pipelines is never far from the agenda in such cases). Yet while Georgia can rightly feel aggrieved at the unwanted intrusion of Russia, in other cases Russian support is actively sought – Armenia, for instance, relies heavily on Russia to provide some degree of security guarantee. In general, while countries in the CIS region and in the West may raise concerns over Russia's intentions in its aggressive conduct of peacekeeping operations in the various armed conflicts seen in the region since 1991 or its attempts to assert influence in the former Soviet republics, the reality is that, on the whole, outside powers such as the USA or Western European countries have shown little interest in engaging with this region. This might change, however, given the enormous investments being made by Western oil and gas companies in the Caspian Basin and elsewhere, and given the perceived threat posed by terrorist groups based in Afghanistan and other locations in Central Asia.

Further afield, Russia's relations with China have faltered at times because of fears in Siberian and Far Eastern parts of Russia over the predicted influx of Chinese migrants from the overpopulated Chinese areas that border sparsely populated Russian regions. At the same time, Russia has not held back from selling considerable quantities of arms to China, with this commodity also the source of a healthy trade with India, bringing in valuable export earnings for the beleaguered Russian economy. The situation with Russo–Japanese relations, however, is still overshadowed by what seems at times an intractable dispute over a group of islands to the north of Japan (in Russian they are called the Kuril islands), which were occupied by Soviet forces after the surrender of Japan in World War II. For both sides the islands hold considerable symbolic value (with the Russian leadership reluctant to be seen to be giving in to the demands of Japan), but until the problem is resolved in Japan's favour (by the return of the islands), Japan will continue to hold back on economic investment in Russia – a serious blow indeed, given the potential effect that interaction with the Japanese commercial world could mean for Russia.

This case highlights the dilemma that often seems to affect the ability of the Russian government to define what its foreign policy priorities should be. On the one hand, there is still a strong pull, fed by inertia from the past, and pressure from nationalist sentiments in the Duma and elsewhere, to continue with the notion that Russia is still a great power, relying first and foremost on its military strength to assure this status. And on the other is the more pragmatic stance, that Russia's interests would be best served by attempting to integrate more fully in the world, not expecting to be given special treatment because of its past status, but prepared to be treated as just another country, ready to contribute as well as to take and committed to playing the game by the same rules as everyone else. Despite the ongoing need to provide assertive rhetoric that seems to go in the opposite direction, by the start of the 21st century there were signs that Russia was finally coming to terms with the changes that have taken place since 1985. This is to be expected, of course – after all, it took Britain and France decades to get over the effect of the end of their role as centres of empires.

Russia's image

In 2000 the Russian government launched a programme, under Press Minister **Mikhail Lesin**, to improve Russia's image abroad, and counter what is felt to be the negative views on Russia that are presented in Western media. To some extent, one can sympathize with this aim – in Hollywood action movies the one-dimensional stereotypes of the Cold War have given way to one-dimensional and ubiquitous characters from the world of

Russian organized crime, while in the news media, Western TV, radio and newspapers often focus only on the problems to be found in Russian society, through a somewhat superficial analysis of the situation. The cheap and crude stereotypes presented in the worst coverage of Russia in the West certainly do give a distorted and often very inaccurate picture of life in Russia.

Of course, this does not imply that problems should not be investigated – there is no escaping the fact, for example, that Russia's human rights record in Chechnya (and in certain spheres in Russian society as a whole) cannot be defended, no matter how much effort is put into image making. But it would help if at times in such coverage, and, indeed, in the statements of Western political leaders, a greater attempt were made to avoid taking the moral high ground and lecturing to the Russian side, as if Western states and societies had nothing to learn themselves from their own past and present faults. A 'holier than thou' approach to international relations can often lead to a more entrenched attitude from those being criticized, rather than a shared reflection on common shortcomings and constructive solutions.

Having said that, there is still, of course, plenty of informed coverage of Russian affairs in the Western media, with some TV companies investing considerable effort into producing insightful, balanced yet revealing documentaries about life in Russia. True, many of these documentaries also tend to concentrate on the problems that the country has encountered and this can skew the image that audiences receive of Russia, as the more positive – yet perhaps for TV executives more boring – aspects of society can often be left in the background of such programmes. But at least these documentaries do indicate an enduring fascination with Russia in the West and provide a starting point for audiences to find out more about the country.

People to people: contact with the world

The best way to do this, naturally, is through direct personal contact. We are living in an era of unprecedented interaction between Russians and people in the West: apart from those foreigners who visit Russia for vacations, there have been increasing opportunities to study and work in Russia. Meanwhile, after being cut off for so long through the policies of isolation and restrictions on travel, Russian citizens now enjoy far greater opportunities to travel to different countries (although visas need to be obtained for many destinations, including the European Union, the USA and Canada and this can prove problematic from time to time). Nowadays, the main obstacle to going abroad is not the political stance of Moscow, but the need for hard currency – with salaries in Russia far lower, on the whole, than in the more affluent West. For many Russians the prospect of travelling to Western Europe, North America or other expensive regions can still be a distant one.

However, as we saw in Unit 10, foreign travel is far from being the reserve of just rich 'New Russians,' with package holidays to Mediterranean destinations proving increasingly popular. More and more young people are taking advantage of opportunities to study abroad, through exchange programmes or by funding themselves and many Russians are to be found working in a wide variety of professions throughout the world, but especially in Western Europe and North America. In fact, the exodus of educated young professionals has led to consistent talk of a 'brain drain', as some fear that Russia will suffer in the years to come as it proves ever more difficult to replace the skills and expertise of those who have left. And the influx of Russians to the West has also been given further momentum by the sharp increase in the number of marriages between Russians and foreigners (as in the case of the authors of this book!).

In certain major cities in North America and Western Europe sizeable Russian or Russian-speaking communities have grown up or joined those established by previous waves of Russian émigrés. The Russian population in New York is able to enjoy all the comforts of home, with Russian bakeries, shops and restaurants and food and other supplies even flown in from Russia. In London, the Russian community has its own newspaper (with online version) and radio station, while similar communities exist in Paris, Berlin and elsewhere.

The future?

The pace and scope of the changes that have taken place in Russia since 1985 have been staggering and have often left the politicians, media and academic analysts, not to mention the general public at home and abroad, reeling in their wake. Who could have predicted that Communist rule in Eastern Europe would fall like a pack of cards in 1989 or that the apparently mighty Soviet Union would vanish into thin air at the end of 1991? The transition to democracy and market economy in

Russia has been far from straightforward, of course, with political instability, economic crises, mounting social problems, a crime epidemic and conflicts in Chechnya and elsewhere the visible and disturbing signs of the turmoil that has been produced as Russia struggles between its Soviet past and the search for a path to take it forward.

But over a decade on from the emergence of the New Russia, it is essential to reflect not only on the problems associated with transition, but also on how much has been achieved – a democratic tradition has been set in motion through presidential, State Duma and various regional elections, while the mass media have enjoyed unprecedented freedoms and influence, civil liberties are being strengthened, the practices of the free market are being adopted and the country has opened up as never before to the outside world. To be sure, there is still much to be done in taking these developments further and consolidating them, and concerns are rightly raised about the level of commitment shown by some in Russia towards the principles of democracy and liberty. But the rising generation in Russia is growing up in a very different country to the one which their parents or even their older brothers and sisters knew and it is these young people who will be the ones who decide, in the years ahead, what they want Russia to be. The signs are that they want Russia to be able to stride into the future proud of its achievements and its potential, but ready to play a full part in the world. In the light of everything that has gone before, this will truly be something to celebrate.

GLOSSARY

великая держава (f.)	*great power*
внешняя политика (f.)	*foreign policy*
Европейский Союз (m.)	*European Union*
ездить за границу (vb.)	*to travel abroad*
Международный валютный фонд (m.)	*International Monetary Fund*
международные отношения (pl.)	*international relations*
мир (m.)	*the world; peace*
мировое сообщество (n.)	*international community*
Организация Объединённых Наций (f.)	*United Nations Organization*
отношения с Западом (pl.)	*relations with the West*

Союз Независимых Государств (СНГ) (m.)	Commonwealth of Independent States (CIS)
эмиграция (f.)	emigration
утечка мозгов (f.)	brain drain

Taking it further

Russian communities in the West

A good way to take your interest in Russia further might be to make contact with your local Russian community – try searching for details on the internet or asking the department of Russian at a nearby university for advice. The online Russian newspaper of London's Russian community is located at

www.russianlondon.com/

Travel to Russia – studying, working and living in Russia

There are many package and tailor-made holidays available through general and specialist travel agents. Independent travel requires more effort on your part, as you'll need to arrange a visa and somewhere to stay in Russia – but don't let this put you off, as such arrangements are pretty straightforward nowadays. See a good travel guidebook on Russia for details.

There are also plenty of opportunities for studying the Russian language and other subjects in Russia – try an internet search for courses that appeal to you. Job opportunities for Westerners in Russia are growing all the time, with major (and not so major) companies, international organizations, the mass media and various non-governmental organizations – see newspapers and recruitment websites for details.

Russia's international relations

There are dozens of books out there on Russian foreign policy and the policies of Western governments towards Russia. For a critical view of US policy, see Cohen, Stephen, *Failed Crusade: America and the Tragedy of Post-Communist Russia* (New York: W. W. Norton & Company, 2001). For a general overview of the subject, see Hopf, Ted (ed.), *Understandings of Russian Foreign Policy* (Philadelphia: Penn State University Press, 1999).

To keep up to date with developments, try the English- or Russian-language websites of Russian newspapers, listed on

www.smi.ru

the website of the *Sovet po vneshnei i oboronnoi politike* (Council for Foreign and Defence Policies) at

www.svop.ru/

(in Russian), or the US-based Center for Defense Information's Russian pages at

www.cdi.org/russia/

taking it even further

And finally... in this last Taking it further section we give details of books and websites that cover a broad range of topics relating to Russian language, life and culture. As ever, this is just a tiny selection – there are plenty more sources to help you go on discovering Russia for many years to come!

Books

Barker, A. (ed.) *Consuming Russia: Popular Culture, Sex and Society Since Gorbachev* (Durham, NC: Duke University Press, 1999).

Bowker, M. and Ross, C. (eds) *Russia after the Cold War* (London: Pearson Education, 2000).

Dixon-Kennedy, M., *Encyclopaedia of Russian and Slavic Myth and Legend* (Santa Barbara, CA: ABC Clio, 1999).

Gerhart, G., *The Russian's World: Life and Language* (2nd edn) (Fort Worth, TX: Harcourt Brace Publishers, 1995).

Hellberg-Hirn, E., *Soil and Soul: The Symbolic World of Russianness* (Aldershot: Ashgate, 1998).

Hosking, G., *Russia and the Russians* (London: Penguin, 2001).

Lincoln, B., *Between Heaven and Hell: The Story of a Thousand Years of Artistic Life in Russia* (London: Penguin, 1999).

Marsden, P., *The Spirit Wrestlers* (London: Flamingo, 1999).

Rzhevsky, N. (ed.) *The Cambridge Companion to Modern Russian Culture* (Cambridge: Cambridge University Press, 1998).

Stites, R., *Soviet Popular Culture* (Cambridge: Cambridge University Press, 1992).

Thubron, C., *In Siberia* (London: Penguin, 2000).

Websites

The following are all 'megasites', which provide lots of links to web pages on a huge range of Russia-related topics:

Little Russia in USA **http://russia-in-us.com/**

Reesweb **www.ucis.pitt.edu/reesweb/**

Russia on the Net **www.ru/eng/index.html**

Sher's Russian Index **www.websher.net/inx/link.html**

Slavophilia **www.slavophilia.com/**

Some typical Russian dishes

If you're feeling hungry after reading the book, why not try
making these simple, classic Russian dishes?

Борщ

На 4-6 порций:

500 г кусочков говядины или куры*

2 л холодной воды

300 г свежей свёклы (натёртой на крупной тёрке)

1 большая луковица (мелко порезанная)

2 ст. л. томатной пасты или почищенных и мелко порезанных помидоров

2 среднего размера картофелины (почищенных и нарезанных соломкой)

2 ст. л. подсолнечного масла

½ ч. л. сахара

сок ½ лимона

соль и перец

2 лавровых листа

петрушка (мелко порезанная)

сметана

Приготовление:

Положите мясо в кастрюлю и залейте холодной водой. Доведите до кипения. Накройте крышкой и варите на медленном огне до готовности, снимая пену по необходимости (1-2 ч для мяса и 30-40 мин для куры). Разогрейте масло в большой сковороде, добавьте свёклу, лук, томатную пасту или помидоры, сахар, лимонный сок и соль. Тушите помешивая 20 мин. Когда мясо готово, положите картошку и потушенную свеклу в бульон. Добавьте лавровый лист и посолите и поперчите по вкусу. Варите еще 5 мин на медленном огне. Посыпьте свеженарезанной петрушкой перед подачей на стол. Подавайте со сметаной и чёрным хлебом.

* можно использовать овощной бульон

Borshch (Beetroot soup)

Ingredients
(serves 4–6)
500g stewing steak (cubed) or beef shins (sliced)
  or chicken pieces *
2 l cold water
300g fresh or pure cooked beetroot (coarsely grated)
1 large onion (chopped)
2 tablespoons tomato paste or 2 fresh peeled and chopped
  plum tomatoes
2 medium potatoes (peeled and diced)
2 tablespoons sunflower oil
$^{1}/_{2}$ teaspoon sugar
juice of $^{1}/_{2}$ a lemon
salt and pepper
2 bay leaves
fresh flat-leaved parsley (chopped)
smetana (sour cream)

Put the meat into a large saucepan together with the cold water.
Bring to the boil, skim with a draining spoon if necessary, cover
and simmer on a low heat for up to two hours until the meat is
tender (30–40 minutes for chicken). Heat the oil in a large frying
pan and briefly fry the chopped onion on low heat until the
onion is transparent. Add beetroot, tomato paste (or tomatoes),
sugar, lemon juice and salt. Reduce heat and cook for 20
minutes (5 minutes if using cooked beetroot), tossing frequently.
When the meat is ready, add the potatoes and the cooked
beetroot to the stock. Add bay leaves, and season to taste. Cook
for 5 minutes on low heat. Serve with fresh parsley, *smetana* and
black bread.

* Can also be made using stock cubes or without meat, using vegetable stock

Ватрушка

Для теста:

4 ст. л. (горкой) муки

4 ст. л. сахара

4 ст. л. сметаны

2 ст. л. растительного масла

1 яйцо

½ ч. л. соли

1/3 ч. л. соды

Для начинки:

250 г творога

2 ст. л. сахара

2 ст. л. сметаны

1 яйцо

1-2 ч. л. изюма (по желанию)

Приготовление:

Замесите тесто в большой миске. Перемешайте творог с сахаром, сметаной и яйцом в другой миске. Тонко раскатайте тесто в лепёшку. Сделайте краешек, загибая и защипывая тесто. Выложите начинку на тесто. Разровняйте ложкой и смажьте тонким слоем сметаны или растительным маслом. Впекайте на смазанном противне в духовке (180-200°С) пока творог не зарумянится: около 30 мин.

Vatrushka (Sweet cheese tart)

Ingredients
For the dough
4 heaped tablespoons plain flour
4 tablespoons sugar
4 tablespoons *smetana* or crème fraiche
2 tablespoons vegetable oil
1 egg
$^{1}/_{2}$ teaspoon salt
$^{1}/_{3}$ teaspoon baking powder

For the filling
250g curd cheese
2 tablespoons sugar
2 tablespoons *smetana*
1 egg
1–2 teaspoons raisins (optional)

Mix the ingredients for the dough in a large bowl. Mix the ingredients for the filling in another bowl. Roll the dough out on a floured surface into a circle as thinly as possible. Make a rim around the circle by rolling up and pinching the dough. Spoon the filling into the centre. With the back of a spoon smooth a little bit of *smetana* or vegetable oil over the top of the filling. Carefully transfer onto a greased baking tray. Bake for around 30 minutes in a preheated oven (180–200°C), until the filling has turned golden brown.